THE MOBILE FRO

A GUIDE FOR DESIGNING MOBILE

Rachel Hinman

Rosenfeld Media
Brooklyn, New York

The Mobile Frontier: A Guide for Designing Mobile Experiences
By Rachel Hinman

Rosenfeld Media, LLC

457 Third Street, #4R

Brooklyn, New York

11215 USA

On the Web: www.rosenfeldmedia.com

Please send errors to: errata@rosenfeldmedia.com

Publisher: Louis Rosenfeld

Developmental Editor: Marta Justak

Interior Layout Tech: Danielle Foster

Cover Design: The Heads of State

Indexer: Nancy Guenther

Proofreader: Dan Foster

ISBN: 1-933820-55-1

ISBN-13: 978-1-933820-55-2

LCCN: 2012935787

Printed and bound in the United States of America

DEDICATION

To my mother, Patricia Tiffany-Hinman. Thank you for your unwavering support and love—and for raising me to believe a woman can do anything she sets her mind to.

HOW TO USE THIS BOOK

Who Should Read This Book?

This book was written for anyone curious about creating compelling mobile experiences. While it is primarily targeted at those who call themselves "designers" or "user experience practitioners," it should prove helpful to engineers, project managers, students, and anyone interested in designing for mobile.

To be clear, this is not a technical book. It does not contain code snippets or provide the ins and outs of designing an application for any particular mobile operating system. There are lots of great books out there that will help you do that—but this is not one of them. Instead, this book has been designed to help you understand what makes mobile user experience unique and fundamentally different than other design spaces. It outlines what I believe is important about mobile user experience while providing frameworks, design exercises, and interviews with mobile experts. My hope is that this book will help you navigate the unfamiliar and fast-changing mobile landscape with grace and solid thinking while inspiring you to explore the possibilities that mobile technology presents.

What's in This Book?

Section One: What Makes Mobile Different?

The first part of this book will introduce you to the key characteristics that define mobile user experiences today. Chapter 1, "Casting Off Anchors," is an introduction to the mobile frontier. Chapter 2, "The Emergent Mobile NUI Paradigm," Chapter 3, "Peanut Butter in Denver," and Chapter 4, "Shapeshifting," are dedicated to providing you with information on what makes mobile user experience and design different than other design spaces.

Section Two: Emergent Mobile Patterns

Chapter 5, "Mobile UX Patterns," will discuss what people who have begun to settle the mobile frontier are currently doing. This chapter will discuss five emergent mobile UX (user experience) patterns you can lean on as you begin to craft your own mobile experiences.

Section Three: Crafting Mobile Experiences

Chapters 6, "Mobile Prototyping," 7, "Motion and Animation," and 8, "Awakening the Senses," in this section will give you design exercises, prototyping methods, and design guidelines to try once you begin crafting mobile experiences.

Section Four: The Future of Mobile UX

Finally, Chapter 9, "New Mobile Forms," is all about the edge of the mobile frontier. It's the "deep space" stuff that a few brave souls have already begun to explore and pioneer. It's the stuff that will likely become our future very soon.

What Comes with This Book?

This book's companion Web site (rosenfeldmedia.com/books/mobile-design/) contains some templates, discussion, and additional content. The book's diagrams and other illustrations are available under a Creative Commons license (when possible) for you to download and include in your own presentations. You can find these on Flickr at www.flickr.com/photos/rosenfeldmedia/sets/.

FREQUENTLY ASKED QUESTIONS

Why is mobile UX such a hot topic right now?

For what felt like the longest time, mobile UX was considered a small and obscure design space that most designers felt obliged to learn more about but loathed participating in because of all the inherent design constraints. The release of the first iPhone in 2007 changed all that. The iPhone demonstrated to the mobile industry and the world what was possible when innovative mobile technology was paired with a stellar user experience. The iPhone was more than an innovative product; it was the first mobile device that got people—regular, everyday people (not just the geeks)—excited about using a mobile phone. Now, as increasingly more people are experiencing what it's like to access and interact with information from nearly anywhere, through devices that are beautifully designed, mobile is no longer a niche topic. There's never been a better time to design mobile experiences. See Chapter 1 for more.

What makes mobile user experience and design different?

Practitioners of mobile UX design often cite context as the biggest difference between designing for mobile experiences and other design spaces. Developing an understanding and empathy for the depth, breadth, and design implications of the mobile context is quite possibly the most essential skill necessary in creating great mobile experiences. If you're a practicing designer, chances are that *context* is your design blindside. Most designers have been steeped in a tradition of creating experiences with few context considerations, although they may not realize it. Books, Web sites, software programs, and even menus for interactive televisions share an implicit and often overlooked commonality: use occurs in relatively static and predictable environments. In contrast, most mobile experiences are situated in highly dynamic and unpredictable environments. See Chapter 3 for more information on designing for the mobile context.

What modifications to my existing design processes do I need to make to create good mobile experiences?

Mobile UX professionals use many of the same tools and processes as other UX professionals. Designers new to mobile UX must learn to calibrate their design decision-making skills to a new medium—and prototyping is essential in developing those decision-making skills. Although prototyping is considered a luxury for many PC-based experiences, it is an absolutely *essential* part of creating compelling tablet and mobile experiences. The reason is simple. Chances are, if you are new to mobile, your design experience and instincts aren't very well tuned to mobile. Unlike the PC, the mobile design space is relatively new, and design patterns have yet to be formally codified. In lieu of experience and heuristics, the best way to develop these skills is to practice turning the brilliant ideas in your head into tangible experiences you and other people can engage with.

Prototyping can become your saving grace in this regard. See Chapter 6 for tons of info on prototyping methods.

How do I design for touchscreen experiences?

One of the issues that makes designing for touchscreen experiences challenging for designers is that most of us have been steeped in a tradition of creating experiences using GUI (graphical user interface) principles. With the widespread uptake of mobile phones and tablets outfitted with touchscreens, we're currently in the midst of a UI paradigm shift. Designers and UX professionals must now learn to create experiences that leverage NUI (natural user interface) principles. This includes learning the key differences between GUI and NUI, as well as understanding how to optimize experiences for touch. Chapter 2 will help you understand what makes NUI interesting and different, and Chapter 8 will give you valuable info on how to optimize screen-based experiences for touch UIs.

Should I design a native mobile app, a mobile Web app, or a mobile Web site?

Many experts in the mobile industry have deeply held philosophical viewpoints on this question and have been willing to fight verbal cage fights with those whose opinions differ. The short answer is: "It depends." Chapter 4 covers some of the pros and cons of each approach. A word of caution: While this is an important implementation question to answer, it's not necessarily the first question you should be asking at the beginning of a mobile user experience project. Ultimately, your goal should be to create a great user experience. Technology and implementation choices can help guide your design and decision-making process—but they should not dictate it. More on identifying mobile needs in Chapter 3.

What does the future hold? What's next for mobile user experience?

In the near future, many designers and UX professionals will focus on pioneering the parts of the mobile frontier that have already been discovered. And that is a good place to be. But there's a vast space just beyond what's been discovered that some brave souls have already begun to explore. There are three mobile trends I've been tracking that I believe will have a profound impact on the future. These themes will not only redefine mobility, but they'll also irrevocably alter the relationship we have with computing. They are: the shifting boundary between computers and the human body, the shifting boundary between computers and the environment, and mobile experiences for emerging markets. These topics will all be covered in Chapter 9.

CONTENTS

How to Use This Book   iv

Frequently Asked Questions   vi

Foreword   xiv

SECTION ONE: WHAT MAKES MOBILE DIFFERENT?

CHAPTER 1

Casting Off Anchors
Preparing to Explore the Mobile Frontier   1

The Golden Age of Mobile   4

Casting Off Anchors from the Past   6

Section One: What Makes Mobile Different?   7

Section Two: Emergent Mobile Patterns   8

Section Three: Crafting Mobile Experiences   8

Section Four: The Future of Mobile UX   9

The Mobile Sinners   10

CHAPTER 2

The Emergent Mobile NUI Paradigm
Traversing the GUI/NUI Chasm   11

The Emergent Mobile Paradigm   13

A Paradigm Shift Is Underway   14

The Evolution of User Interfaces   19

The Emergent Mobile NUI Paradigm   23

Past and Present Computing Paradigms   28

Future Computing Paradigms   30

Summary   33

Expert Interview: Mike Kruzeniski   34

CHAPTER 3

Peanut Butter in Denver
Demystifying the Elusive Mobile Context   **39**

It Was a Dark and Stormy Night…   41
Developing Empathy for Context   42
Reduce Cognitive Load and Opportunity Cost   51
Mobile Context Design Tips   54
Mobile Context Design Method: Brainstorming
   in the Wild   56
Mobile Context Framework: Nouns and Relationships   57
Peanut Butter in Denver?   59
Mobile UX Beachhead   60
Summary   63
Expert Interview: Alex Rainert   64

CHAPTER 4

Shapeshifting
Convergence and Multidevice Experiences   **69**

What Is Convergence?   70
Convergence and Mobility   72
What Is a Device Ecosystem?   76
Mutual Reconfiguration and Multidevice Experiences   82
Identifying Ecosystem Relationships Through
   Participatory Design   85
Creating Experiences That Scale   90
Mobile Web Site, Web App, or Native App?   98
Summary   103
Expert Interview: Stephanie and Bryan Rieger   104

SECTION TWO: EMERGENT MOBILE PATTERNS

CHAPTER 5

Mobile UX Patterns
Designing for Mobility   **107**

The Structure of a Design Factor	108
Mobile Design Patterns	110
Mobile UX Pattern #1: "The Cloud" and Applications as Natural Set Points for Mobile Experiences	111
Mobile Pattern #2: Good Mobile Experiences Progressively Reveal their Nature	121
Mobile Pattern #3: Content Becomes the Interface	128
Mobile Pattern #4: Use Uniquely Mobile Input Mechanisms	134
Mobile Pattern #5: Say Good-Bye to Done	138
Summary	141

SECTION THREE: CRAFTING MOBILE EXPERIENCES

CHAPTER 6

Mobile Prototyping
Tools and Methods for Designing Mobile Experiences   **143**

The Design Process	145
Prototyping	147
Genres of Mobile Prototyping	151
Tactical Prototyping	153
Experiential Prototyping	162
Three Prototyping Truisms	172
Summary	175
Expert Interview: Julian Bleecker	176

CHAPTER 7

Motion and Animation

A New Mobile UX Design Material — **181**

Principle 1: Squash and Stretch — 184

Principle 2: Anticipation — 186

Principle 3: Staging — 187

Principle 4: Straight Ahead and Pose to Pose — 188

Principle 5: Follow-Through and Overlapping Action — 190

Principle 6: Slow In and Out — 191

Principle 7: Arcs — 193

Principle 8: Secondary Action — 194

Principle 9: Timing — 195

Principle 10: Exaggeration — 196

Principles 11 and 12: Solid Drawing and Appeal — 198

Methods for Specifying Motion in Your Work — 198

Summary — 201

CHAPTER 8

Awakening the Senses

Touch, Gesture, Voice, and Sound — **203**

Touch — 205

Gestures: Let's Get Physical! — 215

Voice and Sound — 226

Swing for the Fences When Thinking about
  the Senses — 232

Summary — 233

SECTION FOUR: THE FUTURE OF MOBILE UX

CHAPTER 9

New Mobile Forms
Pioneering the Mobile Frontier   **235**

The Shifting Boundary Between Computers and
the Human Body   237

The Shifting Boundary Between Computers and
the Environment   239

Mobiles and Emerging Markets   242

Pioneering the Mobile Frontier   247

Index   249

Figure Credits   261

Acknowledgments   262

About the Author   264

FOREWORD

So here's a little fact that feels surprising: Today on our small blue planet, more people have access to cell phones than to working plumbing. Think about that. Primitive plumbing has been around for over a thousand years. Modern working plumbing has been around for at least 200 years longer than the fleeting few years since 1984 when Motorola first ripped the phone off the wall and allowed us to carry it around.

Most people find plumbing useful. Apparently, many millions more find cellular phones indispensible. Whenever big parts of modern life—the Internet, video games, search engines, smartphones, iPads, social networking systems, digital wallet payment systems—are so useful that we can no longer imagine life without them, we act as if they will forever be the way they are now. This childlike instinct has its charms, but it is always wrong and particularly dangerous for designers. People who think deeply about the built world necessarily must view it as fungible, not fixed. It is the job of thoughtful designers to notice the petty annoyances that accumulate when we use even devices we love—to stand in the future and think of ways to make it more elegantly functional, less intrusive, more natural, far more compelling. In the best such cases, designers need to surprise us—by radically altering what we think is possible. To create the futures we cannot even yet imagine.

But the future is a scary place replete with endless options, endless unknowns. Of course, like everyone else, designers don't have a crystal ball. There is a constant risk that we will make assumptions that turn out to be either too bold or too timid. Designers must rely instead on methods to think through which evolutionary and revolutionary shifts are most likely—among an infinite array of possibilities.

In *The Mobile Frontier,* Rachel Hinman has tackled one of the most vital issues in the future of design: *How will our lives change while we are on the go?* She has used her vast prior experience in working to shape the future for Nokia, then added disciplined methods to do us four vital favors:

Reveal the structures of current and coming mobile interfaces...

Just as cars have gone through several design eras (remember tailfins?), *The Mobile Frontier* has clarified four waves of successive strategies that make a device successively easier and more pleasant to use. Whether you are a designer or simply an enthusiast, this is a revelation. It shows how the metaphors and strategies for how to use a device evolve as there is more processing power, memory, and display capabilities available to make a device better behaved.

Uncover patterns in how we behave when we are mobile...

When you observe people deeply enough, you discover something fundamental. While there are an infinite number of things people theoretically might do with mobile devices, inevitably the real activities we choose to do can be distilled into clear patterns with a few themes and variations. *The Mobile Frontier* has made these clear, so that the challenge of thinking about mobility becomes vastly more interesting, more tractable, and far easier to either improve or reinvent.

Provide strategies for designing better mobile experiences...

Whenever we want to improve or reinvent a category, there are some methods that are better than others. *The Mobile Frontier* helps lay out active design and prototyping strategies that make the otherwise daunting task of building new interface alternatives likely to succeed instead of fail. This allows designers to proceed with courage and confidence, knowing they can reliably imagine, develop, and test alternative interfaces, in order to get the future to show up ahead of its regularly scheduled arrival.

Speculate about what will come next...

Finally, *The Mobile Frontier* bravely peers down a foggy windy road to guess what lies around the corner. This is a task always doomed to failure in detail, but Rachel does a brilliant job of giving us the broad outlines. This is essential for helping us get past the trap of merely filigreeing around the edges of the known, to instead imagine the breakthroughs still to come.

Collectively, these four deep insights advance the known boundaries of understanding today's mobile devices and experiences. Thus, they help usher in the vastly new ones sure to emerge soon. Here's why that matters: We are only three decades into one of the most important revolutions the world has ever seen. In design development terms, that is a mere blink. Just as the mobile device world has zipped past plumbing like a rocket sled would pass a slug, we simply must see ourselves at the very beginning of this revolution. With mobile devices, we are today where automobiles were when the Model T was the hottest thing on wheels. We will see vastly more change than most of us can possibly imagine. Through our mobile devices, we will find new advances in learning, security, community, interaction, understanding, commerce, communication, and exploration.

Rachel Hinman is helping us make all that come along a little sooner, a lot easier, and far more reliably. See for yourself. Better yet, join in. Get a move on. *Oh, and bring your devices. Let's make 'em more amazing.*

—Larry Keeley
President and Co-Founder, Doblin, Inc.

CHAPTER 1

Casting Off Anchors
Preparing to Explore the Mobile Frontier

The Golden Age of Mobile   4

Casting Off Anchors from the Past   6

Section One: What Makes Mobile Different?   8

Section Two: Emergent Mobile Patterns   8

Section Three: Crafting Mobile Experiences   8

Section Four: The Future of Mobile UX   9

Excerpt: *The Mobile Sinners*   10

Whenever I think of mobile user experience, I think of frontiers rather than the latest mobile app, the hottest mobile operating system, or debates over mobile apps versus mobile Web. Instead, for me, images of astronauts exploring lunar landscapes or the brave pioneers who settled the Wild West come to mind. Much like outer space or the western half of the U.S., I picture the mobile design space as a frontier that people can explore and invent new and more human ways for people to interact with information.

By definition, a *frontier* is simply the term used to describe the land that lies beyond a settled geographic region. Unlike similar words such as *wilderness*, *sticks*, or *outback*, the term *frontier* is subtly but significantly different in that it conjures up romantic notions that have long held the human imagination. A frontier represents more than a piece of land—it's a word that symbolizes optimism, unlimited opportunity, and the shedding of current restraints. Frontiers inspire in us the sense that anything is possible.

In reality, thinking of the mobile user experience as an unsettled frontier is a romantic notion that at times can be difficult to sustain. Instead of an idyllic landscape of unfettered land, today the mobile industry looks a lot more like Figure 1.1.

FIGURE 1.1
Iconic image of the Oklahoma Land Rush of 1889.

On April 22 of 1889, an estimated 50,000 people lined up on the edge of an unsettled frontier in the United States to participate in a land run, later known as the Oklahoma Land Rush. On that day, the two million-acre restricted frontier known as the *Unassigned Lands* was opened for settlement by the U.S. government. In essence, the government gave away the land for free; all that settlers had to do was grab it. So picture 50,000 men and women mounted on their horses waiting for hours for a symbolic gunshot to be fired. Once that shot was fired, the race was on. They were free to claim their land. I've long loved this image because it captures what I imagine those settlers felt on that day—the frenetic energy of unbounded optimism.

Right now, the mobile industry feels a lot like this picture. Just like the Unassigned Lands, the mobile industry is a frontier that people want to talk about, hear about, speculate about, and grab a piece of for their very own. Mobile feels like an unsettled landscape that is there for the grabbing.

The design and user experience community is not immune to this sense of boundless opportunity. Everyone wants to get in on the action! Designers and user experience (UX) professionals are clamoring to get up to speed on designing for the latest mobile operating systems, while technologists fight holy wars over which mobile OS is superior. Philosophical debates rage over which design approach is superior: mobile Web sites or native applications. When it comes to mobile user experience, the design and UX community feels a lot like that picture: Mobile is where the action is.

Maybe you've been swept up in that energy already. Perhaps you picked up this book because you're simply chomping at the bit to build a mobile application. Or maybe you hope this book will tell you how to tailor your existing Web site to a mobile device. Yes, this book will offer some insight into how to do those things, but there are other things I think you need to know first. It's easy to get caught up in the mobile land rush and reduce the mobile experience to a new method or tool you need to learn or a technical platform you need to get up to speed on. Allowing the hype to reduce the mobile experience to just one of these areas puts you at risk for losing sight of quite possibly the most important and exciting part of what's currently happening.

Those simple mobile devices you hold in the palm of your hand are offering a new way to think about computing. Unfettered from the keyboard and mouse, mobile devices give you the opportunity to invent new and more human ways for people to interact with information, and with each other.

You may wonder, "Why now? Mobile phones have been around for a long time. Why has mobile become this frontier of opportunity now?"

For what felt like the longest time, mobile UX was considered to be a small and obscure design space that most designers felt obliged to learn more about but loathed participating in because of all the inherent design constraints. Widespread adoption of new and more intuitive mobile devices has changed all that. Now, as increasingly more people are experiencing what it's like to access and interact with information from nearly anywhere, mobile is no longer a niche topic. There's never been a better time to design mobile experiences.

The Golden Age of Mobile

When I began working in the mobile industry seven years ago, mobile experiences truly stunk (as evidenced by Figure 1.2). At that time, a common industry credo was the more features, the better. Subsequently, mobile user experiences were abysmal. They were bloated with features, their user interfaces were confusing and unintuitive, and most users struggled to figure out how to make a simple voice call. There was no joy of use for mobile phones in those days. It was the age of the "Frankenphone." Device experiences were truly miserable

FIGURE 1.2
Before the iPhone was the age of the Frankenphone. Mobile phones were so bloated with features that users struggled to figure how to make a simple voice call.

But one little product changed all that. That product was the iPhone.

Steve Jobs, then CEO of Apple, Inc., unveiled the iPhone, as seen in Figure 1.3, to the public on January 9, 2007. The phone was not available in the United States until June of that same year. Throughout the United States, thousands of customers lined up outside Apple stores waiting to purchase the device, as shown in Figure 1.4. It was something the mobile industry had never seen before.

FIGURE 1.3
The passionate reaction to the launch of the iPhone resulted in sections of the media christening it the "Jesus phone."

FIGURE 1.4
People in New York City waiting in line for the first iPhone in 2007.

Unlike its predecessors with bloated feature sets, the iPhone was a mobile device with a simplified bundle of truly useful applications. Instead of confusing hard keys and buttons, the iPhone had a seductive touchscreen paired with a visually elegant and intuitive interface. Not only was the iPhone a gorgeous product, but it also had something previous mobile devices did not have: The iPhone had a great user experience. The iPhone demonstrated to the mobile industry and the world what was possible when innovative mobile technology was paired with a stellar user experience. The iPhone was more than an innovative product; it was the first mobile device that got people—regular, everyday people (not just the geeks)—excited about using a mobile phone. The iPhone grew to symbolize the shedding of current restraints, newfound innovation, and a sense of unlimited opportunity in the mobile industry.

Much has happened since the iPhone's release in 2007. Unlike other industries that are shrinking or flat, the mobile industry has experienced explosive growth and interest. There are now a plethora of tools and resources available that make it relatively easy for people from almost any walk of life to develop mobile applications. From tiny devices worn on the body to tablet-sized devices such as the iPad, people are pushing the boundaries of scale and form, constantly challenging what constitutes a mobile device. Since the iPhone was released, touchscreens on smartphones have become standard, clearing the path for designers to direct their creative energies toward developing new and emergent interface paradigms.

Unlike the Frankenphone days when little to no attention was paid to user experience, people now care and even talk about mobile user experience and its importance. Basically, the iPhone ushered in the golden age of mobile, when almost anything seems possible. The mobile space has entered into a new era of fast-moving innovation, investment, and creativity. There has never been a better time to begin exploring this new and exciting design space.

The iPhone is the product that opened up the mobile frontier for the rest of us.

Casting Off Anchors from the Past

Humans have two legs, making us inherently mobile beings. Yet for the past 50 years we've settled into a computing landscape that assumes a static context of use. While the wildly successful desktop paradigm enabled more people to interact with computers than its predecessors, it came with its own set of limitations. For example, countless design details—from input mechanisms and device form factors to assumptions about user engagement and interface design—have been made with a common and unfortunate assumption: That users have their butts in chairs and their eyes glued to computer screens. For all its success, the desktop paradigm was never designed to accommodate our pesky human desire to move and roam around the world. Mobility, which involves the ability to compute in mobile contexts, is an inherent human need that has been largely unaddressed for a very long time.

Mobility is an exciting concept, but busting out of this current desktop computing landscape isn't as easy as it may sound. Like any frontier pioneered and settled before, the land of desktop computing has some advantages that are difficult to leave behind. Widespread acceptance and understanding of the paradigm, common and well-documented UI conventions, standard input mechanisms, or the vast bodies of academic research and design heuristics—those benefits of the desktop computing world don't exist for mobile yet. Instead, mobile user experience is a nascent and largely unexplored field. Participation requires designers to explore a largely unsettled frontier with few familiar guideposts. It requires the casting off of many anchors and conventions we've inherited from the past 50 years of computer science and traditional design.

So why do it? Why leave all this established stuff behind and risk it? Much like the lure of creating a new life in the western frontier or discovering new worlds in deep space, humans have an uncanny drive to discover new ways of doing things. Mobile user experience is no exception. Mobile experiences offer the opportunity to break free of the current constraints of the desktop paradigm and define a new way to experience information. These experiences provide an opportunity to acknowledge and accommodate the human desire to physically move. Instead of being trapped behind a desk, mobile devices give people the ability to compute while participating in the world around them.

The only way to truly recognize this opportunity is to take a journey into the mobile frontier. And that is why I wrote this book. It's a guidebook that will help you explore the mobile frontier that lies ahead.

As with any journey, there are some things you need to know before you begin. I've organized this book into four sections.

Section One: What Makes Mobile Different?

Like a cultural book you buy before visiting a foreign country, the first section of this book will introduce you to the key cultural dimensions that define mobile user experiences. Chapter 2, "The Emergent Mobile NUI Paradigm," Chapter 3, "Peanut Butter in Denver," and Chapter 4,

"Shapeshifting," are dedicated to providing you with information on what makes mobile user experience and design different than other design spaces and include the following:

- Information about the NUI mobile paradigm
- Tips for how to design for the mobile context
- Emergent patterns for multidevice experiences

Section Two: Emergent Mobile Patterns

Similar to the first pioneers who began to settle a frontier, Chapter 5, "Mobile UX Patterns: Designing for Mobility," will give you insight into what people who have begun to settle the mobile frontier are currently doing. This section will discuss five emergent mobile UX patterns you can lean on as you begin to craft your own mobile experience:

- Coverage of the two natural set points for mobile experiences
- A set of emerging application types
- How to make content become the interface
- Information on uniquely mobile input mechanisms
- Tips for how to leave tasks behind and say "goodbye to done"

Section Three: Crafting Mobile Experiences

Section three of this book will cover the "stuff to see" and "things to do" part of this guidebook. The three chapters (Chapter 6, "Mobile Prototyping," Chapter 7, "Motion and Animation," and Chapter 8, "Awakening the Senses") will give you design exercises, prototyping methods, and design guidelines to try once you begin crafting mobile experiences, and cover the following topics:

- Information on how to leverage senses other than sight when creating mobile experiences
- Tactical and experiential prototyping tools and methods
- A set of animation principles that will help breathe life into your mobile design work

Section Four: The Future of Mobile UX

Finally, Chapter 9, "New Mobile Forms," is all about the edge of the mobile frontier. It's the "deep space" stuff that a few brave souls have already begun to explore and pioneer. It's the stuff that will likely become our future very soon, as shown by these areas:

- Information about the shifting boundary between computers and the body

- Information about the shifting boundary between computers and the environment

- Mobile experiences for emerging markets

So throw on your space suit or circle your wagons (whichever frontier exploration metaphor you identify with most), because the mobile frontier awaits.

The Mobile Sinners

Excerpt from science fiction writer and author of the seminal design book, Shaping Things, *Bruce Sterling, who is seen addressing the crowd at a Mobile Monday in Amsterdam in 2008 (Figure 1.5).*

The rapid development of cell phones is killing early cell phones much faster than it's killing any of the early, older legacy technologies.

I think that is a real principle…something you have to understand if you're going to be in this line of work. It's very romantic. It's very fast moving.

You are building dead lumps of plastic.

When people come out and they show you an iPhone, or an Android, they are showing you larval versions of something much more sophisticated. Both those devices are going to be dead. Deader than hammers, deader than anvils. You can use a hammer and an anvil; those two devices will have no use.

The world you are building right now is the ground floor for something much larger—and the soil beneath that ground floor is violently unstable.

You're really like people building on Vesuvius.

FIGURE 1.5
Bruce Sterling, science fiction writer and author of the seminal design book, *Shaping Things.*

These things you are putting into people's hands—they are not phones. I want you to stop talking about that. You're putting banks into people's hands. You're putting health clinics into people's purses. You're putting consumer encyclopedias onto everything that has a bar code.

That is not a phone…even with an "i" in front of it. That's not what you are doing. You're allowing people—even small children—never to get lost again. Ever. That's a transformed society.

And what will be built on top of that is much weirder than the transformation you are forcing onto other people right now.

If you live close to the volcano, I want you to think hard about the values you want to save and stop worrying about the plastic ware.

CHAPTER 2

The Emergent Mobile NUI Paradigm

Traversing the GUI/NUI Chasm

The Emergent Mobile Paradigm   13
A Paradigm Shift Is Underway   14
The Evolution of User Interfaces   19
The Emergent Mobile NUI Paradigm   23
Past and Present Computing Paradigms   28
Future Computing Paradigms   30
Summary   33
Expert Interview: Mike Kruzeniski   34

I have long had a love–hate relationship with the 38 Geary bus in San Francisco. Every ride is an uncensored snapshot into the underbelly of humanity. Crowded, smelly, and always driven by a seriously pissed-off Muni driver, it's the only public transportation option to downtown San Francisco from my old neighborhood, the Outer Richmond.

While the 38 Geary has been the backdrop for some of my most interesting urban stories, I'll remain forever in debt to that bus line for the observational fodder of mobile technology use it has provided.

Nothing will drive people into the world of their mobile devices faster than a stinky, slow-moving, and insanely crowded bus. Just like Alice falling into that rabbit hole to escape the injustices of her life, it was my daily rides to work on the 38 Geary that made me realize mobile phones aren't just communication devices, they're portals into another world. They are a tiny world that people can escape into until they reach their destination (see Figure 2.1).

FIGURE 2.1
People are physically on the bus; mentally they are in the world of their mobile devices.

After all, why put up with the awkward experience of listening to some drunken passenger recite his personal manifesto when you can escape into the sonic world of your latest playlist? Or how about avoiding a socially awkward conversation with the crazy person sitting next to you by melting into the world of the Internet through your mobile device's browser. And it's easy to ignore getting repeatedly bonked on the head by handbags and backpacks of fellow passengers if you are enmeshed in your phone's email inbox.

It was my daily commute on the 38 Geary that made me realize mobile devices are little worlds unto themselves. Every day I would observe how my fellow passengers were physically on the bus with me but mentally in the world of their mobile phone.

They were in another paradigm. And so was I.

The Emergent Mobile Paradigm

Paradigms are conceptual frameworks. They offer a way of seeing the world and all the implications that come with it. They are foundational points of view that profoundly shape how we perceive and interact with the world. There are social paradigms, like two-parent families; religious paradigms, like Christianity; and computing paradigms, like the mainframe or desktop. Paradigms create patterns, and humans instinctively rely on paradigms to make sense of their world, relate to each other, and solve problems.

Paradigms in and of themselves can be lofty, abstract, and difficult to pin down precisely. It's the implications of a paradigm that are the salient things we can touch, feel, and experience. Implications are the roles, rules, tools, expectations, assumptions, metaphors, and behaviors that reflect a paradigm in real life. Take, for example, Wonderland—the setting for Lewis Carroll's *Alice in Wonderland*, which depicted an alternate paradigm with its own set of roles, rules, behaviors, and assumptions (see Figure 2.2). Implications aren't abstract—they have form and substance, or they can be experienced—and are therefore the things we can design.

FIGURE 2.2
Wonderland, the setting of Lewis Carroll's children's novel *Alice in Wonderland*, is an alternate paradigm—a world where playing cards are animated and animals can talk.

The concept of paradigms, and more specifically the concept of shifting paradigms, is the first topic to be covered in this book because we are currently in the midst of a computing paradigm shift. From headlines like, "The PC is Dead" and "The Dawn of the Post PC Era" in major news publications, to the predictions of business analysts and academics, a clear and consistent signal is coming through: The desktop computing paradigm is losing its dominance. While we can recognize and celebrate the contribution this once groundbreaking paradigm offered, it's undeniable that a new computing paradigm is emerging. It's a paradigm that allows us to interact with information from anywhere. It enables us to use senses other than sight to navigate and interact with information. And it's a paradigm that will likely supplant the desktop paradigm in the coming decade.

It *is* the emergent mobile paradigm.

A Paradigm Shift Is Underway

Canadian media philosopher Marshall Mcluhan famously said, "We shape our tools, thereafter our tools shape us." Like culture, media, and art, computing paradigms reflect the things that society cares about. There is meaning embedded in form, and let's face it, there were a lot of expectations and assumptions embedded in the desktop paradigm. While some of these expectations and assumptions helped make the paradigm successful, that same paradigm also constrained our expectations and the role that computers have had in our lives.

The desktop paradigm is a classic example of a benefit married with constraint. The benefit of the desktop paradigm was that it mapped the computing experience to objects and experiences in the real world. Unlike the previous command-line interface, which used abstraction and language, the desktop paradigm's graphical user interface mirrored office experiences by allowing users to create "documents" that could be stored in "folders" or thrown away in the "trash." These design decisions made the computing experience more intuitive for a wider audience of users. However, it decidedly constrained our thinking about the role computers can have in our lives. In fact, it has caused people to automatically associate computing with "work" (see Figure 2.3).

Notions of computing have grown far beyond the confines of "the office." Computers have deeply infiltrated our daily lives. They are in our homes, our schools, and our cars. Computers have replaced scrapbooks and photo albums and now serve as the de facto storage for our digital photos. Computers have made physical CD and record collections obsolete and made it possible to buy individual songs instead of complete albums. Computers have become our go-to solution for bouts of boredom, providing us with hours of digital games, Web surfing, and even television shows and movies. Online media have threatened the very existence of their analog equivalents. Products like the Amazon Kindle and iPad's iBooks have been positioned to challenge printed books. All these examples point to a clear pattern: The computer has grown beyond the confines of the desktop paradigm (see Figures 2.4–2.7). Our expectations are changing about the role that computers can have in our lives. It's only natural that the paradigm that supports computing will change as well.

FIGURE 2.3
While the desktop computing paradigm made it easier for users to engage with computers, it also constrained the role that computers can have in our lives.

FIGURES 2.4–2.7
Products like the iPod, coupled with services like iTunes, have made CD collections obsolete. E-readers such as the Amazon Kindle are challenging paper books and fundamentally changing the reading experience.

Paradigm shifts happen when enough people recognize that the underlying values, beliefs, and ideas that any given paradigm supports should be changed or are no longer valid. While GUI, WYSIWYG (what you see is what you get), files, hierarchical storage, and the very metaphor of a desktop were brilliant inventions, they were created before the PC was ubiquitous, email was essentially universal, and the World Wide Web became commonplace. Clear and compelling evidence indicates that the static computing paradigm is reaching (or has reached) the end of its shelf life.

Free from folders, files, and keyboards, a new paradigm is emerging that allows users to access information seamlessly from anywhere.

It *is* the new mobile paradigm.

Widespread Adoption of Mobile Devices

In recent years, mobile devices have taken the world by storm. CCS Insight reported in 2010 that there were more than five billion mobile phone connections worldwide. A billion of anything is difficult to visualize, but to put these numbers into perspective, the statistic of five billion phones means that in 2010 there were more than three times as many phones as personal computers in the world. Analysts at Wireless Intelligence predict that we will have six billion connections worldwide by the middle of 2012. While the market for personal computers continues to grow, mobile phone sales and mobile data usage is outgrowing their PC equivalents nearly 3 to 1.

FIGURE 2.8
The DynaTAC 8000X was the first mobile phone that could connect to the telephone network without a mobile operator and could be carried by the user.

Explosive growth isn't the only thing happening in the mobile landscape. Mobile phones have come a long way since the first Motorola DynaTAC was released in 1984 (see Figure 2.8). Gone are the days when mobile phones were solely used to make voice calls. People now are using mobile devices to crowd-source information about political upheaval and natural disasters. Mobile phones are allowing people to stuff an encyclopedia's worth of information inside anything with a bar code. Mobile money services are virtually putting banks into people's hands. GPS functionality, embedded in almost every smartphone manufactured today, will eventually make it so that people—even small children—will never get lost again. Mobile phones aren't really phones anymore. They are fast becoming the primary way that people interact with information.

In light of all the statistical data and anecdotal evidence, it may be difficult to believe that anything is limiting the potential of mobile technology. But there is one limiting factor: It's our fixation with the desktop paradigm and its graphical user interface.

Reaching the Edge of What GUIs Can Do

The graphical user interface (GUI), also first developed at PARC, was instrumental in the widespread success of the desktop paradigm. In its day, GUI provided something truly new to users—the ability to interact with a computer through means other than text. The Apple Macintosh, released in 1984, was the first commercially successful product to use a GUI. It created a virtual world for information to live in and be interacted with, including a visual interface and interaction language that represented information as objects with physicality and rules of physics that mirrored the real world. Graphical user interfaces initially and aptly reinforced the desktop metaphor: files and documents would sit on top of a computer desktop just like pieces of paper that sit on desktops in the real world.

Since 1984, GUIs have dominated the technology landscape. Our experiences with computers, netbooks, PDAs, mobile phones, and even navigation systems in cars have been defined by the principles of graphical user interfaces. Documents have morphed into Web pages, reinforcing GUI notions of containment and space. We continue to depend on the GUI visual language of iconography and beveled buttons and controls as cues for interaction. And even though the metaphor becomes brittle on small devices, we continue to rely on GUI's folders and files as the default organizing principle for information. GUI isn't just second nature; it's become an entrenched way of thinking about digital experiences.

The desktop paradigm has become so entrenched in how we think about computing that many designers and users aren't even conscious of it. In fact, it's so engrained in how we conduct our daily lives that it's difficult for some people to even bring new technology into their lives. This recently became very clear to me while conducting a research study on tablet usage.

During the study, I spoke with 18 iPad owners with the goal of understanding how regular people were using this new, innovative tablet computer. One particular participant, Kyle, was able to articulate the "engrained thought process" of the PC paradigm succinctly. During the interview, he shared how he had eagerly waited in line at the Apple store to purchase the first release of the iPad and how, over a year later, he was still thrilled with his purchase. During his last semester of college, he shared how he had "trained" himself to use his iPad as his primary portable computer. He then explained how it was a "personal test" to see if he could "wean" himself off using a laptop. "Trained" and "weaned" were interesting word choices, so I asked Kyle to elaborate. To which he replied:

"…well, you see, that laptop is portable. But an iPad…an iPad is mobile. Laptops and iPads are similar, but there are important differences, and you have to train your mind to think about them differently.

I think people are attached to the idea of laptops. They want the "feeling" of a computer because it's familiar and makes them feel at home and like they know what something is. With the iPad…it's a totally new device that people are going to use differently. Even though there were touchscreens out there before the iPad, this was actually the first time I used a touchscreen this big. So to me it's a totally new device. It's a truly mobile computer. It's like you have to train your mind to think of it differently."

While some participants in our study seemed haunted by the memory of laptops past, Kyle was the first person who seemed to best articulate the subtle yet significant difference between laptops and tablet computers. While current tablets feel almost tailored for content consumption (reading email, watching Netflix, browsing the Web), I believe the more significant role they are serving is to introduce people to the possibilities of mobile computing: To wean us off a paradigm we know and love (the PC) and introduce us to a new one…a mobile one. For all its strengths, the desktop paradigm is a static one, and the world is longing for a mobile paradigm. We've reached the edges of what GUI can do (see Figure 2.9).

FIGURE 2.9
Many graphical user interfaces, like the Microsoft Word UI shown here, have become bloated and difficult to use. With all the features displayed, there's hardly any room left to just type! We've reached the edge of what GUIs can do.

If we've reached the edges of what GUIs can do, what's next for UI design? What does the future hold and what will be mobile's role? Looking to the past often gives insight into how the future will unfold.

The Evolution of User Interfaces

Just as it's believed that animals and humans evolved from cells in some primordial soup, the characteristics of interfaces have evolved by building on what came before while simultaneously offering higher levels of sophistication.

Evolution is a natural process for any kind of human expression. The history of art, for example, did not radically change from one period to the next, but rather evolved slowly. Art started out very primitive—flat and lacking dimension, like paintings from the medieval period (see Figure 2.10). Then art evolved into depictions of form that closely mirrored how humans perceive it, such as paintings from the Renaissance period (see Figure 2.11). Later, artists turned to emotional representations, like the ones found in the Impressionist period. Then artwork became abstract and conceptual, like modern Abstract Expressionism. The development of a child's drawing skills often recapitulates the history of art.

FIGURES 2.10 AND 2.11
Medieval art was highly symbolic and lacked dimensionality. In contrast, Renaissance art celebrated depicting form in a way that closely mirrored how humans perceive it.

If we look to examples of human expression, like art history or children's artwork as precursors, we can trace the history of computing and interface paradigms and identify how they have evolved in order to predict how interfaces will evolve in the years to come.

In 2008, I attended a conference in which Dennis Wixon, a research manager for Microsoft Surface, presented a talk entitled "A Brave NUI World" (he's the co-author of a book with the same title). In the talk, Dennis spoke at length about natural user interface (NUI) design principles (see Figure 2.12). However, the part of his talk that was most interesting to me was how he framed the presentation from a historical perspective. He explained how NUIs are a natural evolution of the interface paradigms that preceded them. Dennis explained that looking to the past can help us predict what the future has in store.

According to Dennis, the past, present, and future of interface paradigms and their characteristics look something like this:

- Command line interfaces

- Graphical user interfaces

- Natural user interfaces

- Organic user interfaces

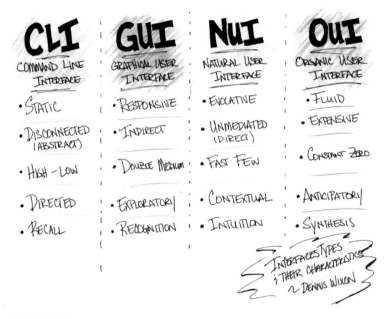

FIGURE 2.12
Sketch note of talk given by Dennis Wixon tracking the evolution of interfaces: interface types and their characteristics.

Command Line Interfaces

Command line interfaces (CLI) are primarily text-based interfaces built around the psychological function of recall (see Figure 2.13). Users must remember commands and use the text-based interface to enter commands in order to direct the computer's functionality. The experience of using CLIs can feel disconnected and abstract. Commands such as *start, show, copy,* and *rename* create a high–low interaction experience for users: CLIs have a high number of commands, but a low number of ways to interact with the system. CLIs reflect ideas and attributes of ancient Greek Classicism by creating a static paradigm built on the premise of classification.

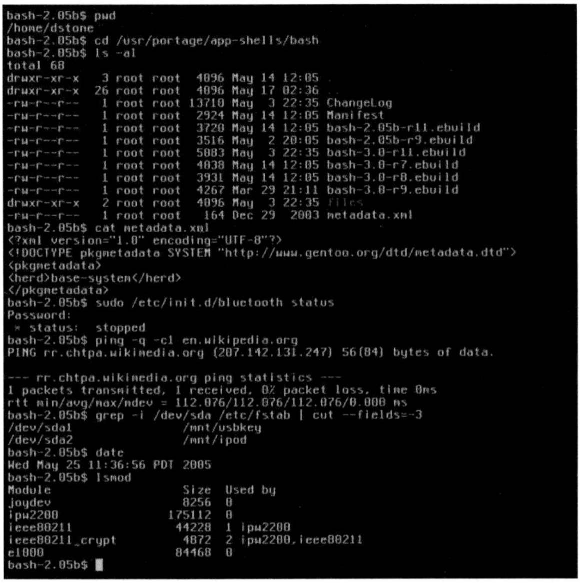

FIGURE 2.13
The UNIX Shell, still used today, is an example of a command line interface.

Graphical User Interfaces

Unlike command line interfaces that are primarily text-based, graphical user interfaces (GUIs) use graphics to represent information objects (see Figure 2.14). GUIs are built around the psychological function of recognition: Users can pull down a menu and "recognize" items in that menu. Instead of remembering system commands from CLIs, GUI users are able to explore what the computing system offers. Design principles like WYSIWYG (what you see is what you get) allow users to see all their options through icons, floating tool palettes, and pull-down menus. This results in a double medium interaction experience for users.

GUI systems have a high number of available commands. This system is complemented by indirect responsive interactions through a mouse and keyboard. Unlike the classification of CLIs, graphical user interfaces reflect ideas and attributes of Newtonian science by focusing on how things are constructed and work, and by relying on the principles that all things are positioned in absolute time and space with absolute qualities.

FIGURE 2.14
Early personal computers for both Mac and Windows used graphical interfaces.

Natural User Interfaces

Building on the GUI notion that a graphic or an icon represents an information object, natural user interfaces (NUIs) depict information as objects in space. NUIs leverage human intuition; instead of what you see is what you get, NUIs rely on our innate sense of the physical world where what you *do* is what you *get*. Unlike GUIs that reflect the notion that objects are positioned in absolute time and space with absolute qualities,

FIGURE 2.15
Microsoft's Surface Table is an example of a natural user interface.

natural user interfaces are highly contextual. NUI systems understand and are responsive to the environments in which they are located. NUI interactions are fast and few, and are based on the natural properties of the object and how you would expect those objects to behave. Because of touchscreens, interactions are unmediated, allowing users to interact with information in a direct and natural way (see Figure 2.15). NUI systems are based on principles of contextualism, where there are no absolutes. Instead, events are analyzed in context and interpreted according to a frame of reference.

Organic User Interfaces

User interface experts like Dennis Wixon predict that organic user interfaces (OUIs) will supersede NUIs. Organic user interfaces use the metaphor of an organic system: Everything is interconnected and fluid. Instead of form following function, form follows flow. Organic user interfaces negotiate user actions based on context. Unlike GUIs, where the mouse and keyboard input actions for the user and there is a clear division of input/output, with OUIs, input will equal output (see Figure 2.16). OUIs will use nonplanar objects to both input and output actions onto the same object. With OUIs, function will equal form. Interactions will be seamless because the form of an object clearly will determine its ability to be used as an input, providing users with fluid interactions.

FIGURE 2.16
Credit-card mock-up with organic user interface on a bendable display.

The Emergent Mobile NUI Paradigm

In January of 2007, a product was released that would mark the beginning of a transformative trend in both computing and user interface paradigms. The iPhone, with its responsive multi-touchscreen, intuitive UI, and gestural interface became the first commercially successful consumer electronic device that gave people a taste of a new type of interface— the natural user interface (see Figure 2.17). Suddenly people could interact directly with information through a touchscreen instead of a keyboard and mouse. Instead of endless lists and pull-down menus, applications were streamlined and felt more intuitive. With features like zoom and pinch, the iPhone's UI expressed almost supernatural characteristics. Rather than being chained to a static and bulky computer workstation, users could easily compute while on the go. The iPhone marked the beginning of an important moment: The rise of the mobile computing paradigm and the natural user interface.

Just like the Apple Macintosh computer released in 1984 ushered in the age of the graphical user interface, Apple's iPhone was an iconic product

FIGURE 2.17
The iPhone was the first device that gave a large-scale consumer audience the opportunity to experience the magic of natural user interfaces firsthand.

that served as an indicator of the natural evolution of the next wave of user interfaces. The fast and steady uptake of touchscreen devices in all shapes and sizes since 2007 indicates a fundamental change is afoot. We've reached the edges of what graphical user interfaces can do. A natural evolution has started, and GUIs will be supplanted by NUIs in the foreseeable future.

Stuck in the GUI/NUI Chasm

Although the desktop computing model still dominates the computing landscape, rapid and widespread uptake of mobile devices and touchscreen tablets are indicators that a mobile UI paradigm shift is currently underway. In the U.S. alone, researchers have predicted that tablets with touchscreen interfaces will grow 400% in 2012. They also predict that by 2014, 20% of the U.S. population will use touchscreens with natural user interfaces as their primary computing device. Once the preserve of high-end mobile devices, touchscreen devices with NUI interfaces are becoming standard for even affordable, midrange mobile phones. Users are enchanted by the intuitive experiences that touch interfaces enable. NUIs are hard for users to resist. Their growth is inevitable.

While NUI domination may seem inevitable, today we are situated in a strange GUI/NUI chasm. While there are similarities and overlap between graphical user interfaces and natural user interfaces, there are obvious differences in the characteristics and design principles of each. What makes a GUI experience successful is very different from the attributes that make a NUI experience successful. This is where much of the design confusion comes into play for both designers of NUIs and users of NUIs. We're still stuck in a valley between the two paradigms. Just as we look back today on the first GUIs with nostalgia for their simplicity, the NUI interfaces we see today in mobile devices and tablets are larval examples of what NUIs will grow to become. NUIs are still new—the design details and conventions are still being figured out by people just like you.

Mastering NUI Fundamentals

Mobile experiences are a good place for designers to start if they are keen on getting a better understanding of how to craft compelling NUI experiences. Since designers and user-experience professionals have spent the lion's share of their careers creating experiences built on GUI principles, NUIs are a new paradigm that will require some learning. Understanding the fundamental difference between the two types of interfaces and learning how to optimize for touch can be challenging since the tenets of the graphical user interface are likely ingrained into our instincts and behaviors. However, feeling comfortable with NUIs is an important skill to hone as you begin to explore the mobile frontier. The following are the eight basic design principles any successful NUI experiences should reflect.

Eight Principles of Natural User Interfaces

1. Principle of Performance Aesthetics

Unlike GUI experiences that focus on and celebrate accomplishment and task completion, NUI experiences focus on the joy of doing. NUI experiences should be like an ocean voyage; the pleasure comes from the interaction, not the accomplishment, as shown in Figure 2.18.

2. Principle of Direct Manipulation

Unlike GUI interfaces, which are enabled by indirect manipulation through a keyboard and mouse, natural user interfaces enable users to interact directly with information objects (see Figure 2.19). Touchscreens and gestural interaction functionality enable users to feel as if they are physically touching and manipulating information with their fingertips. Instead of *what you see is what you get* (WYSIWIG), successful NUI interfaces embody the principle of *what you do is what you get*.

3. Principle of Scaffolding

Successful natural user interfaces feel intuitive and joyful to use. Information objects in a NUI behave in a manner that users intuitively expect. Unlike a successful GUI in which many options and commands are presented all at once and are depicted with very subtle hierarchy and visual emphasis, a successful NUI contains fewer options with interaction scaffolding. Scaffolding is a strong cue or guide that sets users' expectations by giving them an indication of how the interaction will unfold (see Figure 2.20).

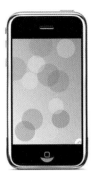

FIGURE 2.18
Part instrument, part composition, and part artwork, the iPhone application Bloom enables users to create elaborate patterns and unique melodies by simply tapping on the screen.

FIGURE 2.19
The scrolling gesture is an example of the principle of direct manipulation.

FIGURE 2.20
The graphics that surround objects as they are placed on a Surface table are an example of scaffolding. They are a strong visual cue that gives users an indication of how the experience will unfold.

Good NUIs support users as they engage with the system and unfold or reveal themselves through actions in a natural fashion.

4. Principle of Contextual Environments

One of the great things about natural user interfaces is that they are dynamic and can locate themselves in space and time. Unlike GUIs that will present a user with the same set of options regardless of the context, NUIs are responsive to the environment and suggest what the next interaction should be.

5. Principle of the Super Real

Successful NUIs extend objects in a logical way into the world of magic, unlike GUIs that contain information in a cascading series of windows that resemble sheets of paper. With features like stretch to zoom, the UI elements of NUIs not only look real, but we also perceive them to be super real as their character can change in a way that is almost magical (see Figure 2.21).

6. Principle of Social Interaction

Unlike GUIs that are highly visual and often require a great deal of cognitive focus to use, NUIs are simpler and require less cognitive investment. Instead of getting lost in a labyrinth of menu options, menus on NUIs are streamlined, enabling more opportunities for users to engage and interact with other users instead of the system's interface. As opposed to GUI laptops, which are optimized for individual use, systems with larger NUI formats, like the Microsoft Surface Table or tablets similar to the iPad, lend themselves to social computing experiences (see Figure 2.22).

FIGURE 2.21
Gestures like "pinch/zoom" are a logical extension into the world of magic.

FIGURE 2.22
Matt Jones of BERG Design Consultancy created a UI iPad sketch that explores the passable and shareable nature of the iPad as an object tailored for multiple users.

7. Principle of Spatial Relationships

Unlike GUI systems, where an icon serves as visual representation of information, NUIs represent information as objects. In the world of successful natural user interfaces, a portion of an object often stands for the object itself. NUI objects are intelligent and have auras, as shown in Figure 2.23.

FIGURE 2.23
NUI objects have auras, like attraction affordances pictured in this Surface Table application.

8. Principle of Seamlessness

GUIs require a keyboard and mouse for interaction with computing systems. Touchscreens, sensors embedded in hardware, and the use of gestural UIs enable NUI interactions to feel seamless for users because the interactions are direct (see Figure 2.24). There are fewer barriers between the user and information.

FIGURE 2.24
Coverflow UI on the iPhone is a seamless way to navigate content.

Past and Present Computing Paradigms

The interaction design duo of Bill Verplank and Bill Moggridge created a framework to describe three firmly established computing paradigms: Computers as person, tool, and media.

Computers as Person

Initially, computers were conceived of as "intelligent agents" or "electronic brains." This paradigm supported the notion that computers could replace

the need for humans to perform mundane tasks. Systems designed in this ilk would commonly have anthropomorphic metaphors such as interfaces that "listen" or "hear" human commands. Research areas like computer visioning, artificial intelligence, and robotics continue in the tradition of the "computer as person" paradigm.

Key Values

- Computers as assistant or servant
- Command and control
- Computers can replace people

Expressed in Interactions Through

- Voice commands
- Text/language interfaces
- Text input programming

Examples

- Microsoft Office's Clippy
- Command-line interfaces
- Voice-driven interfaces

Computers as Tool

The notion that computers act as a tool that augments human intelligence emerged in the 1970s and has been best exemplified by the desktop metaphor and the graphical user interface. Instead of replacing people, the "computer as tool" paradigm reflects our ability to view computers as we would a hammer or a pen—as a tool for completing tasks. This paradigm supports the notion that computers exist to enable people to be more efficient through their own agency. It celebrates values like utility, task completion, and efficiency.

Key Values

- Computers should empower us
- Utility and usability
- Computers are useful/efficient

Expressed in Interactions Through

- Metaphorics
- "The desktop"
- Graphical user interface

Examples

- Microsoft Office
- Email
- Folders and files

Computers as Media

It wasn't until the widespread proliferation of the Internet that the "computers as media" paradigm got traction and became convincing. Instead of tools for efficiency, computers in this paradigm bear a likeness to televisions and radios in that they distribute media. Instead of helping people complete tasks, computers provide content that can be watched, read, heard, engaged with, and enjoyed. This paradigm celebrates values like engagement, expression, content distribution, play, and access. In this paradigm, content can be prismed through a variety of devices—televisions, computers, mobile phones, and portable media players. As such, anything

that can deliver content and provide an engaging and immersive experience is "a computer."

Key Values

- Computers should entertain us

- Expression and engagement

- Play and persuasion

Expressed in Interactions Through

- Web pages

- Content stores (iTunes, Netflix)

- GUI/NUI hybrid interfaces

Existing Examples

- YouTube

- Online publications

- Wii

Future Computing Paradigms

There are three similar yet distinct future paradigms I've been tracking that I believe will become important and emergent in the years to come: Computers as organic material, computers as infrastructure, and computers as social currency.

Computers as Organic Material

What if everything in the environment was embedded with computing power? Or if computing and information had organic qualities? Similar

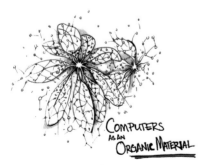

to Verplank and Moggridge's "computer as life" metaphor, the "computers as organic material" paradigm predicts a fluid, natural, almost biological perspective of our relationship to computers and information. Instead of media streaming through "dumb terminals" such as computers, TVs, and mobile devices, computing and information are ambient forces woven into the fabric of the world. Sensors are everywhere; computers are embedded into everything in the environment. Monolithic devices are not only de-emphasized, but they are supplanted by an ecosystem of smaller, more portable devices or large public monitors built into the environment.

Instead of focusing on devices, people focus on data and information. People come to understand data and data patterns as if they were a biological form. The dynamic and life-like qualities of data are celebrated. Systems allow information to form and reform by connecting to other data, making computer experiences contextual and adaptive. Computers can anticipate human intent, making interactions "quiet" and "dissolving into human behavior."

Key Values

- Computing is embedded into the fabric of the world

- Computing is quiet and seamless

- Data empowers us to make better decisions

Precursors

- Oyster Card
- NFC
- Nike+
- GPS
- RFID

Computers as Infrastructure

What if computing power and information were like water and electricity? The "computer as infrastructure" paradigm prediction is based on the idea that eventually we'll live in a world where computing power and information are a man-made utility built over or into the environment. We assume it is always there, waiting for us to engage with it. Just like plugging in a hairdryer or turning on a water faucet, people can "tap into" computing functionality through physical mechanisms in the environment like RFID, NFC, and free public WiFi. Interactions become about orchestrating networks, people, and objects through physical computing and tangible interactions. Similar to the hand gesture we make to indicate "I'm on the phone," our interactions with this infrastructure become so pervasive that gestures and mechanisms embedded into the environment serve as a way to communicate our behavior.

Key Values

- Computers and information access are utilities

- Computing is physical and tangible

Precursors

- Smart environments

- Organic interfaces

- Sensors embedded into textiles

- Biometrics

- Glucose sensors inserted into skin

- Plants and bridges that Twitter

Computers as Social Currency

Since humans are inherently social critters, we're innately attuned to understand how our actions and behaviors are perceived by our family and friends, our tribes, and our society. What if the focus of computing and information consumption became yet another form of social expression? The

"computers as social currency" paradigm prediction amplifies Yuri Engstrom's theory on object-centered sociality, our use of book covers, and the inherent shame we feel for perusing Perezhilton.com. In this future paradigm, computing reflects social behavior. Computers, data, and information are social objects that people use to form connections with others and to express their identity and values in the world. What we own and consume matters greatly. People become highly conscious of their content consumption and computing ecosystems because computing behaviors are expressions of class, education, socio-economic status, and social standing within a given society or tribe.

Key Values

- Computers and information consumption are a reflection of social identity.

- I am what I consume.

Precursors

- Apple Fanboys

- Facebook

- "Checking-in" to FourSquare

- LinkedIn

- The digital divide

Summary

While we can laud the wildly successful desktop computing paradigm, it's clear that a computing paradigm shift is underway. It's time to embrace what's next. Have no doubt: Mobile *is* what's next. It's a new, dynamic computing paradigm that will liberate us from the static desktop and graphical user interface of the past. Instead of GUI, this new mobile paradigm will undoubtedly be expressed through NUIs.

The desktop paradigm and the principles that guide graphical user interface design are deeply entrenched into our perceptions about computing and our instincts around designing technology experiences. Recognizing that this fundamental paradigm shift in computing and interface design is underway is an essential first step in exploring the mobile frontier that lies ahead. The next step is getting a handle on what practitioners of mobile user experience cite as one of the most important and defining skills required to design successful mobile experiences: understanding context.

- We are in the midst of a computing paradigm shift. Clear and compelling evidence indicates that the static desktop computing paradigm is reaching the end of its shelf life and will be supplanted by a new mobile one. We're reaching the edge of what GUIs can do.

- The characteristics of interfaces have evolved by building on what came before, while simultaneously offering higher levels of sophistication. Looking to the past can help us predict the form interfaces will take in the future.

  - *Past:*
    Command line interfaces
    Graphical user interfaces
  - *Future:*
    Natural user interfaces
    Organic user interfaces

- The iPhone was the first device to give a large-scale consumer audience the opportunity to experience the magic of natural user interfaces firsthand.

- While "NUI domination" may seem inevitable, today we are situated in a GUI/NUI chasm. People are excited by NUIs, but are proficient and familiar with GUIs. NUIs are still new; their design details and conventions are still being figured out.

- Feeling comfortable with NUIs is an important skill to hone as you begin to explore the mobile frontier. Make sure that you follow the eight basic design principles any successful NUI experience should reflect.

Expert Interview: Mike Kruzeniski

Creative Director at Microsoft in the Windows Phone Design Studio

Mike Kruzeniski, pictured in Figure 2.25, is currently a Creative Director at Microsoft in the Windows Phone design studio, leading the Communications and Apps teams, as well as collaborations with Nokia. He's been an active member of the mobile design industry since he began his career with Nokia in the Insight and Innovation team in Calabasas, California.

How did you find your way into the mobile user experience space?

Mobile phones became really important to me when I moved away from home for the first time. I was studying Industrial Design in college, and it was the first time I'd ever lived far away from home. Needless to say, my mobile phone became a very, very important part of my life for keeping in touch with friends and family back home.

FIGURE 2.25
Mike Kruzeniski, Creative Director at Microsoft in the Windows Phone design studio.

Most of my school projects managed to have a lot to do with the mobile or communication products. That just became a recurring theme. While pursuing my Master's degree in Sweden, mobile communication was a theme both personally and in my work. All those experiences in school, thinking about the importance of communication and mobile devices, led to my first job, which was with Nokia in 2004.

So I guess you could say I found my way into mobile experience from this simple circumstance many people face—I left home and mobile phones played a big part in helping me stay in touch with my family and friends. It made me realize how important phones and communication in general are to people. My interest started there, and it really hasn't stopped since.

You've been thinking about mobile UX for a long time now. What's changed the most since you began your career in 2004?

One of the most significant changes has been the rising importance of software. The focus of the mobile industry for many years was the physical device. Form factors were the thing. It was transformers and flips and three-way slides and candy bars. We focused a lot on the physical form factors of the device, and the software was always secondary. It's not just about phones anymore. It's about software—apps and operating systems—and hardware, companion products, and accessories. It's not enough anymore to simply have a great mobile device. You have to be thinking about the entire ecosystem of related products and experiences.

I don't think anyone in the mobile industry anticipated the role software was going to play in mobile user experience until the iPhone was released. Industry veterans kind of looked down on the iPhone because they felt it was a dumbed-down phone, in terms of feature specs. A lot of people also were very skeptical of touch interfaces, since it had been tried with very little success. But Apple showed the opportunities that were being missed because of poor, difficult-to-use, fragmented software. Apple created a great product and a software foundation they could build on.

You mentioned Apple played a big part in shifting the mobile landscape in a profound way with the release of the first iPhone. Since your role at Microsoft is to create products that will compete with the Apple platform, what are some of the ideas that you've integrated into products like Windows Mobile 7 and the Kin that make those experiences different?

One of the main concepts we focused on with both the Kin and Windows Mobile 7 was to create a truly content-driven interface. While the iPhone is beautiful, its UI and the UI of many other devices is built on the desktop metaphor. Most of the mobile interfaces we see in the market today are built upon entrenched metaphors inherited from the PC—folders, icons, desktop spaces, and chrome elements that are rendered to represent real materials. The focus of visual UI design has been on polishing metaphors rather than exploring other approaches: more detail, more shine, more texture, more depth, more shading, more transparency. It's as if we are trying to rebuild the physical artifacts around us inside of our computers. But that approach makes less sense today than it did 30 years ago. What people care about now is content. While metaphors have been helpful in the development of software, I feel like they are failing to serve us the same kind of value now. I think UI metaphors—especially for mobile—are dead. For so much digital content, there is no good metaphor to render anymore—the content is just information, text, and images—so new approaches to visual UI design are needed.

In an age where our interactions are information-based rather than tool oriented, a visual communication language that is hinged on arcane artifacts is no longer relevant. The value of interfaces today is the information it wants to present, not the physical vessel [in which] the information once resided.

Inventing new interaction paradigms for mobile sounds like a creatively liberating yet highly intimidating task. Where have you gotten ideas and inspiration for shifting out of old computing metaphors?

In 1999, Jakob Nielsen said "Anything that is a great print design is likely to be a lousy Web design. There are so many differences between the two media that it is necessary to take different design approaches to utilize the strengths of each medium and minimize its weaknesses." I disagree. The design principles established through the history of print design are also true for interaction. In our exploration of the differences, we've forgotten how much they are the same. They are both about clarity in communication and simplicity through systems. I believe mobile interaction designers can learn from print design and apply many of the same principles to interactive experiences.

Instead of carrying on what we see as outdated metaphors, the Windows 7 team tried to take a different approach. We drew inspiration from print design (see Figure 2.26), and that's what lead us to Metro, which is the typography-based design language used for Windows Phone 7. Instead of icons on a desktop, Metro focuses on typography and features large text that catches the eye and runs off the page. Instead of drop shadows and bevels or skeuomorphic controls, we really focused on a UI that was about featuring and presenting the user's content. We've made a conscious effort to strip out icons and tools wherever we can, and create a UI that was elegant and focused on the content (see Figure 2.27). We designed Metro to be sleek, quick, modern—and a real departure from the icon-based interfaces that we are more used to seeing.

FIGURE 2.26
Metro, the visual language of Windows Phone 7, was inspired by print design and iconography from the International Style.

FIGURE 2.27
Metro focuses on typography and features large text that catches the eye and runs off the page. Instead of gimmicky UIs with drop shadows and bevels or skeuomorphic controls, Microsoft focused on a creating a mobile UI that was content-centric.

Is there an example of a current mobile interface that you believe is an indicator of what mobile interfaces in the future will be like?

To me, Photosynth (depicted in Figure 2.28) was—and still is—an incredible and relevant UI. It is one of the most beautiful pure examples of a content-centric interface. The UI is just the photos, a small palette of actions, and whatever input device is connected (the keyboard, a mouse, or touch).

FIGURE 2.28
Photosynth software takes a collection of photos of a place or an object, analyzes them for similarities, and displays them in a reconstructed three-dimensional space. You can see where pictures were taken in relation to one another and find similar photos.

UI tools fade until you need them; otherwise, you are just sort of moving around in the photos. It's almost uncomfortable the first time you see Photosynth as a UI designer because it seems that there is no interface—the interface is just the content. But when you push yourself to approach UI in this manner, you focus on designing the interaction instead of the interface. It's a subtle yet very important difference that I think will distinguish interfaces from the last 10 years to the interfaces of the next decade. What do you get if you approach communication in the same way as Photosynth?

Over the last 20 years, there has been one reigning user interface paradigm. I think right now we're in a period of intense change. Sometimes, when that intense change is happening it feels like "Oh, my God! When is all this change going to stop?" It can be overwhelming. But that's what makes mobile such a fun and exciting design space to be in. Some things will stick, some won't, and we'll discover more along the way. But, basically, I just want to continue to improve the experience of communicating. It's great to be able to play a role exploring and guiding how that experience will evolve.

CHAPTER 3

Peanut Butter in Denver
Demystifying the Elusive Mobile Context

It Was a Dark and Stormy Night…   40
Developing Empathy for Context   41
Reduce Cognitive Load and Opportunity Cost   51
Mobile Context Design Tips   54
Mobile Context Design Method: Brainstorming
    in the Wild   56
Mobile Context Framework: Nouns and Relationships   57
Peanut Butter in Denver?   59
Mobile UX Beachhead   60
Summary   63
Expert Interview: Alex Rainert   64

P ractitioners of mobile UX design often cite context as the biggest difference between designing for mobile experiences and other design spaces. But what does "the mobile context" really mean?

In 2006, I worked on a research project designed to answer that very question. We recruited 10 participants and asked them to photograph their surrounding environment each time they used their mobile device. The research team hoped these photos would reveal a pattern and that somehow through analyzing all these diverse images—like the ones shown in Figures 3.1–3.4— we could crack the code of the mysterious and elusive mobile context.

FIGURES 3.1–3.4
Pictures of the mobile context from a diary study on mobile Internet access.

A week later, we were drowning in a sea of photographs. Some photos were predictable on-the-go shots often associated with the mobile context: the inside of a supermarket, interiors of buses or trains, and photos taken by users while rushing down the street. Other environments were surprising: the interior of a public restroom, a bedroom, the interior of a church. After many days of sifting, sorting, and clustering photographs, the research team came to a sobering conclusion:

Mobile context = anywhere and everywhere.

It wasn't the earth-shattering, code-cracking conclusion we'd hoped for. It did, however, underscore one of the most fundamental aspects of designing for mobile user experiences. Unlike the static and predictable PC context, the mobile context is a lot like life. It's unpredictable, ambiguous…it's everywhere. The sheer number and variety of environments depicted in the photographs we received emphasized one of the most magical aspects of mobile user experience that is still true today. The ability to access, consume, share, and create information from anywhere, anytime—untethered from a keyboard or mouse—is a latent human need that mobile technology has only just begun to solve.

It Was a Dark and Stormy Night…

"Let me give you some context." It's the phrase that frames any great story from gossip to epic parables. Behavior doesn't happen in isolation. Instead, much of life is a reaction to the world around us. Experiences occur in place and time and under dynamic social conditions. Context, which is the set of circumstances or facts that surround a particular situation, profoundly shapes our daily experiences.

Without understanding context, many of our actions and behaviors would fail to make sense. Developing an understanding and empathy for the depth, breadth, and design implications of the mobile context is quite possibly the most essential skill necessary in creating great mobile experiences. Unfortunately it is a skill that most designers haven't had the need to develop…until now.

If you're a practicing designer, chances are that *context* is your design blindside. Most designers have been steeped in a tradition of creating experiences with few context considerations, although they may not realize it. Books, Web sites, software programs, and even menus for interactive televisions share an implicit and often overlooked commonality: Use occurs in relatively static and predictable environments. In contrast, most mobile experiences are situated in highly dynamic and unpredictable environments, as depicted in Figure 3.5.

Put simply, what makes mobile difficult (and different) is that people move.

FIGURE 3.5
The mobile context can be anywhere, as demonstrated by a man texting while biking in Vietnam.

Developing Empathy for Context

Compelling mobile experiences share a common characteristic—they are empathetic to the constraints of the mobile context. Underneath all the hoopla that mobile folks make about the importance of context is the recognition of a skill that everyone interested in this medium must develop: both empathy and curiosity for the complexity of designing for everywhere. It's not a skill most people grow overnight, but rather something we learn through trial and error. And like any skill, the learning never stops.

Throughout the course of my career, there are three design principles that have emerged through my own painful process of developing this skill. I've found them to be invaluable for coping and dealing with "the everywhere" that is the mobile context of use. They are the following:

- Focus on creating experiences that are uniquely mobile.
- Design for partial attention and interruption.
- Reduce cognitive load and opportunity cost.

Focus on Creating Experiences That Are Uniquely Mobile

Remember a time not so long ago when the Internet was new? Companies big and small clamored to create some semblance of a "Web presence." A common strategy for grappling with this new and unknown medium was to translate or replicate known experiences online. This approach resulted in a number of missteps. Retailers quickly learned that the Web was not a great place to sell low-value items with high shipping costs online, like laundry soap, for example. Users quickly learned to ignore brochureware (Web sites that were produced by taking an organization's printed brochure and translating it directly to the Web), as shown in Figure 3.6, and instead flocked to sites that embraced the interactive and dynamic capabilities inherent to the burgeoning Web medium. The most confusing translations were those that attempted to replicate analogous real-world environments online, such as depicting a Web site as physical space or attempting to render Web pages as tangible pages like those of a book.

These early Web experiences evidence a common pattern that's frequently repeated when new technology is introduced. Driven by habit and cognitive comfort, humans often replicate previous experiences with new technology, rather than inventing new experiences that leverage the inherent characteristics afforded by the new technology. Marshall McLuhan referred to this as the rear-view mirror effect.

FIGURE 3.6
Brochureware Web sites are often developed as a direct translation of existing printed promotional materials.

McLuhan noted that,

> "...even in situations in which a spirit of exploration and freedom exist, where faculty are free to experiment to work beyond physical and social constraints, our cognitive habits often get in the way...it is the rear-view mirror effect....We see the world through a rear-view mirror. We march backwards into the future."

Even in an industry like mobile where innovation abounds, the rear-view mirror effect is all too often at play. Much effort, for example, has been directed at porting experiences, such as email and browsing the Internet to the mobile environment—experiences that were born in and borrowed from the PC. While these experiences have value, they fail to leverage the inherent characteristics of mobile. They are replications of previous technology experiences in a new medium.

When the rear-view mirror is in effect, creating mobile experiences is akin to pushing water uphill. The characteristics that define mobile experiences will feel like frustrating, unworkable constraints. Part of creating experiences that are empathetic to the mobile context is learning how to focus on what mobile can do well. *Don't waste your time retrofitting old experiences into the new mobile medium.* Instead of pushing water uphill, you should focus on creating experiences that are uniquely mobile.

The first step toward creating uniquely mobile experiences is learning to identify the difference between a solution and a need. Early in my career I worked on a classic rear-view mirror project. I was part of a design team charged with designing an email application for a mobile device. This project took place during a time before touchscreens and QWERTY keyboards were standard issue for smartphones. Text input could only be entered through a mobile device's numeric keypad through predictive text technology referred to as T9, much like Figure 3.7. The design team I was a part of used standard design processes and methodologies for this project—personas, task flows, wireframes, prototyping, and so on.

FIGURE 3.7
Text messaging and email are similar solutions that fulfill the same human need.

We created an on-device prototype of our email application, tested it with users, and were somewhat blindsided by the results. Almost every participant echoed a similar sentiment throughout testing, "Why would I email someone from my mobile phone when I can just text them?"

Throughout the design process, we had assumed that people had a real need for email on their mobile device. If someone had asked us, "What is the user need your project is fulfilling?," we would have answered, "Email, of course!"

The thing is…email isn't a need. Email is a solution. Text messaging is also a solution. People *need* conversations. People *need* to communicate through text. Had our team been able to identify the difference between needs and solutions, we might have identified that the user needs we were designing for were already being filled by text messaging.

Identifying the difference between needs and solutions is tricky because most people are pragmatic by nature and speak in terms of solutions. Even users often speak in terms of solutions: "I want a phone with an MP3 player," or "I want an Internet browser on my phone." And sometimes selecting appropriate solutions is the design task many of us will face. But sometimes…it's not. In fact, if you want to create uniquely mobile experiences, you'll need to learn how to weed through all the solution-speak and find what is central to every solution: The human need it serves.

The key difference between a need and a solution is that when you hear a need described, it should tickle the problem-solving part of your brain. It should open your mind to multiple possibilities instead of providing you with a singular answer. Table 3.1 is a list of solutions that fill an underlying human need. Needs inspire multiple solutions while solutions provide a singular answer to a need.

TABLE 3.1

SOLUTION VS. NEED	
Solution	Need
Database of doctors' names and addresses	Find a doctor near me.
Map	Get from point A to point B.
Calendar	I need to know what may happen. I need to plan ahead.
Email	I need to communicate.
Facebook Updates	I need to feel connected.
LinkedIn	I need to manage my professional identity.
Search	I need to answer a question.
Picassa	I need to share.

Mastering the skill of identifying the underlying needs your mobile experience can serve is critical for avoiding the rear-view mirror effect. Once needs are identified, you can be more inventive and creative in your design approach, and you're free to leverage the characteristics inherent to mobile.

Mastering Constraints

The second step toward creating a uniquely mobile experience is understanding and mastering the constraints inherent to mobile. Any design activity, from furniture design to system architecture, has inherent constraints. Being able to artfully embrace constraints is the stuff that makes for great design. Whether it's the small size of the mobile device's screen or the highly variable environments of its use (or a user's patience level), mobile UX is riddled with design constraints that many new mobile designers struggle with (see Figures 3.8 and 3.9). The three most important constraints that have the most impact on mobile user experience are the following:

- **Device constraints:** The limitations of a small and portable form factor.

- **Environmental constraints:** Highly variable context of use.

- **Human constraints:** Varied cognitive abilities caused by social dynamics, cultural influences, and ergonomic limitations of mobile devices.

FIGURES 3.8 AND 3.9
The PC experience has very different device, environmental, and human constraints than mobile. Small screen size, highly variable context of use, limited user attention levels, and limited/erratic network access are a few of the constraints inherent to mobile.

What's complicated about these constraints is that they're not discreet and constant. They are dynamic and interrelated. Compare the constraints of mobile versus the constraints of the PC in Table 3.2.

Regardless of the technology platform being used, it's helpful to keep a running list of the characteristics innate to mobile that can be leveraged in the experiences you create. I recommend looking at these less as constraints and more as design opportunities waiting to happen.

TABLE 3.2

MOBILE UX CONSTRAINTS		
Mobile Device Constraints	**Mobile Environment Constraints**	**Mobile Human Constraints**
Small form factor	Can be used in almost any environment.	Easy to lose.
T9 and/or QWERTY alphanumeric input	Can be stored in almost any environment.	Language and metaphors aren't always appropriate for some cultures.
Small screen	Screen glare can occur in bright sunlight.	Focus required for cognition.
Camera/video	Sensitive to wear and tear (dropping in water, dust, etc.).	Alphanumeric input is challenging.
Battery operated	Use is prohibited in some environments.	Socially awkward or unacceptable to use in some circumstances.
Cellular, WiFi, and bluetooth network access	Unable to use because of lack of network connectivity.	Small text and graphics are sometimes difficult to read.
Microphone	Electricity is scarce in some environments.	Difficult to hear in some contexts.
Speaker	Financial constraints are based on location (roaming charges, data costs).	Use places high demands on working memory.
Headphone jack		
Sensors		
Accelerometer		

I once had the pleasure of interviewing Jack Dorsey, one of the founders of Twitter, for a mobile project. The interview was full of great quotes, but my favorite was his response to his strategy for designing Twitter within the constraints of mobile:

> "...there's something enchanting about the constraint of 140 characters."

I've long remembered that quote because it epitomizes the spirit of creating experiences that are uniquely mobile. Attributes such as a small screen size, limited text input, and inconsistent network access might at first feel unworkable and frustrating. However, with time you'll begin to see these as creative fodder. Instead of fighting with these attributes, you should leverage them. Use them to invent new interactions and experiences. Focus on what can be uniquely mobile, as shown in Figures 3.10 and 3.11.

FIGURES 3.10 AND 3.11
Unlike an email application, Shazam, an audio search application that allows
users to identify tunes anywhere using their mobile phone, is a perfect example
of a "uniquely mobile" experience.

Design for Partial Attention and Interruption

A key constraint most users are confronted with on a daily basis is allocating
their two most precious resources: their time and attention. While it's
possible for users to become engrossed in a mobile game or reading
on a Kindle, a key difference between mobile experiences and their PC
counterparts is the expectation of engagement. It's expected that desktop
experiences be immersive. In fact, many of the metrics used to measure the
success of PC-based Web sites, such as page views and average time on site,
are built on this assumption. Mobile experiences are different. Immersive
isn't always desirable. Because of their design, coupled with the complexity
of the mobile context, it's likely that a user will be interrupted while using an
experience you've designed. Expecting mobile experiences to be completely
immersive in the way a desktop experience is can be unrealistic. Instead, be
sympathetic to the conditions of the mobile context and design with partial
attention and interruption in mind.

A metaphor that helped me tune my sympathies to the time and attention
constraints of a typical mobile user has been to compare PC and mobile
experiences to a pair of similar yet fundamentally different water activities:
scuba diving and snorkeling.

PC experiences are scuba-like because they are designed to be immersive. Just as a wet suit and a tank of air enables scuba divers to plunge deep into the ocean and become immersed in the exploration of a different world, the large screen and static environment implicit during PC use enables users to become immersed in the rich, graphical world behind their computer monitor. Just as it's easy for scuba divers to maneuver through the water, it's easy for PC users to move through content quickly and easily with the precision afforded by a keyboard and mouse (see Figures 3.12 and 3.13). Overlapping windows and visual cues allow for easy exploration of multiple applications and documents at one time. Just like the world beneath the ocean, the PC invites exploration and discovery. Engagement is prized.

Mobile is akin to snorkeling because attention is divided. Similar to snorkelers who float on the surface of the water and must ride with the ebb and flow of the ocean, mobile users often need to access content while in an uncontrollable and unpredictable environment. Snorkelers tend to dip in and out of the water in search of interesting seascapes, just as mobile users "dip in and out" of content and information. The dynamics of both snorkeling and mobile experiences make it inherently difficult for users to get totally immersed. Slow connection speeds and small screen sizes do not allow users to multitask or become engrossed.

FIGURES 3.12 AND 3.13
PC experiences are immersive, akin to scuba diving. Users often dip in and out of mobile experiences, akin to snorkeling.

Multitasking and Task Switching

I've long loved the scuba/snorkeling metaphor because it depicts differences in expectations and behavior based on the environment. Because environment shapes behavior, users have developed a host of coping strategies to manage the demands of the wild and unruly mobile context. There are innumerable strategies, but the three behaviors I think are most significant to mobile UX are multitasking, task switching, and continuous partial attention, as is aptly shown in Figure 3.14.

FIGURE 3.14
An example of multitasking—a woman snapping digital photos while talking on the phone.

Despite research that indicates its ineffectiveness, multitasking (the handling of multiple tasks at the same time) is a common part of everyday life. People are motivated to be productive and efficient, so it's common to use a mobile device while doing other activities, such as making dinner, driving a car, or socializing.

Because mobile devices are multipurpose (music player, voice calls, text messaging, etc.) and people use them everywhere, the possibility of interruption during use is very high—either by the physical environment or other functions of the device. As a result, users of mobile devices are often in a state of juggling big and small tasks, a behavior known as *task switching*. Whether it's an incoming call or the arrival of a bus, users of mobile devices must often reshuffle what they're doing based on incoming information and changes in the environment.

In addition to multitasking and task switching, the prolific use of "always-on" communication technologies such as email, IM, and text messaging has brought about the phenomenon of continuous partial attention. Coined by Linda Stone, continuous partial attention is the practice of skimming the surface of the incoming data, picking out the relevant details, and moving on to the next stream. It's a behavior where users pay attention, but only partially, and it is motivated by a desire to be a live node on the network.

The implication of these three behaviors is that mobile experiences should be designed for partial attention and interruption. Instead of forcing users to dive deep into menu structures, you must get people to the content and functionality they want intuitively and quickly. Instead of attempting to present all possible menu options, you can allow users to "opt in" to information while simultaneously giving them the opportunity to intuitively dive more deeply into the content. That way, you make it easy for people to pause and pick up an experience where they left off.

Reduce Cognitive Load and Opportunity Cost

The third and last design principle for creating mobile experiences that are empathetic to context is to make every effort to reduce cognitive load and opportunity cost required. Cognitive load has to do with understanding the impact context has on a user's ability to focus (their working memory). Opportunity cost has to do with understanding user motivation—why a user will choose to engage with a mobile experience based on the other options at their disposal.

Working memory is a mental workspace where humans analyze, manipulate, and synthesize information. Working memory helps us make sense of the world as we compare what we see to what we know. The children's game *Memory*, depicted in Figure 3.15, was designed to improve working memory skills. The demands we place on working memory are referred to as *cognitive load.* Some tasks like counting make few demands on working memory, while others like problem solving make greater demands. As cognitive load increases, our ability to process information in working memory decreases. Several factors, such as age, processing speed, and domain expertise affect the constraints of working memory. Similar to "working memory" in a computer, when a user's working memory is tapped out, he is often unable to complete a task and will likely feel frustrated.

FIGURE 3.15
The game *Memory* is a matching game designed to improve children's short-term memory skills, thus increasing their cognitive load thresholds.

Two key factors that are significant to mobile UX and affect cognitive load are distractibility and interruption. The more a user is distracted or interrupted, the more difficult it becomes for him to complete a task. People who seek refuge in a quiet place in order to write in a journal or read a book are in a sense increasing the capability of their working memory. The mobile context, however, is riddled with distractions and interruptions. The cognitive load exacted on users by mobile experiences is innately greater than most PC experiences because the mobile context is dynamic and full of potential distractions and interruptions. Creating mobile experiences with an appropriate level of cognitive load is a sensibility most designers new to mobile must develop. It requires evaluating your work throughout the design process in a variety of mobile contexts.

Opportunity cost can be defined as the costs related to the next-best choice available to someone who has picked among several mutually exclusive choices. For example, a person who decides to quit his job and go back to school to increase his future earning potential has an opportunity cost equal to his lost wages for the period of time he is in school. Opportunity cost is assessed not only in monetary or material terms, but also in terms of anything that has value. Assessing opportunity cost is fundamental to assessing the true cost of any course of action. For example, in a restaurant situation, the opportunity cost of eating steak could mean not enjoying the salmon.

Opportunity cost in the mobile context is not fixed. Instead, it is constantly in flux because it's based on a combination of need, motivation/urgency, environment, and alternatives—dimensions that are always in flux. Take, for example, the opportunity cost associated with using an application for public transportation, such as the iPhone BART application shown in Figure 3.16.

If a user is at home on a Saturday morning, leisurely planning a shopping trip to a local shopping district, her opportunity cost might look something like this:

- **Need:** Transportation to the local shopping district

- **Motivation/Urgency:** Low

- **Environment:** Home

- **Alternatives:** Online schedule through PC, driving, showing up at the station and asking an attendant, calling a friend

However, if that same user is rushing out the door on a Monday morning, late for a job interview in an unfamiliar neighborhood, her opportunity cost might look slightly different:

- **Need:** Transportation to an unfamiliar neighborhood

- **Motivation/Urgency:** Very high

- **Environment:** On the street, rushing to the station

- **Alternatives:** Maps at the BART station, showing up at the station and asking an attendant or fellow passenger, calling a friend

An understanding of the limits of a typical mobile user's cognitive load impacts a myriad of design decisions from information density to navigation and functionality. Thinking through the possible opportunity costs of an interaction is a significant step toward ensuring that your work is empathetic to the mobile context. For example, the opportunity cost of using a mobile application that provides routes and schedules for a public train, as shown in Figure 3.16, is much higher if a user is running late for work as compared to that same user checking schedule information on a leisurely Saturday morning. However, a good rule of thumb is that clear and simple is almost always better. Striving for intuitive menu options, screen layouts with low information density, and functionality that is edited to only the essentials are a few of the ways you can ensure that your mobile design work reduces cognitive load and opportunity cost. Think one big idea per screen and remember that in mobile, clarity trumps density.

FIGURE 3.16
The opportunity cost of a mobile experience, such as this mobile application for a public train, will vary depending on the user's context.

Mobile Context Design Tips

Admittedly, designing for the "everywhere-ness" of the mobile context can be overwhelming. The following are some tactical tips for creating mobile experiences that are empathetic to the mobile context.

1. **Trim the fat.**

    Edit, edit, edit! Users want and expect interface options to be edited to what is essential and relevant in a mobile context—shoot for low information density with extraneous information cruft removed (see Figure 3.17).

2. **Design for "glance-ability."**

    Users don't want to be immersed in the tiny world behind the LCD of their mobile phone. Avoid creating visually greedy interfaces that require high levels of focus and attention to use. As users drill down and dive deeper into a mobile experience, attention may increase. Information density can grow correspondingly. For example, the dynamic tile home screen of the Windows Mobile 7 interface depicted in Figure 3.18 provides users with a glance-able view of their communication channels.

FIGURE 3.17
Trimming the fat is a necessary part of creating mobile experiences. PC experiences have a relatively large amount of screen real estate, which allows designers to annotate expectation. In mobile, options have to be readily apparent.

FIGURE 3.18
Playing to the notion of continuous partial attention behavior, this UI feature allows users to feel connected without diving into the world of their mobile device.

3. **Reduce digging.**

   Instead of drilling down into deep menu structures, as illustrated in Figure 3.19, users want tailored interactions that get them to the content and functionality they're seeking intuitively and quickly. Show restraint. Get your users to their information with as few screens and transitions as possible.

4. **Grease the skids of natural connection points (phone number).**

   Information may naturally reside in one application silo but can be used as interaction triggers for functionality that resides in multiple applications. Anticipate the possibilities. Clear the path for anticipated interactions.

5. **Enable "picking up where you left off."**

   Because the potential for interruption in the mobile context is high, users will likely need to pause or abort a mobile interaction midstream. Make it easy for them to pick up where they left off, regardless of context or device, as shown in Figure 3.20.

6. **Use time as an organizing principle.**

   Email, text messages, and Twitter and Facebook feeds share a common trait—they use time as an organizing principle. When people are interrupted or returning to a task, time is a natural and intuitive way for users to reorient themselves within an experience. If appropriate, consider the use of time-based organizing conventions such as timelines, lists, and streams as a way to easily reorient users within a mobile experience.

FIGURE 3.19
The deep menu structure found on the Nokia N95 forces users to dig and burrow into the UI in order to access functionality.

FIGURE 3.20
Users of the Netflix application can start watching a movie on their PC, pause, and pick up where they left off on their mobile device.

Mobile Context Design Method: Brainstorming in the Wild

In addition to heuristics such as design principles, your design process also plays a role in creating mobile experiences that are empathetic to context. A good sense of the limitations the mobile context places on your mobile design work is a sensibility very few people have naturally. This lack of sensibility is exacerbated by the unfortunate fact that the activity of design often occurs in a static context such as a desk, an office, or conference room. Judgments made about context from these common work environments are approximations at best.

A method that's proven helpful in alleviating this problem in my own work is conducting ideation sessions "in the wild." Armed with post-it notes and sharpies, I've conducted brainstorming sessions on the street, in coffee shops, and in grocery stores as seen in Figures 3.21–3.23. The quality of the ideas from these "ideation in the wild" sessions always trumps their conference room counterparts because the ideas themselves are inspired by and born in a more realistic environment for a typical user.

FIGURES 3.21–3.23
How many times have you attended ideation sessions in windowless conference rooms? I've attended more than I can count and have come to the unwavering conclusion that a conference room is exactly the wrong environment to conduct brainstorming sessions for mobile UX.

Ideating in the wild has many benefits.

- Environments inspire ideas. Being out in the world and engaging with the environment and people can become a catalyst for your creativity.

- Being out in the world and engaging with it gives you a more realistic sense of a typical user's cognitive limits and makes you better able to gauge his willingness to engage with the experience you're conceiving.

- Brainstorming in the wild makes it difficult to ignore the inherent constraints and demands of the mobile context because you are feeling them for yourself instead of projecting and estimating.

A logistical recipe for conducting an ideation session "in the wild" is almost as simple as boiling water. Just tell attendees to wear comfortable shoes.

Mobile Context Framework: Nouns and Relationships

A framework I've developed to decrypt the complexity of context is to think about mobile's "everywhere-ness" in terms of grammar. Everything can be categorized as a common noun: people, places, or things. What breathes life into nouns is their relationship to other nouns in the world. In the world of mobile UX, relationships can be described and categorized into four basic types: semantic, social, spatial, and temporal. Getting a handle on the mobile context is about developing an understanding of the implicit human relationships between users and the people, places, and things (the nouns) that make up the world, as seen in Figures 3.24 and 3.25.

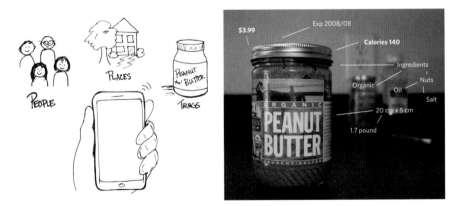

FIGURES 3.24 AND 3.25
Getting a handle on the mobile context is about developing an understanding of the implicit human relationships between users and the people, places, and things (the nouns) that make up the world.

The nouns are the easy part of this framework; the relationships are the tough part because they are dynamic and fluid and never happen in isolation. All four relationships are likely in play during any mobile UX interaction. Just as a musician artfully inflects emphasis on particular chords of a song, mastering context is about understanding which relationships to emphasize and when.

Understanding relationships will help you understand the mobile context.

My favorite food is peanut butter. Using the context framework, peanut butter is obviously classified as a thing. While my love of peanut butter is unwavering, my relationship to it varies depending on space, time, social conditions, and semantics. If the real potential for mobile user experiences is to invent new ways for people to interact with information, the information needs of the user and which information to emphasize with regard to peanut butter will vary wildly depending on context.

Spatial Relationships

Consider the information needs you might have for a jar of peanut butter sitting on the shelf at a supermarket. Now imagine the information needs you might have for a jar of peanut butter sitting on a kitchen shelf. The information needs are different because of your spatial relationship.

Temporal Relationships

I could eat anything that contains peanut butter at almost any time of day or night. Most people are more discriminating, though, because of their relationship to time. For example, receiving a phone call in the middle of the night, spotting a wonky dialog box in the middle of completing an online purchase, and eating tofu with peanut sauce for breakfast have one thing in common: bad timing.

Social Relationships

Online personal ads, Facebook posts, and talking about peanut butter cookies with a fellow customer in line at Starbucks all share a similarity. They exemplify the use of our relationships to people, places, and things in the world for social purposes. Sharing information—like a passion for a thing like peanut butter—serves as our common ground. Humans use and reinforce common ground to facilitate conversation, manage identity, and deepen relationships to other people in the world.

Semantic Relationships

Semantic relationships have to do with the words we use to identify and describe nouns. When people learn a language, they are learning the semantic relationship between a word or a group of words and the person, place, or thing that particular word is associated with. It's important, for example, to know the word associated with peanut butter when traveling to a foreign country like China, as peanut butter is difficult to pantomime.

Peanut Butter in Denver?

Imagine you just arrived by airplane to an unfamiliar city, such as Denver. As you collect your suitcase in baggage claim, you're struck with an insatiable craving for peanut butter (see Figure 3.26). How would you use your mobile device to find peanut butter?

This example underscores one of the most important shortcomings of how we experience technology today. Currently, technology experiences are good at "things" and leveraging semantic relationships. Place and spatial/temporal relationships, however, are relatively unexplored. Accessing information as it relates to place, space, and time—such as finding peanut butter in Denver—remains elusive. The legacy of the PC is likely to blame for this inadequacy.

FIGURES 3.26
How would you use your mobile device to find peanut butter? Accessing information as it relates to place, space, and time—such as finding peanut butter in Denver—remains elusive.

Whether writing a paper or surfing the Web, PC experiences have important contextual commonalities. It's safe to assume that a PC user's context of use will be seated in a relatively predictable environment with few spatial or temporal considerations. Keyboards make it easy to rely heavily on text-based semantic relationships for interaction. Google search—the seminal interface of the Internet—leverages these characteristics and relies almost solely on the use of semantic relationships for its success. Subsequently, many of the technology experiences we are most comfortable with today have been tailored to leverage semantic relationships to people and things.

These assumptions, however, become brittle when applied to mobile. The mobile context is highly variable. Text input requires much focus. Applying PC context assumptions to mobile experiences all too often results in a marginalized experience for users. One of the biggest challenges for mobile user experience is coming to terms with the legacy of the PC and having the courage to invent new ways for people to interact with information and make it feel intuitive for them in a mobile context.

Mobile UX Beachhead

If the PC is good at "things" and semantic relationships, its blindside is place, as well as spatial and temporal relationships. While information about right here, right now remains elusive in the static context of the PC, mobile is especially well suited to explore information along these dimensions. People carry their mobile phones everywhere, and most modern devices have features that enable users to place themselves in space and time. That's why instead of getting caught up in the complexity of designing for everywhere, designers should focus on what mobiles can do well. There is a beachhead for mobile UX: place and spatial–temporal relationships. Instead of repurposing experiences from the PC, mobile experiences present the opportunity to unlock the power of place and invent new ways for people to explore their spatial and temporal relationships to information.

Some great precursor mobile experiences are leading the way in defining this new place and temporal–spatial frontier. Shazam is a perfect example of a mobile application that leverages place and our "right here, right now" relationship to sound. The application IntoNow, seen in Figure 3.27, applies the same principle to television shows. The application analyzes the audio generated from a user's television and identifies the exact episode being watched. It then provides data and links associated with the show that can be shared with a user's social network.

FIGURE 3.27
The mobile application IntoNow analyzes the audio generated from a user's television and identifies the exact episode being watched.

Simply moving data between two mobile devices, such as contact information or an invitation to connect through a social network, can prove challenging. This can be especially frustrating when both devices share the same location and have a strong spatial and temporal relationship. Applications such as Bump, as shown in Figure 3.28, allow users to transfer data between two devices that are in close proximity to each other by simply bumping their phones against each other. When applied to applications like LinkedIn, the interaction mimics business card exchange, without the physical business cards.

Connect instantly with nearby LinkedIn iPhone Users

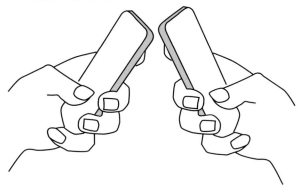

FIGURE 3.28
When the "bump" gesture is applied to applications like LinkedIn, the interaction mimics business card exchange, without the physical business cards.

The application GeoLoqi also allows users to leverage location information with features such as "Geonotes," proximal notification, and real-time map sharing. The application allows users to attach geotagged reminders to a place, enabling them to send information to their future selves. Users can leave themselves a note and receive it next time they're at the grocery store.

While embracing the spirit of invention is a key part of mobile UX, simply adding dimensions of space and time to experiences borrowed from the PC can dramatically improve a mobile experience. Maps are a great example. Looking up maps on a PC requires users to know and input their location in time and space. Modern smartphones know this information and leverage it, enabling users to never feel lost again (at least in the geographic sense), as shown in Figure 3.29.

Admittedly, designing for the "everywhere-ness" of the mobile context can be overwhelming, but it is one of the most significant and defining aspects of mobile user experiences. As you begin to design mobile experiences, the notion of "context" will likely be your blindside. Instead of repurposing PC experiences, it's important to remember that mobile UX presents the opportunity to invent new ways for users to interact with information. Focusing on what mobile can do well—place + spatial–temporal relationships—can help you focus your work and break down the complexity of the mobile context. Being aware of context will likely be one of the most important skills to develop as you explore the mobile frontier that lies ahead.

Just as people use their mobile devices everywhere, they are growing to expect their mobile devices will be able to interact with almost anything. Instead of monolithic experiences with a PC, people want experiences that traverse seamlessly across all the devices in their ecosystems. The next chapter will cover this emergent but important aspect of mobile user experience: convergence and the need to design for multidevice experiences.

FIGURE 3.29

Unlike mobile, looking up maps on a PC requires users to know and input their location in time and space.

Summary

- Practitioners of mobile UX design often cite context as the biggest difference between designing for mobile experiences and other design spaces. *Mobile context = anywhere and everywhere.*

- If you're a practicing designer, chances are that *context* is your design blindside. Most designers have been steeped in a tradition of creating experiences with few context considerations, though they may not realize it.

- Three design principles that will prove helpful in ensuring your work is empathetic to the mobile context are

  1. Focus on creating experiences that are uniquely mobile.

  2. Design for partial attention and interruption.

  3. Reduce cognitive load and opportunity cost.

- Here are six tips to remember when designing for the mobile context:

  1. Trim the fat.

  2. Design for glance-ability.

  3. Reduce digging.

  4. Grease the skids of natural connection points.

  5. Enable "Picking up where you left off."

  6. Use time as an organizing principle.

- Go wild! Take to the streets! Conduct your brainstorming/ideation sessions someplace other than a conference room or your desk.

- Get a handle on the mobile context by developing an understanding of the implicit human relationships between users and the people, places, and things (the nouns) that make up the world. Those relationships can be spatial, temporal, social, and semantic.

Expert Interview: Alex Rainert

Head of Product at foursquare

Alex is Head of Product at foursquare (see Figure 3.30). Alex brings 12 years of product development experience and a multidisciplinary background to his work, with a focus on mobile, social, and emerging technologies. Previously, he co-founded Dodgeball, one of the first mobile social services in the U.S., which he sold to Google in May 2005. He is a lifelong New Yorker currently living in Brooklyn with his wife, daughter, and dog. Alex holds a master's degree from New York University's Interactive Telecommunications Program and a bachelor's degree in philosophy from Trinity College.

FIGURE 3.30
Alex Rainert, Head of Product at foursquare

How did you find your way into the mobile user experience space?

I started getting interested in mobile when I attended New York University's Interactive Telecommunications graduate program. I went to ITP in 2003 and 2004 when, believe it or not, Friendster was still en vogue. At that time, mobile technology was still super frustrating but just starting to turn the corner to be a little bit more consumer friendly. ITP is an environment where students are encouraged to play around with the newest technology as part of the curriculum.

I've always been interested in the idea of mobility and presence and how you can alter and enhance the way people interact with the world around them through technology in a non-intrusive way. At ITP, I started working with Dennis Crowley on an application called *Scout*. When students arrived at school, they had to swipe their ID cards to enter the building. We designed Scout around that core interaction. When students entered the building and swiped their card, Scout would drop them into a virtual space and then other students could query that space with questions like, "Is there anyone on the floor right now who knows action script?" Scout used the idea of presence and social connection to enhance the way students were interacting with each other based on space. In a lot of ways, foursquare has been a natural extension of that idea. We've tried to take something simple like a check in and build a rich experience around that.

One thing that has been challenging—both with the early version of Scout and now foursquare—is that when you're designing mobile experiences, it often feels like you're trying to build things that help pull people over that hump to appreciate the richer experience that can come from designing around the intersection of mobile, social, and place.

How do you pull people over that hump so that they can realize the value of the types of mobile experiences you're designing?

Part of pulling people over the hump is staying focused. The foursquare team is a group of people who have an incredibly active relationship with our phones. It's easy to forget that not everybody has that type of a relationship with their mobile devices, and we have to always make sure we're designing for those outside of our power-user set.

The app, foursquare, (depicted in Figure 3.31) has always been a social utility at its core—find out what your friends are doing, tell your friends what you're doing. We use levers like game mechanics (encouragement though points, the leader board, badges), recommendations, and specials to encourage engagement with the app. The challenge is tweaking all those different levers without losing site of what is central to the app's experience—social and place.

FIGURE 3.31

"From day one, we've been building the foursquare experience for people to share things in the real world—to share experiences—and everything we've done has gone into that."

Now that people can carry around these powerful devices and have access to rich content like maps, images, and video, it's easy to think, "Oh, you can watch videos on it" or "We can create an augmented reality lens to enhance people's view of the world." We don't want people to open up foursquare and be buried in there or force people to look ridiculous waving their phone in the air to see things. That's definitely not the kind of experience we're trying to create. We want to build something that people can pop open anywhere in the world and provides a quick, valuable interaction, and then it's done. They can close it and get back to enjoying what it is they were doing.

From day one, we've been building the foursquare experience for people to share things in the real world—to share rich experiences—and everything we've done has gone into building towards that vision. We feel that's our beachhead—to keep plugging away and being able to focus on that area is our competitive advantage.

There seems to be a theme in your professional history. Dodgeball, Scout, and foursquare all combine mobile, a sense of place, with a social layer. Where does that interest come from?

I think part of it is my personality. I'm personally drawn to things that bring people together. I love that a big part of my job is building the team that builds the product. I've been managing a softball team for 12 years, and I run a football office pool. I know the latter two are sort of trivial examples, but it's coordinating groups of people around a thing, and that thing can be a fantasy baseball league, or that thing can be going out for happy hour. That's something that's been true about me my whole life.

Do you think the fact that you have spent so much time in New York City has influenced your thoughts about mobile design?

Definitely. New York is a unique place to design things around real-time place-based social interactions. Designing mobile experiences in New York is very much a gift, but it's also a challenge not to get too swayed by that. Currently, foursquare has over 10 million users. We have to design for the next 40 million users and not the first 20 million if we want to build the type of experience that I think we can, and a lot of those 40 aren't necessarily going to be urban dwellers.

You've been involved in the mobile industry for quite some time now. What do you think have been some of the biggest changes you've experienced?

One big change is how easy it is to create experiences that use the social graph. With Dodgeball, there was no social graph to speak of. If you wanted to create a social experience, you basically had to rebuild it from scratch. There weren't really graphs you could leverage like you can now with things like Twitter and Facebook. Now that it's easier to bootstrap a friend graph, we can focus all our efforts on the experience we want to design on top of that. The fact that there's a standard social graph designers can use to build social experiences is definitely a high barrier to entry that's been removed.

Also, the sheer number of people with high-end mobile devices is another big change. When I think back to the days of Dodgeball, we decided not to build the experience for devices like Windows mobile phones or smartphones, because the reality was that not that many people were carrying those phones. Despite the fact that it was a bigger challenge to build a rich mobile experience on lower-end phones, we focused on SMS (Short Message Service) because it was something everyone could use and because we felt strongly that if you're building something social, it's not fun if it's something that most people can't use. Now, higher-end mobile devices are much more common and are becoming people's preferred device. Now, even if people are given the choice of having an experience on their laptop or having an experience on their phone, people are starting to choose the experience on their phone because it's always with them. It's just as fast. It's just as nice looking. That just really opens the door for designers and engineers to build great mobile experiences.

What mobile design topics interest you the most?

I'm really interested in designing experiences that leverage mobile devices as location-aware sensors. There's something really powerful about the idea that the phones people carry with them can act as sensors alerting people about interesting things in their environments. Devices can know about the people you've been at places with, the things you've done and shared…even the speed at which you're moving. That opens up the opportunity to build experiences that are even less disruptive than the experiences we have now. Now, it's still very much like, "Let me open up Google maps and get directions to go do such and such."

Granted, this all has to be done with the user's privacy always kept front of mind, and I think the technology is finally getting to a point where we can find that balance and design an incredibly engaging augmented experience while respecting a user's privacy. Ultimately, I think we'll settle into some place where people will feel comfortable sharing more information than they are now, and I'm interested in seeing the kinds of mobile experiences we can create based on that information.

It seems weird to think that in our lifetime, we had computers in our homes that were not connected to a network, but I can vividly remember that. But that's something my daughter will never experience. I think a similar change will happen with some of the information sharing questions that we have today.

There's a weird line, though. Those kinds of experiences can get creepy super fast. I think the important thing to remember is that some problems are human problems. They're problems a computer can't solve. I'm definitely not one of those people who says stuff like, "We think phones will know what you want to do before you want to do it." I think there's a real danger to over rely on the algorithm to solve human problems. I think it's finding the right balance of how you can leverage the technology to help improve someone's experience, but not expect that you're going to wholeheartedly hand everything over to a computer to solve. It's a really difficult dance to try and be the technology in between human beings. However, no matter how far the technology goes, there's always going to be that nuance that needs to be solved by people.

CHAPTER 4

Shapeshifting

Convergence and Multidevice Experiences

What Is Convergence?	70
Convergence and Mobility	72
What Is a Device Ecosystem?	76
Mutual Reconfiguration and Multidevice Experiences	82
Identifying Ecosystem Relationships Through Participatory Design	85
Creating Experiences That Scale	90
Mobile Web Site, Web App, or Native App?	98
Summary	103
Expert Interview: Stephanie and Bryan Rieger	104

Shapeshifting—a theme common in fairy tales and folklore—is an idea that has held my imagination since childhood. Whether it was the Wonder Twins transforming into their appropriate animal/water duo that would save the day or the regular guy who turned into a savage werewolf at the sight of a full moon, the idea that a person or a thing could actually transform into something entirely different still remains both compelling and mysterious to me (see Figures 4.1–4.3).

When I think of the topic of convergence and designing for multidevice experiences, I automatically think of shapeshifting. In my mind, *convergence* is what allows digital experiences to change shape and form in order to accommodate the multitude of devices that have become commonplace in our lives.

FIGURES 4.1–4.3
Wonder Twins, Mystique, and werewolves are examples of shapeshifters—a being (usually human) who has the ability to change its shape into that of another person, creature, or entity.

What Is Convergence?

Convergence is what enables experiences to shapeshift between different devices and environments. Instead of a user interacting with his mobile device as one isolated experience and then interacting with another device (such as a personal computer) as a totally separate, isolated experience, convergence allows these experiences to be connected *and* have continuity. Instead of experiences being trapped on a device, they can move fluidly through multiple devices. There is a growing expectation among users that our digital content will follow us seamlessly from device to device. Convergence is enabling that to happen.

The best example of a truly convergent experience that I've found is from a Super Bowl commercial for NFL Mobile Television, as shown in Figures 4.4–4.11. The commercial depicts a guy watching the same football game from multiple devices in multiple environments throughout game day.

FIGURES 4.4–4.11

These stills from an NFL Mobile television commercial depict a great example of convergent experiences. Instead of camping out in his living room all day, the main character can be mobile and follow the big game from any device in his ecosystem.

Convergence and Mobility

One aspect of the NFL Mobile Television convergence example that I love is that it underscores why convergence is an important and timely mobile UX topic. Instead of camping out in his living room all day watching the game, the central character in the commercial can be both mobile—walking around and participating in the world—*and* connected to the content that's important to him. People are growing to expect their digital content to follow them seamlessly through the world, and mobile devices are enabling this to happen.

Mobile Devices Are Enabling Convergence

In addition to enabling these seamless, multidevice experiences, convergence is a timely and important mobile UX topic at this time because of two other, equally significant reasons:

- **What constitutes a "mobile device" is rapidly evolving.**

  Today, the character in the convergence commercial can watch his football game from two mobile devices in his ecosystem—his smartphone and his tablet. On what mobile devices will he watch the game six months from now? Or two years from now? While there may be great cognitive comfort in defining mobile devices as pocket-able, handheld devices predominantly used for voice calls and data consumption, that notion is changing. In reality, the definition of a mobile device is expanding to encompass devices that are much larger (tablets), much smaller (FitBits), and objects that are questionably devices at all (smartcards such as Hong Kong's Octopus card) at a rate must faster than any technology prior to this time. As the definition of "mobility" rapidly expands, designers must work outside the contours of their typical comfort zones. They must learn to step up to the challenge of working with new and experimental form factors, hardware configurations, and interface paradigms with the spirit of creativity and discovery—or they will get left behind.

- **UX professionals must now design for ecosystems.**

  Gone (or at least rare) are the days when UX professionals could design for single, siloed experiences (such as a desktop Web site or an app mobile phone) with little regard for the other devices a user might possess. As Moore's law charges forward and computational power becomes less and less expensive, people are acquiring more and more devices. Users are no longer interested in single, siloed experiences. Instead, they have grown to expect experiences that traverse multiple devices and contexts seamlessly. Users insist that their experiences be integrated and accessible in a wide variety of environments, screen sizes, and network connections. They want their devices to be aware of and talk to each other. This significant shift in user expectation means that designers can no longer focus on single device experiences and expect to meet or exceed user expectation. Designers must now account for the interconnectedness of information and subsequently design for ecosystems.

Three Levels of Convergence

One of the key challenges in creating seamless, multidevice experiences is adjusting our own deeply ingrained ideas and expectations about devices. A long-held belief has been that everything we know about devices—from the technology used to create them, to the activities undertaken on them, to the media consumed on them—was intrinsically tied to the device, when in fact it was not. Devices are merely conduits for experiences. The needs, activities, and media are actually often independent of the device.

Our perceptions are changing, though. As mobile devices become more prevalent, Internet access becomes more widespread, and media gets prismed through a variety of technology channels, users are getting introduced to the notion of convergence on three key levels that are separate but interrelated, as shown in Figure 4.12.

- Technology convergence
- Media convergence
- Activity convergence

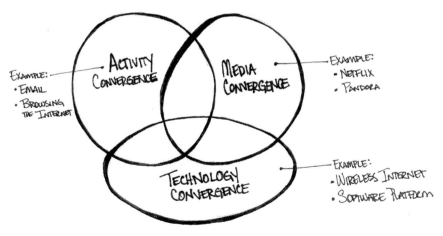

FIGURE 4.12
Levels of convergence.

Technology Convergence

When a user buys an Android tablet so that it will work with his Android phone, he is orchestrating *technology convergence.* Technology convergence occurs when a set of devices contain a similar technology and "play well" with each other (see Figure 4.13). In this type of convergence, the underlying technology enables experiences to move seamlessly across multiple devices.

Examples: Wireless Internet, Bluetooth, or a software platform like Android.

FIGURE 4.13
While interacting with a tablet, a smartphone, and a television are vastly different experiences, the Android operating system is used to create all three.

Media Convergence

When a user watches a reality television show, follows along on the show's Twitter stream, and downloads the TV network's iPad app, he is experiencing *media convergence.* Media convergence occurs when content is prismed through multiple devices or touchpoints (see Figure 4.14). The content and interactions often respond appropriately to the context (smartphone vs. big screen TV, etc.), but the focus is on the through-line of the content through the ecosystem of devices.

Examples: Pandora, Netflix, Bravo TV.

Activity Convergence

When a user undertakes the same activity, such as email, on multiple devices in his ecosystem, he is engaged in *activity convergence.* Activity convergence enables the user to perform an activity, regardless of the device (see Figure 4.15). The key to this type of convergence is figuring out how to allow users to complete a task or achieve their goal in a way that is intuitive, given the high degree of variance between types of devices and the vast number of use contexts.

Examples: Email, browsing the Internet, looking up a restaurant on Yelp.

FIGURE 4.14

Bravo is a cable television channel. Media convergence enables users to consume Bravo content from a variety of outlets: TV, Web sites, mobile applications, and through social media points like Facebook and Twitter.

FIGURE 4.15

Apple's email application is an example of activity convergence. Users can engage in the activity of reading and responding to emails from a variety of devices. Apple's email application keeps all the experiences up to date and in sync.

The key to these three types of convergence is the notion of a through-line. The through-line is what enables continuity of an experience, regardless of the device. It's the user's mental cue that allows the experiences to transcend devices. Through-lines are the hook that allows the technology to fall away and enables people to focus on what matters to them. Technology platforms are the through-line for technical convergence, media is the through-line for media convergence, and tasks/goals are the through-lines for activity convergence.

These are preliminary examples of current converged experiences. As our perceptions about device experiences shift and a future of seamless experiences between devices unfolds, there will likely be many more. The important idea is that convergence is no longer a lofty, abstract word used to describe a future that few people could imagine. Convergence is actually happening. It's something users are growing to expect.

How do designers steeped in a tradition of designing for a single device begin designing for this new, interconnected device landscape? If convergent experiences are the goal, then ecosystems are the means of production. Ecosystems are the pieces and parts designers can use to craft new multidevice experiences.

Ecosystems are the medium of the new converged digital landscape.

What Is a Device Ecosystem?

FIGURE 4.16
Coral reefs are considered to be complex marine ecosystems because the plant life supports the animal life and vice versa.

Similar to the term "convergence," a digital ecosystem is yet another abstract and ill-defined term that has been used and abused by many. What exactly does the term *digital ecosystem* mean and why does it matter to mobile UX?

In the world of biological sciences and ecology, an ecosystem is a term used to describe the interactions between a community of living organisms and their nonliving environment in a geographically bound area (see Figure 4.16). Instead of focusing on one aspect of a geographic area—such as the plants or the animals—ecosystems account for all the organisms (large and small), as well as nonliving components of the environment with which organisms interact (such as air, soil, and sunlight). The study of biological ecosystems entails understanding relationships: How different life forms help sustain one another.

Just like a biological ecosystem, a digital ecosystem is the term used to describe the interactions between the pieces, services, systems, and processes of a digital environment. An ecosystem is all the stuff that makes an experience work. It includes all of the relevant digital touchpoints (hardware, content providers, Web sites, mobile applications, and so on), the people that interact with them, and the business processes and technology environments that support them (see Figure 4.17)

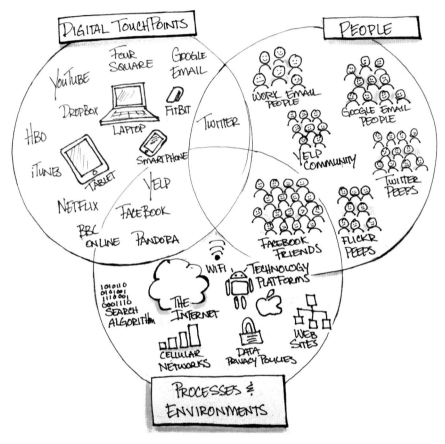

FIGURE 4.17
An ecosystem includes the digital touchpoints, the people that interact with them, and the business processes and technology environments that support them.

- **Touchpoints:** Touchpoints in a digital ecosystem include everything that people within a system come in contact with—hardware, software, Web sites, and services.

- **People:** The "people" part of an ecosystem includes all the users who interact with a system, encompassing everyone from the users and developers of a system to the people within an organization who build and maintain a system.

- **Processes and Environments:** The stuff that's categorized as "processes and environments" within a digital ecosystem can generally be described as the stuff that makes the ecosystem run efficiently. It includes underlying technology, such as wireless Internet or cellular networks, as well as processes, such as membership features or privacy policies.

Generally speaking, touchpoints are what designers and UX professionals are privy to because it's what they can create and design. Whether it's designing the pages of a Web site or the interface for a mobile application, most designers feel more comfortable designing digital touchpoints.

But the people, processes, and environments are what make experiences happen for a user—and understanding and designing the interactions with these processes and environments is essential to creating good ecosystem experiences for users. Unfortunately, our current working processes aren't tailored for designers to give much consideration to anything that's not a touchpoint. Device ecosystems are changing that.

Why Ecosystems Matter

In the past, designers were often responsible for creating one instantiation of an experience—such as a Web site—and they could assume that users would interact with that Web site through a browser on a personal computer. Creating an attractive, well-organized Web site optimized for a PC was the scope of their responsibility.

Today, that no longer holds true.

Now, in addition to a PC, users might view that very same Web site through a mobile browser on a smartphone or a tablet. In addition to a Web site, they may expect the company to have a custom mobile application that provides a tailored experience for a mobile phone or tablet phone and tablet computer. They may even browse the Internet on their television and expect the Web site experience to be navigable from their TV's remote control. They will also likely expect all these experience to interrelate to one another and have continuity. Gone are the days of designing simple Web sites solely for a PC. Users now have an ecosystem of devices for consuming and interacting with content. Instead of designing sites or single experiences, designers must design entire systems.

You may think, "Yeah, but my job is just the mobile part. I'm only responsible for the mobile Web site." However, what you are designing is part of a bigger picture. If you don't have a sense of the bigger picture, the mobile experience you create will suffer.

Even if, as a designer, you are only responsible for creating a mobile experience, a user's engagement with an experience is no longer isolated to one device. Designers are no longer designing "screens" or "pages." Instead, they are designing flexible systems that must accommodate multiple content relationships. Today, designers must get out of the "screen" or "page" mindset and start designing for systems.

Just like runners in a relay team similar to those pictured in Figure 4.18, you have to know what the other experiences are in order to catch and hand off the baton. Understanding not only the device experience you're designing, but also the other devices in a user's ecosystem will enable you to identify and design for attributes that are unique to the mobile experience and create a mobile experience that will scale and play well with other devices.

FIGURE 4.18
Just like runners in a relay team, designers must be conscious of and understand the role of other devices in a user's ecosystem in order to catch and hand off the baton, thereby enabling seamless multidevice experiences.

Designing for Ecosystems: Where to Start?

Where does a designer steeped in the tradition of creating "screens" or Web "pages" begin to design for these flexible content systems? My recommendation is to start with your users. Recruit some people who use your product or service and ask them to make a map of their device ecosystem. It's a great contextual research exercise that will help you get a handle on the touchpoints, people, processes, and environments they interact with everyday. When it comes to ecosystems, one of the best ways to get the lay of the land is to ask your users for a map (see Figures 4.19 through 4.21).

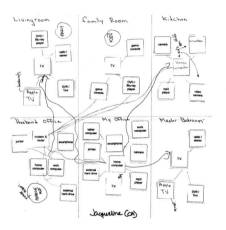
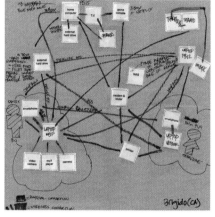

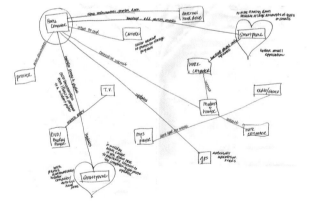

FIGURES 4.19–4.21
These images represent device ecosystem maps drawn by users of mobile devices.

Diagram Your Ecosystem

1. Provide participants with a large sheet of paper.

2. Ask them to draw images that represent all devices they own or interact with in a given day.

3. Next, ask the participants to list five things they do (activities, tasks, etc.) with each device.

4. Ask them to list what sites, services, or communities they use to accomplish their tasks. This part of the exercise should answer, "How does that work?" "What site, application, or service do you use to make that happen?"

5. Next, ask your participants about the infrastructure they use to make those experiences happen. Do they have an account with a network provider for their smartphone? Do they have a WiFi connection in their home? Ask them to indicate the underlying infrastructure that makes those devices run.

6. Finally, ask your participants if they had to select the five most important or personally significant things they do (within the context of all the devices in their ecosystem), what would those five things be?

FIGURES 4.22–4.24
Images from an ecosystem drawing exercise with research participants.

The benefit of this exercise is twofold:

1. It's a great "lay of the land" exercise. It will help you get a sense of the depth and breadth of your typical user's digital ecosystem. Knowing this information will help you focus your design efforts.

2. This exercise will provide you with a sense of the different mental models that people currently have for their digital ecosystems. As illustrated in the examples shown in Figures 4.22–4.24, some people naturally communicate their ecosystem based on rooms in their homes, while others choose to communicate their digital ecologies based on the relationships between devices or services. Understanding and building on the natural organizing principles people use for their ecosystems can help you create an intuitive multidevice experience.

Mutual Reconfiguration and Multidevice Experiences

In her book *Human-Machine Reconfiguration: Plans and Situated Actions*, HCI scholar and professor of Anthropology of Science and Technology at Lancaster University, Lucy Suchman challenged common assumptions behind the design of interactive systems by offering a very different way of looking at the fundamental issues of agency and interaction.

Much of the current thought and discourse around human–computer interaction today assumes a very static model between users and their devices. The human (user) is an agent with goals, plans, and intentions who achieves these goals (actions) with messages (interactions) conveyed through interfaces to computers. Under this assumption, the aim of HCI is to narrow the distance between human and machine to make the interface more transparent.[1]

Informed by the discipline of social studies of technology, Suchman's theory of mutual reconfiguration suggests that a person's capacity to act (their agency) is reconfigured when it comes into contact with another thing or person—that human action is constantly constructed and reconstructed from dynamic interactions with the material and social worlds.

As the boundaries between devices and interfaces continue to shift, this idea of mutual reconfiguration has great relevance to the design of mobile and multidevice experiences. Instead of viewing interaction as a static model between a person and device through an unfluctuating interface assigned to a single device, it supports the need for a more fluid interaction model. Suchman's theory reflects the need for interfaces that are dynamic and have the ability to change and reform depending on the environment and social circumstances of the user.

I experienced the phenomenon of mutual reconfiguration firsthand while researching how people use tablet computers. During a research study on iPad usage, my colleague Jofish Kaye and I spoke with over 20 iPad users in the summer of 2011. What we found was that while tablets are widely considered to be "mobile devices," the primary environment where participants reported using their iPad was in their home. However, unlike a PC or laptop computer that lends itself to a seated stance on flat surfaces, participants reported using an iPad while curled up, like they would with a book. Participants found their iPads especially well suited for "comfortable computing": using their tablets in "soft surface" environments that could easily support casual content consumption with some lightweight interactivity (see Figure 4.25).

---

1   Peter Wright, "Reconsidering the H, the C, and the I: Some thoughts on reading Suchman's Human-Machine Reconfigurations" (*Interactions Magazine*, Volume 18, Issue 5, September + October 2011) p. 29.

FIGURE 4.25
Participants used their iPads predominantly in "soft surface" environments. These environments supported "comfortable computing"—casual content consumption with some lightweight interactivity.

At the simplest level, "comfortable computing" was an observation of how the environment currently shapes the way people use tablets. In our iPad study, people used their iPads while curled up in bed or sprawled on the couch. These soft-surface environments configured the users' bodies into comfortable positions—and this in turn influenced/configured how people used the device. While in these "comfortable configurations," users did not want to use their iPads for writing emails, balancing spreadsheets, or other "task-focused" computing activities. Instead, they desired a sense of comfort in the primary uses of their iPads: reaching out to social connectedness on Facebook or Twitter, the storytelling of movies and TV shows on Netflix, and conversations with loved ones on FaceTime.

> More than a conversation at the interface, creative assemblages like these explore and elaborate the particular dynamic capacities that digital media afford and the ways that through them humans and machines can perform interesting new effects. Not only do these experiments provide innovations in our thinking about machines, but they open up as well the equally exciting prospect of alternate conceptualizations of what it means to be human. The person figured is not an autonomous rational actor but an unfolding, shifting biography of culturally and materially specified experiences, relations, and possibilities, inflected by each next encounter—including the most normative and familiar—in uniquely particular ways.
>
> —Lucy Suchman
> Human-Machine Reconfigurations: Plans and Situated Actions[2]

---

2   *Human-Machine Reconfigurations: Plans and Situated Actions (Learning in Doing: Social, Cognitive and Computational Perspectives)*, Cambridge University Press; 2nd edition (December 4, 2006).

What underlies Suchman's theory is the notion of situated cognition—that knowing is inseparable from doing—and that how people understand and interact with the world is situated in activities that are bound to social, cultural, and physical contexts.

Suchman's theory of situated action is especially relevant to the design of convergent multidevice experiences because:

1. **Mental models for ecosystems don't exist yet.**

   Unlike the PC/desktop experience with a relatively known and predictable mental model, most users don't yet have a mental map of how pieces and parts of their digital ecosystems fit together and interact with each other. Subsequently, convergent, multidevice experiences are often achieved through trial and error. Users learn through doing instead of building on existing knowledge.

2. **Ecosystems are growing rapidly.**

   The rate at which new devices and digital services are being added to a user's ecosystem is growing exponentially, creating scale issues for systems that are not flexible enough to accommodate the user's burgeoning ecosystems.

3. **Context matters.**

   Context has a huge impact on the ways that people use mobile devices, and mobile devices are a huge piece of the ecosystem "pie." Suchman's theory is sympathetic to context—it seeks to understand how the environment and social context affect how people interact with technology and design experiences appropriately.

While ecosystems are a growing trend in the digital landscape, designers and UX professionals presently have few design methods, heuristics, or conceptual models to lean on when designing multidevice experiences. Suchman's theory and subsequent design recommendation to employ participatory design methods can help. Instead of thinking of a multidevice experience as a predetermined set of interactions that must be followed, the theory of situated action supports the idea that people learn and acquire knowledge about device ecosystems by thinking on the fly and through trial and error. This approach requires designers to create interactive systems that are less "mapped out" and bound by logic and instead opt for systems that are intuitive, invite exploration, and progressively reveal their nature. The best way to create such a system is to invite users into your design process through participatory design methods.

Identifying Ecosystem Relationships Through Participatory Design

After having a group of users draw a map of their current ecosystem, it's easy to get overwhelmed. While the maps are helpful in providing a "lay of the land" view of the users' digital landscape, they don't communicate or emphasize the most important element of multidevice experiences: relationships.

Similar to a biological ecosystem, a key part of understanding a digital ecosystem entails understanding relationships—the interdependencies between different elements within a system—and how the different parts of the system help relate to and sustain each other. For example, the experience of a digital touchpoint such as Twitter would fail without the participation of your friends and the Internet. The relationship between the touchpoint, friends, and the Internet is a significant relationship for the Twitter experience (see Figure 4.26). Using a digital touchpoint like an iPad would be a lot less fun without iPad applications, the iTune store, and the millions of applications developers who create them. The relationship between the iPad device, the iTunes store, and applications is a significant relationship for the iPad experience (see Figure 4.27). Instead of being overwhelmed by all the pieces and parts of a digital ecosystem, identifying and understanding the critical relationships within an ecosystem will allow you to focus your design efforts.

FIGURE 4.26
The Twitter/Twitter Community Relationship: Another important interdependent ecosystem relationship exists between Twitter and Twitter users. Making it easy to identify and interact with people in the Twitter community should be a key design consideration for any experience that integrates Twitter data.

FIGURE 4.27
The iTunes/iPad Relationship: There's an important interdependent ecosystem relationship between the iPad, the iTunes store, and iPad applications. Identifying and prioritizing relationships in a device ecosystem will help you design for the relationships that matter most.

It's the study of these relationships and interdependencies that is key to multidevice experiences. When these relationships are not supported by good, thoughtful design, multidevice experiences fall flat. Identifying relationships is critical. The best way to distinguish and understand these relationships is to watch users identify and enact them through participatory design.

Participatory Design

Unlike other approaches to design, participatory design assumes that users should play an active role in the creative process. The theory behind participatory design methodologies assumes the following:

- All people are creative.

- All people have dreams.

- People can project their needs onto ambiguous stimuli.

- People are driven to make meaning and will fill in what is unsaid or unseen.

Participatory design presupposes that in the right context, users can envision the future by identifying *defining moments*. In the context of designing for digital ecosystems, defining moments are the interactions that unearth the critical relationships between touchpoints, people, processes, and environments within an ecosystem. Defining moments unearth these relationships and provide an understanding of the nature of the relationship for users.

Role Play and Participatory Design

The stories that users share and the role playing that occurs during participatory design sessions will help you uncover defining moments within a user's multidevice experience. A key challenge to integrating participatory design methods into your creative process is to create a space in which users feel comfortable telling stories about their experiences and can engage in role playing with props. This makes thoughtfulness around the stimuli, props, and environments where the participatory design sessions occur quite possibly the most important part of using this type of method in your design work.

Environments

As referenced earlier in Suchman's theory of situated action, environment and social circumstances deeply affect the way that people engage with a digital experience. This is why it's important to identify the types of environments your users will likely engage in with the experience you're creating and conduct participatory design sessions in those environments. These may include a living room, a crowded bus, or even inside a car. Conduct your participatory design sessions in a variety of environments in order to explore how different social and environmental conditions affect the relationships between elements in an ecosystem. A variety of environments will also help you capture how users communicate with experiences differently depending on the environment (see Figures 4.28–4.31).

FIGURES 4.28–4.31
Identify the types of environments that users may engage with the experience you're creating and conduct participatory design sessions in those environments.

Props

In participatory design sessions, props are the physical representations of intended form factors. Like a blank canvas, they should have a physical form that constrains their function, but the props should be stripped of detail in order to allow participants to discover and determine the crucial design elements throughout the design session. The role of props is to provide a mechanism for participants to enact their ideas, goals, and opinions in a given context. Good props inspire compelling stories and make it easy for users to fill in important design details (see Figures 4.32–4.34).

FIGURES 4.32–4.34
Good props inspire compelling stories and make it easy for users to fill in important design details.

Stimuli

Participants in participatory design sessions have to be the authors of their own experience. However, participatory design sessions have a theatrical aspect to them and not all participants will feel completely comfortable improvising on cue. Stimuli—verbal cues (such as questions or describing the context of use) or nonverbal cues (such as images or words on paper)—can help get the ball rolling for participants and direct the flow of the session and allow designers to get deeper insights on a particular idea. Being thoughtful about which stimuli to use and when to introduce them within the process is crucial for getting the most out of your participatory design session (see Figures 4.35–4.37).

FIGURE 4.35-4.37
Stimuli can help get the ball rolling for participants and direct the flow of the participatory design session.

While companies often like to think that users are fully committed to their digital ecosystem offering, that is rarely the case. In reality, a user's ecosystem rarely aligns neatly to one company. Users may have an HP computer with an operating system designed by Microsoft, an Android tablet, an Apple iPhone, and a Sony PlayStation connected to their 10-year-old TV. People own devices from various manufacturers, run different software on each, and use Internet services from a motley crew of companies. People out in the real world often cobble together their own digital ecosystems based on a variety of factors such as cost, convenience, legacy devices, and sometimes just plain old whim.

The goal of any converged ecosystem from a user's perspective is interoperability, which is the ability of diverse systems and organizations to work together harmoniously. Unfortunately, many companies create barriers to interoperability as a strategy. While capitalism drives innovation, it also creates obstacles. In fact, many manufacturers actively work to prevent people from using devices together as a way of locking people into their products and services. As users march toward a converged future, proprietary formats, limited access to content, and competing standards not only stand in the way…they piss customers off. Lock-in is a difficult UX strategy to pull off and sustain successfully over a long period of time. People should want to use your products and services because of the experiences they provide, not because they feel like they don't have a choice.

Creating Experiences That Scale

Once you've identified the key relationships in a user's ecosystem and the important experiential handoffs, you can start creating digital experiences that scale across devices. While creating a seamless experience is the goal, there are multiple ways to deliver a seamless experience. Part of orchestrating an experience across multiple screens is to understand how the different screens in a device ecosystem can relate to each other.

Until recently, the heart of a typical user's device ecosystem was likely his personal computer. A PC was the center of the experience, and all the other experiences radiated off the PC like a hub and spoke. The common and widespread practice of "synching" a tablet or smartphone to a PC reinforced the assumption that a personal computer was the hub of any family of devices. That notion is rapidly changing. While PCs still play a dominant role in most users' device ecosystems, they aren't always the heart. As mobile devices become more prevalent, new, more distributed relationship patterns between devices are emerging.

The talented folks at Precious Design in Hamburg, Germany identified the following six relationship patterns for screen ecosystems:

- Coherence
- Synchronization
- Screen Sharing
- Device Shifting
- Complementary
- Simultaneity

The following section references and builds on their ideas outlined in their "Patterns for Multi-Screen Strategies" presentation on Slideshare (http://www.slideshare.net/preciousforever/patterns-for-multiscreen-strategies). This section should give you a sense of the different types of relationships you can create between devices in an ecosystem.

Coherence

The coherence convergence pattern is about optimizing digital experiences for specific device characteristics and usage scenarios while simultaneously ensuring there is a sense of continuity of the experience across all the devices. Essentially, experiences are tailored to each device but have some sense of consistency (see Figures 4.38–4.39). The three keys to creating a coherent experience are:

- Identifying the primary use cases for each device.
- Optimizing the design of each experience to map to those use cases.
- Maintaining a unified design language (visual and interaction) that scales across a variety of devices.

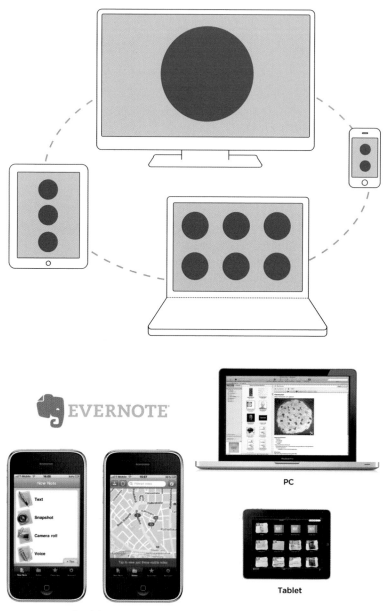

FIGURES 4.38–4.39

Evernote, a digital to-do list and notebook application, is available on numerous platforms and devices. The smartphone apps are optimized for photo and audio input and notes are location tagged.

Synchronization

Similar to keeping devices in sync with your computer, the synchronization screen pattern is all about keeping content in sync, regardless of the device for the sake of task continuation (see Figures 4.40–4.41). If a user starts watching a streaming Netflix movie on his networked TV, this approach allows him to pick up the movie where he left off on any device in his ecosystem.

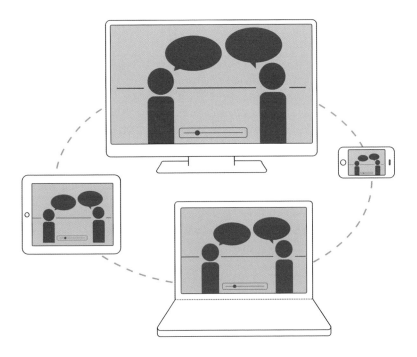

FIGURES 4.40–4.41
Users of Amazon Kindle's ebook can pick up where they left off, regardless of the device.

Screen Sharing

This pattern is about multiple devices sharing the same content source. Similar to a patchwork quilt, each device in the ecosystem displays parts of the whole. Only when all the devices are together can the complete picture emerge, as shown in Figures 4.42–4.43.

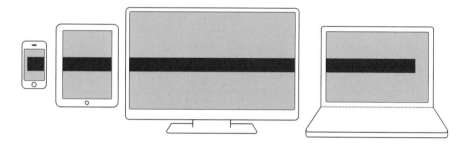

FIGURES 4.42–4.43
Junkyard Jumbotron allows users to combine random devices into one large virtual display. The research project explores how sharing screens affects social interaction.

Device Shifting

This pattern is all about shifting an experience from one device to another or seamlessly and intuitively moving data from one device to another. The pattern plays on the notion that a user can physically "move" content between devices that are in close proximity. Imagine physically "flicking" or "tossing" an image from your phone to your tablet without email or a cable. See Figures 4.44–4.45 for an example.

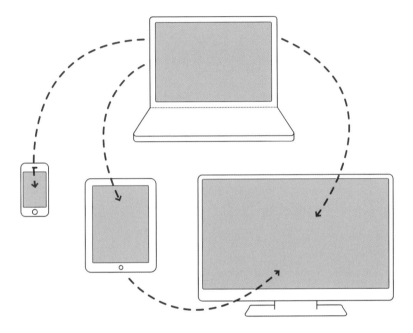

FIGURES 4.44–4.45
With Apple's Airplay technology, a video can be shifted from an iPhone or an iPad to a television.

Complementary

Similar to the relationship between a TV and a remote control, the complementary screen strategy occurs when two screens work together in concert to elevate an experience. Each device plays a specific role, but the roles support each other in a complementary fashion (see Figures 4.46–4.47).

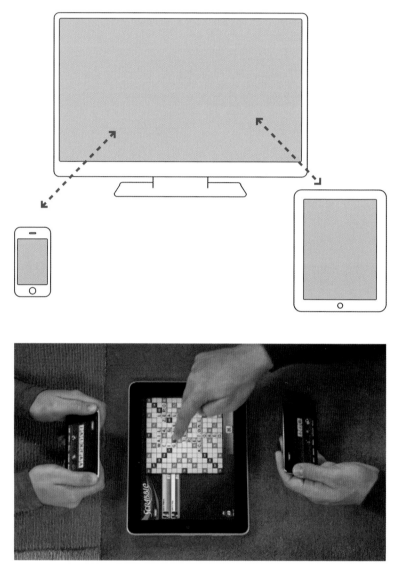

FIGURES 4.46–4.47
The iPad serves as a Scrabble board while the iPhones store an individual player's Scrabble tiles.

Simultaneity

Have you ever used the Internet via a laptop to look up a factoid while watching TV? If so, you've experienced first-hand what has been coined a "simultaneity" screen experience. This pattern is about providing users with two separate but connected experiences that can occur simultaneously (see Figures 4.48–4.49).

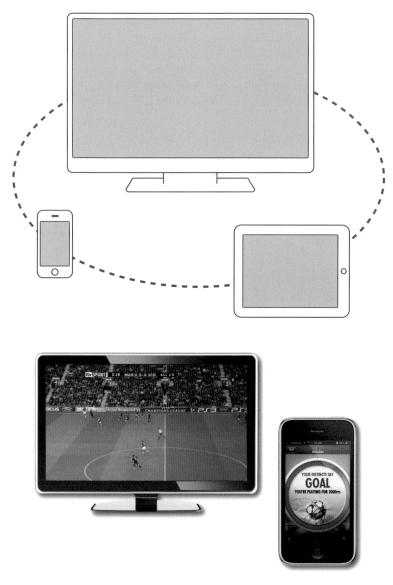

FIGURES 4.48–4.49
During a live football broadcast, users take guesses about the outcome of match situations.

Mobile Web Site, Web App, or Native App?

More people are accessing content on mobile devices than ever before, and that trend shows no sign of slowing down. Analysts predict that in the future, more people will access information through a mobile device than the PC (see Figure 4.50). As designers clamor to "mobilize" information and make it easy to experience on mobile devices, a common question arises: What's the best way to deliver a mobile experience to users? A mobile Web site? A mobile app? Or a native app? And, if so, which technology platform should you build your app on? There's been a lot of debate in mobile UX circles with regard to this basic question: Should I build a native app or a Web app (with HTML5, CSS3, and JavaScript) or a mobile Web site?

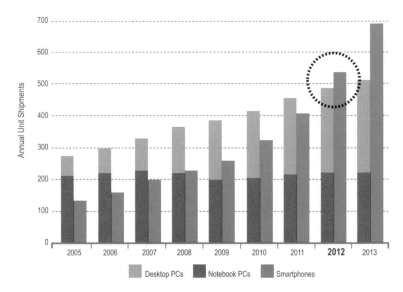

FIGURE 4.50

This chart from Morgan Stanley published on the Web site *Online Marketing Trends* shows the incredible global mobile sales growth. The estimated growth of mobile smartphones is increasing almost exponentially, with 2012 as the inflection year, when there are more smartphones than PCs around the world.

First, you may wonder…What are the differences?

- **A mobile-optimized Web site is an iteration of your PC Web site that has been optimized for the mobile context.** Built using standard Web programming (HTML) and viewed through a mobile device's browser, good mobile Web sites are designed to emphasize the content and features of your Web site that have the most relevance for users in a mobile context. Since most mobile devices come preloaded with a browser, a mobile-optimized Web site is the most accessible way to provide users with Internet content on a mobile device.

- **A native app is a custom-made application users can download onto their mobile phone for frequent use.** Native apps are created using platform-specific software (for example, Android, Apple iOS, Windows, Symbian, and so on), and they often provide more interactive features, which result in a slicker, more dynamic user experience for your users than a mobile Web site. Native apps often hook into the Web and provide Web content, but they are not viewed through a browser. Unlike a mobile Web site, a native app will only work on the software platform for which it was developed. For example, a native mobile application developed for iOS platform will only work on an iPhone. It won't work on other devices.

- **A mobile Web app is a mobile application that users can access via a mobile browser.** It is not a static mobile Web site. It is designed to work like a native app, but it is not accessible via the App store or Android marketplace. You access it from the browser. Some parts of the software are downloaded from the Web each time it is used. It can usually be accessed from all Web-capable mobile devices.

Which Should You Create?

Given the popularity and ever-growing demand for smartphones, a Web site optimized for mobile devices is something any company with a Web presence should have. Unlike native mobile applications, the Web affords you universal access to any device with a browser. Users expect Web content to follow them seamlessly from device to device, so not creating a Web site that's optimized for mobile is a big missed opportunity.

The pros of creating native apps are that they offer more in terms of design options for interaction design and user interface. Native apps are just generally…well, prettier! The big drawback of native apps is that they automatically limit your audience to the mobile phone owners of the platform you decide to design for.

The pros of creating Web apps are the inversion of native apps. Anyone who owns a smartphone with a browser can access the mobile experience you've created. The cons are that the Web doesn't offer the same design options for interaction design and user interface that apps created using native software do.

So which should you choose?

In my opinion, native apps tend to deliver better mobile experiences. From an interaction design perspective, you have more options and more control of the experience. Native apps deliver a richer experience and allow you to access and use leading technologies within the experiences you're crafting. Native apps enable you to hook into a mobile device's capabilities (NFC, camera, GPS, and so on) much more easily than a Web app or a mobilized Web site. That said, designers are creating phenomenal Web app experiences with HTML5, CSS3, and JavaScript. Hopefully, Web app experiences will be able to compete from a design perspective with native apps in the not-too-distant future.

Mobile is changing quickly, so this could change quickly as well. For now, if you have the time and the resources, then you should do both! If not, create a Web site optimized for mobile. (This is just something everyone should do.) Then choose the mobile platform that fits the needs, personality, and demographics of your users. And build a native app that really sings for them.

Responsive Web Design

With the number of devices in a user's ecosystem rapidly increasing, so too are the number of screens affixed to those devices. All these many screens come in varying sizes, screen resolutions, and orientations. Some are in landscape, others in portrait, and some support both. Plus, new devices with new screen sizes are being developed every day, and each of these devices may be able to handle variations in size and functionality. How do you design for all these variables?

Creating a different version of a Web site for each and every device would be too time consuming to even consider.

Responsive Web design is a Web design and development approach that asserts that a site should respond to the screen size, platform, and orientation of the device. As a user moves from his laptop to an iPad or to a smartphone, the Web site should automatically reform to accommodate the screen size and functionality of the device. (In other words, the Web site should respond to the device and the user's preferences.

FIGURE 4.51
Ethan Marcotte's book outlines how you can craft beautiful Web experiences that are responsive to the screen size of a user's device.

The practice of creating a responsive Web site consists of using a mix of flexible grids and layouts, images, and an intelligent use of CSS media queries. Ethan Marcotte wrote a great how-to book about responsive Web design. In it, he outlines how you can craft beautiful Web experiences that are responsive to the screen size of a user's device (see Figure 4.51). It can eliminate the need for a different design and development phase for each new gadget on the market.

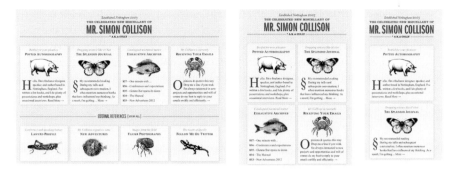

FIGURES 4.52–4.54
Because this site was created using responsive Web design principles, the layout of the Web page responds appropriately to the device's screen size and device context.

Used wisely, responsive Web design is a great method that can improve the user experience of Web sites on a variety of devices. However, it's not a panacea. A Web site created using responsive Web design and development techniques does not fundamentally change the content of a Web site—it only changes the presentation of the content. Remember that mobile needs are often very different than desktop needs (see Figures 4.52–4.54). Responsive Web design doesn't allow you to fundamentally change or drastically edit or reprioritize content based on the needs of your user in a mobile context (see Figure 4.55).

FIGURE 4.55
Facebook's mobile app is tailored for mobile needs. It gives users quick access to the content and functionality that is important to them in a mobile context. Facebook's mobile Web site simply replicates many of the features from the desktop experience.

It's easy to see how content on the first image of the Simon Collision Web site would be illegible when viewed on smaller devices. Because the site was created using responsive Web design, when the browser is minimized or the user is on a mobile device, the layout of the Web page responds appropriately to the device's screen size and device context

> "Great mobile products are created, never ported."
>
> —Brian Fling
> Creative Director at Pinchzoom,
> author of Mobile Design & Development

Once a futuristic topic reserved for business analysts and nerdy technical researchers, convergence is no longer a lofty dream. People are growing to expect their digital content to follow them seamlessly through the world, and mobile devices are enabling this to happen. While mobile devices are an important part of any converged experience, designers can't focus solely on the mobile experience any more than Web site designers can focus solely on the PC experience. This desire for seamless experiences across devices is forcing designers to have a system-wide view of the experiences they create. Just like runners in a relay team, you have to know what the other experiences are in order to catch and hand off the baton.

While this chapter has been all about designing multidevice experiences in which mobile devices are part of a larger ecosystem of devices, the next chapter will focus specifically on what makes mobile experiences unique— mobile UX patterns.

Summary

- Convergence is a timely and important topic in the world of mobility because what constitutes a mobile device is rapidly changing and UX designers must design for ecosystem experiences. There is a growing expectation that digital content will follow the user seamlessly from device to device. Convergence enables that to happen.

- Currently, convergence is occurring on three levels: technology convergence, media convergence, and activity convergence.

- Ecosystems are the medium of the new converged digital landscape. A digital ecosystem includes all the relevant digital touchpoints, the people that interact with them, and the business processes and technology environments that support them.

- A great way to get a sense of the depth and breadth of your users' digital ecosystems is to ask them to draw you a map.

- Lucy Suchman's theory of situated action suggests a person's capacity to act (their agency) is reconfigured when it comes into contact with another thing or person—that human action is constantly constructed and reconstructed from dynamic interactions with the material world.

- There are currently six patterns for multiscreen strategies: coherence, synchronization, screen sharing, device shifting, complementary, and simultaneity.

- Currently, there exists a vigorous debate over whether designers should create a native mobile app, a Web app, or a mobile Web site. There is no right answer…yet.

Expert Interview: Stephanie and Bryan Rieger

PROPRIETORS OF YIIBU

The dynamic duo of Stephanie and Bryan Rieger (see Figure 4.56) own and operate Yiibu, an innovative design consultancy that develops experiences for diverse platforms. Bryan is a designer, writer, and reluctant developer with a background in theatre design and classical animation. Stephanie is a writer, designer, and closet anthropologist with a passion for the many ways that people interact with technology.

FIGURE 4.56
Stephanie and Bryan Rieger focus on designing and developing interactive media experiences that scale across devices.

How did you two find your way into the mobile user experience space?

Bryan: Back in 2000 or 2001, we were both working in the Web, and these intriguing little mobile projects started appearing on our radar. One project that sticks out in my mind was this guy who had made a film and asked the company I was working for to find a way to get the film onto a Palm Pilot. He was able to go to film festivals and show people his work, directly on the conference floor...and actually found distribution for his film by showing it off on that Palm Pilot. It was experiences like that—people whose lives were changed because they were able to carry information around in their pockets—which got us excited about the possibilities of mobile.

Stephanie: We've always been fascinated with how and why people use technology and around that same time we started traveling rather extensively throughout Asia—even living there for a while. Seeing firsthand how differently people in Asia were using mobile technology really intrigued us. The culture was so different—landlines were expensive; everyone seemed to have a phone; there was already this culture of mass experimentation, personalization, and people fixing each other's phones. The uptake of mobile technology by people in all walks of life in Asia was quite stark in comparison to what we were used to in North America.

A lot has changed since 2001. What sticks out in your mind as some of the groundbreaking changes that have occurred since you began your careers in mobile user experience?

Bryan: The Android platform is one groundbreaking change. I think developers and designers really wanted an open platform that everybody could build off of, and Android delivered that. Now, we're just seeing so much experimentation and people running with it and doing all sorts of crazy things, a classic case of unintended consequences—which are often both good and bad.

Stephanie: I think one of the most important changes has been the rapid and widespread growth in access to mobile connectivity. So many more people now carry Internet-connected devices than even three or four years ago. This constant ability to access the Internet (and access each other), not even just on the go, but literally whenever they want—it's almost like a drug. Once people experience that, it's really hard for them to remember that it hasn't always been that way. But while consumers are migrating to mobile for everyday Web use, our content, standards, and ecosystems aren't always ready.

You both advocate building Web experiences with future-friendly principles and progressive enhancement. Why?

Bryan: When the Web started really taking off, nearly everyone's point of reference was a PC with an 800 × 600 screen (or more recently, 1024 × 768). That's just no longer the case. The Web started out with a fairly large viewport, and we all thought that viewport would keep getting larger, but it's now going in all directions. We now have displays the size of a wall, displays the size of a phone, and everything in between.

Stephanie: Putting an operating system with a browser attached to a network on any type and size of device is now insanely easy. It's ultimately a good thing, but an unfortunate consequence is fragmentation. There are millions of devices with very little consistency around standard screen sizes and browser types. There's really no sign this will change anytime soon.

Bryan: Despite the growth of dynamic data and Ajax, I think that most Web design is still a reflection of print. We've been designing for one context, which in the end, isn't much better than creating a PDF document. As the number of access points grow, that approach no longer works.

The biggest mind shift that needs to happen is for Web designers to stop thinking of their work as "designing Web pages" and instead think of it as designing content that can be rendered in multiple contexts—big screen, small screen, all the screens in between, and maybe even no screen.

Stephanie: I think this is difficult for many designers because of the way the Web industry has been structured. There are still people whose entire job is to create visual mockups on a PC and never touch a line of code. They may think they've designed something perfect, but that perfection is tied to a single context. Not only is this approach unrealistic (due to the wide and growing number of devices), but it also doesn't account for the fact that each user journey may include multiple devices.

Bryan: Once a designer accepts that lack of control, it can be very liberating. Instead of focusing so much on the visual presentation of the Web in one context (the PC), designers and developers can start to think about how to render Web experiences in multiple contexts and across multiple devices.

Stephanie: Much Web design still focuses on the design of the overlying view—the container if you will. But the smaller the screen gets, the less we actually see and interact with that container. Often, all we see (and what bubbles up) is the content.

You also advocate a content-out design strategy. Can you describe what a content-out strategy is and how designers can learn to do it?

Bryan: Designing content that looks good on all target devices requires a mixture of flexible design and a solid understanding of a device's capabilities. An approach that's worked well for us is to build a well-structured and flexible base, then enhance the layout using major and minor breakpoints. This approach allows designers to create lovely context-based layouts that move fluidly from one state to another. They won't match specific device sizes but they won't be trying to.

Stephanie: The major breakpoints create the broad stroke changes that are required when moving from the small(er) screen (mobile), to a much wider one (often a tablet-like device), to an even wider one (often a desktop but increasingly there can be higher breakpoints for TVs, etc). These major breakpoints are set using media queries in the document head. The minor breakpoints live within those two to four style sheets and (mostly) provide the tweaks needed to remove awkwardness.

These tweaks most often include adjustments in font size, line length, line height, gutters, padding, and other design elements that make the layout feel more balanced and improve legibility. Other useful tweaks are adjustments of the overall font size to ensure that button/menu touch targets and form elements are large enough to manipulate on touchscreens. If you're going as high as TVs, text may need to be enlarged, but changes don't always follow a predictable upward or downward path.

But while content always guides the design (which also helps prioritize useful stuff like document flow and information design), the end goal should always be an experience that's appropriate to the user's device. This means pairing good design with feature detection to determine a browser's capabilities. This enables you to further enhance the experience with visual and functional enhancements that suit each user's device.

Thinking about the future of mobile, which topics interest you most?

Bryan: Before the iPhone, we had a fantastic range of weird and wonderful devices. Nokia, in particular, experimented quite a bit with mobile as an extension of fashion. When the iPhone came out, there was a different kind of magic to it—magic that was deeply tied to its software, and that was lovely.

But here we are after five years…everyone has mimicked the iPhone form factor, and we're now all left staring at glowing rectangles. These devices may be wonderful blank canvases that morph into whatever you need through software, but much of their outward personality has been lost. People can attach cases to them to personalize them a bit, but there isn't much else they can do.

We often make jokes about zombies walking down the street, staring at a glowing rectangle, but why do they *have* to be glowing rectangles? Seems like a missed opportunity for devices that have become such an important and uniquely personal part of our lives.

CHAPTER 5

Mobile UX Patterns
Designing for Mobility

The Structure of a Design Factor   108
Mobile Design Patterns   110
Mobile UX Pattern #1: "The Cloud" and Applications
    as Natural Set Points for Mobile Experiences   111
Mobile Pattern #2: Good Mobile Experiences
    Progressively Reveal their Nature   121
Mobile Pattern #3: Content Becomes the Interface   128
Mobile Pattern #4: Use Uniquely Mobile Input
    Mechanisms   133
Mobile Pattern #5: Say Good-Bye to Done   138
Summary   141

W hen the topic of design patterns emerges in the context of user experience or interaction design, the work of Christopher Alexander invariably gets mentioned. People love him, and rightfully so. While his theories articulated in *A Pattern Language: Towns, Buildings, Construction* were originally tailored for the field of architecture, they've been widely embraced in the realm of computer programming and interaction design because he expresses design through something described as a pattern language—a language that anyone can learn and speak, as shown in Figure 5.1.

A Pattern Language
Towns · Buildings · Construction

Christopher Alexander
Sara Ishikawa · Murray Silverstein
WITH
Max Jacobson · Ingrid Fiksdahl-King
Shlomo Angel

FIGURE 5.1
Pattern language, a term coined by architect Christopher Alexander, is a structured method of describing good design practices within a field of expertise.

A central idea to Alexander's book was that anyone should be able to design his own house, street, and community—and all that was needed was the appropriate language. Alexander asserted that "patterns" were units of a language and answers to design problems. By articulating these 253 patterns of the built environment, he was in essence giving people a pattern language for that same built environment.

While in graduate school at the Institute of Design in Chicago, I took a class taught by Charles Owen called "The Design and Evaluation of Complex Systems." It was a class dedicated to learning a design process developed by Professor Owens—a process inspired and influenced by Christian Alexander's work that could be used to design anything from an IT infrastructure to a complex legal system. The class was rigorous, highly structured, and at times made me want to pull out my hair in frustration. However, in the years that have passed since graduation, there are aspects of the process I've found invaluable in my mobile UX work. The biggest piece of the process that I find myself turning to time and again is the articulation of design factors (which eerily almost mirror Alexander's articulation of patterns).

The Structure of a Design Factor

Creating a design factor begins by articulating an observation, a question, or a problem; listing ways to react to it; and then outlining an idea for addressing the problem. Similar to use cases, design factors are communicated in written form, using the structure depicted in Figure 5.2.

Observation: A one- or two-sentence description of an observed phenomenon.

Extension: Describe the observation in more detail. Offer supporting evidence.

Design Strategies: Ideas and suggestions about the possible ways to react to an observation and its extension.

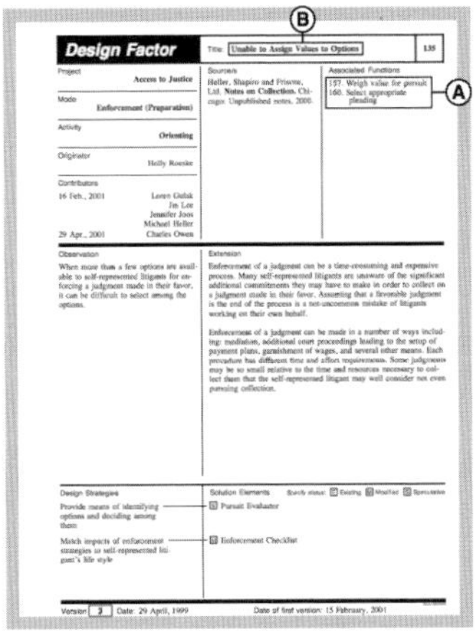

B

Design Factor Title: Unable to Assign Values to Options 135

Project: **Access to Justice**

Mode: **Enforcement (Preparation)**

Activity: **Orienting**

Originator: Holly Roeske

Contributors:
16 Feb., 2001 Loren Gulak
Jin Lee
Jennifer Joos
Michael Heller
29 Apr., 2001 Charles Owen

Sources: Heller, Shapiro and Prisone, Ltd. **Notes on Collection.** Chicago: Unpublished notes, 2000.

Associated Functions:
157. Weigh value for pursuit
160. Select appropriate pleading

A

Observation: When more than a few options are available to self-represented litigants for enforcing a judgment made in their favor, it can be difficult to select among the options.

Extension: Enforcement of a judgment can be a time-consuming and expensive process. Many self-represented litigants are unaware of the significant additional commitments they may have to make in order to collect on a judgment made in their favor. Assuming that a favorable judgment is the end of the process is a not-uncommon mistake of litigants working on their own behalf.

Enforcement of a judgment can be made in a number of ways including: mediation, additional court proceedings leading to the setup of payment plans, garnishment of wages, and several other means. Each procedure has different time and effort requirements. Some judgments may be so small relative to the time and resources necessary to collect them that the self-represented litigant may well consider not even pursuing collection.

Design Strategies:
Provide means of identifying options and deciding among them — Pursuit Evaluator
Match impacts of enforcement strategies to self-represented litigant's life style — Enforcement Checklist

Solution Elements — Specify status: Existing, Modified, Speculative

Version 3 Date: 29 April, 1999 Date of first version: 15 February, 2001

FIGURE 5.2
Example of a design factor from Charles Owens's "The Design and Evaluation of Complex Systems."

Solution Elements: Ideas well enough described to be evaluated as useful.

A favorite example of mine from *A Pattern Language* is the pattern for *Dancing in the Streets.* I've used the design factor format to articulate this design pattern below:

> ***Pattern #63:*** Dancing in the Streets

Title: People are unable or feel uncomfortable dancing in city streets of modern cities.

Observation: Why is it that people don't dance in the streets today?

Extension: All over the earth, people once danced in the streets. In theater, song, and natural speech, "dancing in the street" was an image of supreme joy (as depicted in Figure 5.3). Most cultures have some version of this activity. But in those parts of the world that have become "modern and technically sophisticated," this experience has died. Communities are fragmented; people are uncomfortable in the streets, afraid of one another; not many people play the right kind of music; people are embarrassed. The embarrassment and alienation are recent developments, blocking a more basic need. And as we get in touch with these needs, things start to happen. People remember how to dance; people begin to take up instruments, and many form little bands with no place to play in the urban environment.

Design Strategies: Provide a design pattern that encourages dancing in the streets.

Solution Elements: Along promenades, in squares, and in evening centers, make a slightly raised platform to form a bandstand, where street musicians and local bands can play (as depicted in Figure 5.4). Cover it and perhaps build in ground-level tiny stalls for refreshments. Surround the bandstand with a paved surface for dancing—no admission charge.

FIGURE 5.3
"Dancing in the street" is an image of supreme joy.

FIGURE 5.4
This layout provides
a design pattern that
encourages urban
design to further
encourage dancing in
the streets.

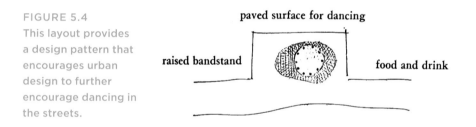

Mobile Design Patterns

Mobile UX has historically been a design space riddled with deeply entrenched user experience problems. This can be attributed to two key issues:

- Mobile UX has had few well-documented design patterns. Designers too often borrow design patterns from the PC instead of designing and documenting new patterns for mobile.

- The few design patterns that *do* exist for mobile are evolving at a very rapid pace.

Relative to a creative discipline like urban planning, mobile user experience is a new design space. It's in its infancy, and just like a newborn baby that triples its birth weight in one year, we should expect to see the rapid and exponential increase in the number of mobile design patterns. While the structure of design factors may seem laborious and text-centric for work that is largely visual, I've found it to be a helpful framework for organizing ideas. During the course of my career in mobile, there are countless user problems I've observed and recorded as design factors. The next section covers five mobile UX patterns I've been tracking that I think are emergent and important:

1. "The Cloud" and Applications as Natural Set Points for Mobile

2. Good Mobile Experiences Progressively Reveal their Nature

3. Content Becomes the Interfaces

4. Uniquely Mobile Input

5. Say Good-bye to Done

MOBILE UX PATTERN #1:
"The Cloud" and Applications as Natural Set Points for Mobile Experiences

Observation: If mobile devices aren't computers, what's the appropriate set point for mobile experiences? If "the desktop" metaphor anchored PC experiences, what will anchor mobile experiences?

Extension: Most any space has a set point, which is an organizing principle that helps people form a mental model of how they think about and navigate that space. Rooms are the set points of homes, neighborhoods and streets are set points of cities, aisles are the set points for most stores, and Web pages are the set points for Web sites. Good set points are intuitive, flexible, and capable of sustaining broad-scale changes. Figuring out the appropriate set point for an experiences is an important design decision because it influences how people engage with a space, how easily they can traverse a space, and sets the tone for future development of a space.

One of my personal favorite anecdotal examples of set points is from anthropology professor Michael Wesch of Kansas State University. During a presentation I attended, Michael shared how during his research in rural New Guinea, he experienced how the introduction of the census changed the way that homes in a village were organized. Before the census, homes were organized in an ad hoc fashion according to the relationships between the people who lived in them. After the census was introduced, people in these villages began to build their home in a more linear, grid-like fashion in order to map to the numbers on the census documents (see Figure 5.5). In essence, introduction of the census caused the set point to change how homes in that village were organized.

FIGURE 5.5
Before the census was introduced in rural New Guinea, homes were organized based on relationships. After the census was introduced, homes were organized in a grid-like fashion in order to map with the census forms.

Set Points and Mobile Experiences

The initial set point for the PC experience was the desktop and accompanying folder/file system. Influenced by notions of containment and place, this set point initially allowed people to traverse their personal file systems with ease. While intuitive, this early set point for the PC was unable to scale and adapt to modern notions of how people use information. Just like hoarders who are unable to purge unnecessary items from their homes, most people who have used computers for any amount of time have saved hundreds upon thousands of files on hard drives and backup drives. These files will likely never be used again, but the task of organizing them is too daunting, and the idea of throwing them away or deleting them is too scary. Instead, people live in their digital mess, victims of a set point that could not scale and sustain change.

Design Strategies: Two set points that are emerging as significant mobile design patterns are the following:

- "The Cloud" as a set point
- Applications as a set point

The growth of the Internet has given rise to a formidable new mobile set point commonly referred to as "the cloud." As an alternative to the burden of storing files locally on your person, cloud services such as Google Docs, Dropbox, and Basecamp enable users to offload storage online. Files stored in "the cloud" through services such as these make sharing and collaboration easier than a desktop, and they allow users to access and manipulate files on multiple devices easily. Instead of storing and managing large media collections, cloud-based services such as Pandora, Netflix, and LastFM enable access to content without the headache of file management and storage. They also give the user a level of social interaction that files trapped on a desktop cannot provide.

"The cloud" is an intuitive and efficient set point for mobile UX interactions. Lugging files around locally forces users to assume the associated risks of data loss through device theft or technical failure. Mobile devices with a desktop set point must physically be larger in size to accommodate larger hard drives for file storage. Because of its legacy as a communication device, mobile phones dovetail nicely with the sharing and community features that cloud-based services provide. Keep the following design considerations in mind when integrating "the cloud" as a design pattern into your work.

Examples of "the Cloud" Design Pattern

Dropbox is a service that uses cloud computing to enable users to store and share content with others across the Internet using file synchronization, so it becomes a solution element, as shown in Figure 5.6.

FIGURE 5.6
Solution element: Dropbox.

1. "THE CLOUD" IS A SERVICE

Unlike locally stored files that are accessed through the device's operating system, the cloud usually presents itself to users as a service. Good services have easy and intuitive ways to manage their relationship with customers, and they offer users help for managing, discovering, and sharing content. If you are integrating the cloud into a mobile experience, think through how your users will be interacting not just with folders and files, but also with a service.

Example: Radio stations that are accessible through the Web are similar to the cloud service Pandora and have similar functionality. They both provide music via the Internet. Yet they provide very different experiences. Similar to analog radio stations, online radio stations have one playlist for all users. Pandora is designed like a service (with profiles, recommendations, etc.), providing users with the ability to tailor their music experience to their tastes.

2. PLAN FOR NON-NETWORK CONNECTIVITY

The underlying promise of any cloud experience is its ability to access your information from anywhere. Unfortunately, mobile network infrastructure doesn't always cooperate and make that dream a reality. An important component of any cloud-based mobile experience is providing a seamless experience even if/when a network connection is disrupted. If your mobile experience is dependent on the cloud, it's important to think about how to provide users with a good experience, even when key functionality is disrupted.

Example: Web applications built using HTML5's Application Cache feature can provide users with minimal functionality when spotty network access strikes.

3. THE PRISM EFFECT

A hallmark of any great cloud experience is that it can be prismed through all the devices in a user's ecosystem. Instead of duplicating the same experience across each device, it's better to take advantage of what each device can do well and design to those strengths. Tablets, for example, are well suited for content consumption, whereas desktop experiences are better suited for content creation through a keyboard and mouse. Experiences should be consistent, but not simply duplicated for each device.

Example: Cloud service Dropbox provides a similar experience across an ecosystem of devices, but tailors each experience to take advantage of the inherent strengths of each device. The mobile experience is tailored for easy access to files, sharing, and seamlessly hooking into files created by the phone without exposing the file system, while the tablet and desktop Dropbox experiences offer a higher degree of file organization and management.

Google Docs integrates with several popular mobile apps such as GoDocs and DocsToGo, making it easy to access documents from multiple mobile devices (see Figure 5.7).

FIGURE 5.7
Solution element: Google Docs.

A service such as Netflix allows users to offload the storage of large media files to the cloud (see Figure 5.8). For a monthly fee, users can enjoy movies from anywhere without the hassle of file management.

FIGURE 5.8
Solution element: Netflix.

While applications play a role in desktop interactions, they are often relegated to the role of a secondary actor. Files are the stars of the desktop experience, whereas applications are merely the tools that make files. In mobile UX, applications are the star, making them a natural set point for mobile experiences. Because many mobile interactions are inherently ephemeral and have no output—no file to save and store—the application becomes a natural set point for the interaction. Files that are created as output on a mobile device, such as pictures taken with a camera phone, are usually saved in either the application itself or a "space" strongly associated with the application (such as a gallery), reinforcing that the application is the set point of the experience, not the file.

Mobile application marketplaces also reinforce the app as the natural set point for mobile experiences. A mobile platform's value and popularity are largely attributed to the depth and breadth of its App Store portfolio. The quantity and quality of mobile applications are a key part of why people buy particular devices. Marketing slogans like, "There's an app for that" reinforce application as a key enabler and natural set point of mobile experiences, as shown in Figure 5.9.

FIGURE 5.9
Marketing messages like "There's an app for that" reinforce applications as a set point for mobile experiences.

Emerging Application Types

Since apps are an important part of mobile experiences, it's good to familiarize yourself with the typologies of applications that are emerging. While this is not a comprehensive set, this list should prove helpful when considering the type of experience you want to create for your users.

Core Application

Core applications encompass apps such as the contact/address book, mail applications, calendar applications, and the voice calling features on the phone. These apps are native to the mobile operating system on the device. Data created by or associated with core applications (such as information from the address book/contact list) can hook into other types of applications (see Figure 5.10). However, inherently changing them or attempting to replace them is difficult to do since they are native to the phone's operating system.

Examples:

- Mail application

- SMS application

- Voice call application

- Camera application

FIGURE 5.10
The iPhone's calendar app is an example of a core application.

Widgets

Widgets are single-purpose applications that supply information with minimal functionality, as shown in Figure 5.11. Widgets are a great application choice if your app has a single purpose with minimal functionality and complexity.

Examples:

- Weather widget

- Calculator widget

- Stock quote widget

- Currency converter widget

FIGURE 5.11
The iHandy Level is an example of a widget application.

Feed-Focused Applications

Feed-focused applications display bite-sized pieces of content in a list fashion, organized by time with the most recent content at the top of the list. This application type is commonly used for experiences with a social networking component, similar to Figure 5.12.

Examples:

- Twitter
- Viddy

- GoWalla
- InstaGram

Consumption-Focused Applications

Consumption-focused applications funnel users to a piece of content (see Figure 5.13). Similar to feed-focused applications, consumption-focused applications offer types of interactivity; however, the main feature of the application is its ability to search for and consume content. Highly visual and evocative, these applications make content the star.

Examples:

- Netflix
- BBC News

- iBooks
- FlipBoard

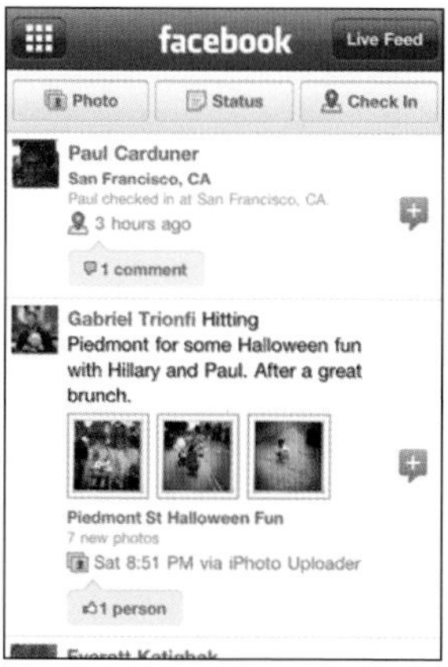

FIGURE 5.12
The Facebook application for the iPhone is a feed-focused app. While you'll find tons of other functionality packed into this social networking app, the News Feed section receives the bulk of user engagement.

FIGURE 5.13
HBO Go for the iPad is an example of a consumption-focused application. While there are in-depth options for interactivity, the main feature of the application is its ability to search for and consume content offered by its premium TV channel.

Search/Find Application

Search/find applications are all about connecting users to products and services near them (see Figure 5.14). Unlike search features on a desktop experience, search/find applications usually leverage the mobile's ability to add the dimension of "place" to data. Not only can users search for information, but they can also search for information that is relevant to them based on their current location.

Examples:

- Yelp

- Google Maps

FIGURE 5.14
Yelp for the iPad is an example of a search/find application. Users can find places to eat, shop, and drink. While there is additional functionality such as reviewing/rating venues and sharing photos, the key attraction for users is the ability to find nearby businesses.

Search/Find/Transact Application

This application type is similar to search/find, as shown in Figure 5.15; however, it adds an extra piece of interaction to the equation—the ability to transact. A great fit for online services, search/find/transact applications are about presenting the information necessary to make a purchasing decision and then funneling users into a purchase flow.

Examples:

- TripAdvisor

- OpenTable

- Shazam

- Amazon

FIGURE 5.15

The Shazam application for the iPad is an example of a search/find/transact application. Users can perform a real-time music search of a song. In addition to providing loads of information about the song, users can purchase the song through iTunes.

FIGURE 5.16

Square for the iPhone is a tool-like app. The iPhone app, along with a free card reader that plugs into the headphone jack, allows users to accept credit card payments.

Tool Application

Tool applications are widgets that have grown up. Similar to a widget, tool applications are very focused (see Figure 5.16). However, tool applications are generally more complex than a widget because they often hook into some of the key features and functionality of the mobile device (such as a photo gallery hooking into a camera application on a phone). Or they simply provide more than the single-purpose functionality of a widget. Tool applications help you get stuff done.

Examples:

- Camera
- QR code application
- Clock
- Nike+

Games are simply fun applications for users to kill time and entertain themselves, like the game in Figure 5.17.

Examples:

- *Angry Birds*
- *Tetris*
- *Plants and Zombies*
- *Solitaire*

FIGURE 5.17
The seminal mobile game *Angry Birds* is a great example of a mobile game application. It's interactive, fun, and a great escape when bored with a few minutes to burn.

MOBILE PATTERN #2:
Good Mobile Experiences Progressively Reveal their Nature

A key difference between designing for PC and mobile experiences is screen real estate. Mobile devices have significantly less screen space to work with than their PC counterparts. Creating successful mobile experiences involves learning how to make interactions unfold, and allowing your mobile experience to progressively reveal its nature to users.

Observation: Designing for mobile is more challenging than designing for a PC because the screen size is much smaller.

Extension: Growing up, my sister and I were big fans of *Shrinky Dink* kits (see Figures 5.18 and 5.19). I fondly remember the many hours we spent meticulously adding color to outlined images of our favorite cartoon characters printed on the weird, slightly slippery *Shrinky Dink* plastic paper. While the activity itself was akin to coloring in coloring books, the final product was infinitely cooler. A standard kitchen oven was all that was needed to unlock the magical powers of *Shrinky Dinks*. Bake the colored paper characters in a hot oven like a batch of cookies, and they'd magically turn into tiny versions of themselves.

FIGURES 5.18 AND 5.19

Shrinky Dinks are a children's toy/activity kit consisting of large flexible sheets that, when heated in an oven, shrink to small hard plates without altering their color or shape. Most sets are preprinted with outline images of popular children's characters or other subjects, which are then colored in before baking.

Shrinky Dinks and Mobile UX

Shrinky Dinks come to mind when I think of the often-cited screen real estate disparity between mobile devices and personal computers; mobile experiences have substantially less screen real estate to work with than their PC counterparts. A common yet unwise method for dealing with less screen real estate is to employ a *Shrinky Dink* strategy: to simply shrink a PC experience, load it onto a mobile device, and call it a mobile experience. While my fondness for *Shrinky Dinks* clearly runs deep, miniaturizing a PC experience for a mobile device is a *bad* idea. It's a surface solution to a structural problem. Successful PC and mobile experiences are built on fundamentally different conceptual models and leverage different psychological functions of the user. Understanding these differences will help you create better experiences for both contexts.

PC Design Patterns: Anchors, Stacking, and Recognition

All PC experiences have a conceptual anchor—the desktop—from which users can navigate. Similar to a Jenga tower or a stack of papers, PC experiences have a conceptual "bottom" and "top" that is anchored to the desktop (see Figures 5.20–5.22). Like stacks of paper placed on a table, the desktop metaphor enables multiple cascading application windows to be open at once. These open windows can be shifted and shuffled (reinforced by functions like "bring to front" or "send to back"). This sense of a static anchor coupled with the capability to layer and cascade application windows enables users to traverse between applications with ease and to multitask.

Users of desktop experiences interact with graphical user interfaces (aka GUIs). Graphical user interfaces are built on the psychological function of recognition, as shown in Figures 5.23 and 5.24). Users click on a menu item, the interface provides a list of actions, the user recognizes the appropriate action, and then clicks on it. GUI's reliance on recognition gave rise to the term WYSIWYG (what you see is what you get). Users can see all their options and minimal visual differentiation between interface elements is commonly used.

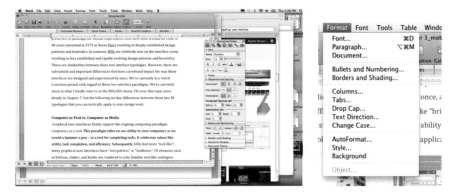

Unfolding, "Topping in" to Information and Intuition

In contrast, mobile experiences—especially those with touchscreens and natural user interfaces—can feel anchorless by comparison. Instead of cascading windows stacked on top of each other, open mobile applications take up the entire screen. Lacking the screen real estate to present all the interface options at once, mobile UIs intelligently truncate and compartmentalize information into bite-size portions that users can navigate in a way that feels intuitive, given the small amount of screen real estate for most mobile devices. If PC experiences are defined as anchored, mobile experiences are about movement and unfolding.

Instead of possessing a strong conceptual anchor, mobile experiences unfold and progressively reveal their nature. While PC experiences present all the content and functionality at once, great mobile experiences allow users to "top in" to information and reveal more content and complexity as the user engages with the application or experiences.

The natural user interfaces (aka NUIs) found on most modern mobile devices are built on the psychological function of intuition. Instead of recognizing an action from a list, users must be able to sense from the presentation of the interface what is possible. Instead of "what you see is what you get," NUIs are about "what you do is what you get." Unlike GUI interfaces with minimal differentiation between interface elements, NUI interfaces typically have fewer options, and there is more visual differentiation and hierarchy between the interface elements (see Figures 5.25–5.27).

 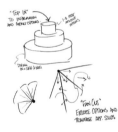 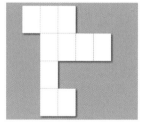

FIGURES 5.25–5.27
Unlike GUIs, natural user interfaces don't have a strong conceptual anchor, which can make users feel anchorless. In order to adapt to limited screen real estate, designers must allow users to "top in" to content, progressively revealing more information as the user engages with the experience.

Design Considerations for Mobile Experiences That Unfold

Patterns are emerging with regard to the way in which mobile experiences unfold. The following examples are patterns I've been tracking.

1. **The Nested Doll pattern.**

    Mobile experiences that employ the nested doll pattern are all about funneling users to detailed content (see Figures 5.28 and 5.29). The nested doll pattern also allows users to toggle easily between an overview screen displaying many pieces of content and a detail-level view of a specific piece of content. It's a pattern that has a strong sense of forward/back movement.

    Nested Doll examples: iPhone email app, BravoTV app, Netflix app

FIGURES 5.28 AND 5.29 The iPhone's email application employs the nested doll pattern. The user is gradually funneled to a detailed view of an individual.

2. **Hub-and-Spoke pattern.**

    Mobile experiences with a hub-and-spoke pattern have a strong central anchor point from which users can navigate (see Figures 5.30 and 5.31). Similar to the model of an airport hub, users can bypass the hub and navigate to other "spokes" of the system. However, users interacting with hub-and-spoke experiences often traverse through the hub of the application several times while engaging with the experience. The hub-and-spoke pattern works best when applied to experiences with large quantities of content or to experiences with several disparate types of functionality.

Hub-and-Spoke examples: Flipboard app, Facebook app, FourSquare app

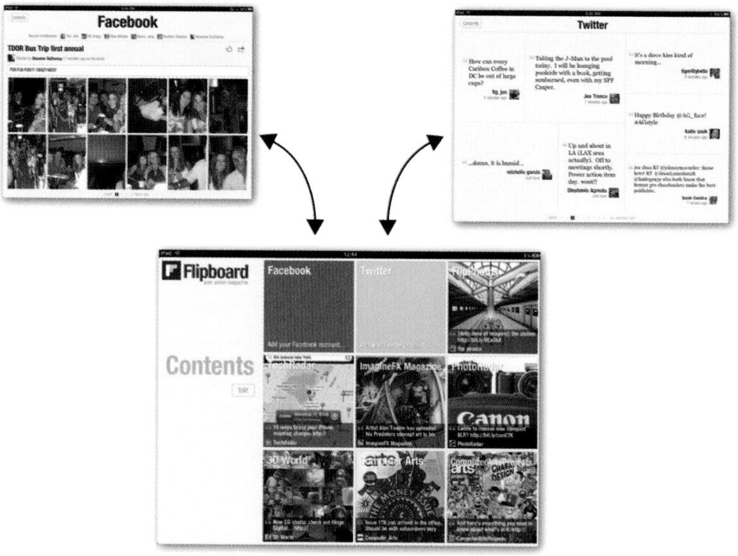

FIGURES 5.30 AND 5.31
Flipboard has a hub-and-spoke unfolding pattern. The "contents" page is the hub, with the various content sources creating the spokes of the experience.

3. **Bento Box pattern.**

Just like a bento box from a Japanese restaurant, this pattern carves up the surface area of a mobile device's screen into small compartments, each portion contributing to the overall experience (see Figures 5.32 and 5.33). This pattern is a good way to express sets of information that are strongly related to each other, and it is more commonly used on tablets than smartphone experiences.

Bento Box examples: Kayak and TripAdvisor applications for the iPad

FIGURES 5.32
AND 5.33
The Kayak application
for the iPad uses the
bento box pattern.
Small pieces of tightly
related information
are displayed on
the screen at one
time, allowing the
user to see the
interrelationships of
information easily.

4. **The Filtered View pattern.**

Similar to the optical refractor used in an optometrist's office, the filtered view pattern enables users to navigate the same data set using different views (see Figures 5.34–5.36). It's a pattern that's especially well suited for navigating large sets of similar media, such as music, photos, video, or movies.

Filtered View examples: iPod app on the iPad or iPhone, CoolIris app, Calendar apps on most smartphones and tablets.

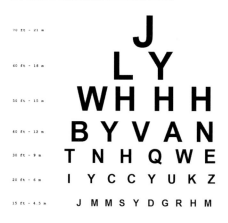

FIGURES 5.34–5.36
Similar to the optical refractor at an optometrist's office, the filtered view pattern provides users with multiple views of the same data. The iPod application for the iPad employs the filtered view pattern.

MOBILE PATTERN #3:

Content Becomes the Interface

Due to the smaller screen size of most mobile devices and the ability to provide gesture-based interactions, trends in mobile UI design focus on the content and allow it to be the star. By stripping away extra UI chrome, content becomes the interface in modern mobile UIs.

Observation: Why do interactions on mobile devices continue to rely on literal analogous representations?

Extension: Browse through the application marketplace of any mobile platform, and you will find countless examples of skeuomorphic UIs—interfaces that attempt to digitally replicate an analogous experience from the real world. Highly rendered buttons, knobs, drop shadows, and beveled edges are hallmarks of the GUI metaphor legacy taken to a hyper extreme. Back in 1973 when scientists at PARC first developed the original graphical user interface, relying on literal analogous metaphors to help users understand the computing experience made sense. Personal computers were a completely new phenomenon, so an interface approach of direct representation was appropriate.

Fast-forward to today and those initial metaphors make less sense, yet remain deeply entrenched in our digital design patterns. While highly rendered buttons with drop shadows and iconography are the easy, widely accepted, go-to approach for most digital experiences, their use makes less sense today than it did 30+ years ago. Heavy-handed metaphors and highly rendered UI affordances become more distracting than helpful. They do little to support digital interactions, take up valuable screen real estate and network bandwidth, and inaccurately depict what modern digital interfaces are capable of.

Examples of Skeuomorphic User Interfaces

A skeuomorph is a derivative object that retains ornamental design cues to a structure that was necessary in the original object (see Figures 5.37–5.39).

FIGURE 5.37

The Amplitude iPad application uses a skeuomorphic design aesthetic, attempting to replicate the dials and knob interface elements of a real-world musical amplifier digitally.

FIGURE 5.38

The Android 3.0 Honeycomb user interface incorporates skeuomorphic design aesthetics in the rending of application icons and folders.

FIGURE 5.39
The iPhone voice memo is a digital example of a skeuomorph. Several elements that were essential to recording equipment are included with no real purpose but to reference an analogous experience.

Design Strategies

A new and important interface trend is emerging that will likely supplant the skeuomorphic design trends of today. This trend assumes that the interactive qualities of an interaction should be embedded within the content itself, not in the superfluous chrome and visual finishing around it. By stripping away the confusion and clutter of traditional interface elements, designers are retooling UIs by placing photos, music, and video at the heart of the user experience and the UI. Two key changes that are enabling this shift from highly rendered, tool-based interfaces to a world where UIs allow the content to become the interface are the following:

- The rise of interconnected information

- NUIs, gestures, and the super real

The Rise of Interconnected Information

When the Internet and all its promise first emerged onto the interaction design landscape, it brought with it the opportunity to invent new models for organizing digital information. As with any new medium, there were a few false starts. Borrowing static metaphors and models from the past was a common and often unsuccessful strategy. However, people quickly began to understand and leverage what made the Internet unique: that the Internet was a new media environment where content was both interconnected and disembodied from physical form (such as the before/after example depicted in Figures 5.40 and 5.41).

Unlike content trapped in the pages of a magazine or book, information on the Web is interconnected. It can be linked to other related content through the use of links and tags. The first flat HTML files that made content and form inseparable have been quickly replaced with new forms of code, such as CSS and DHTML, that separate content from form. The rise of the Internet brought with it a focus on content and the dynamic capabilities of interconnected data. The Internet allowed users to focus and fall in love with content. The Internet made content a star.

FIGURES 5.40 AND 5.41
The Southwest Airlines Web site from 1996 tries to replicate the experience of interacting with an airline agent at a desk. The design of the Southwest Airlines Web site from 2011 leverages what the Web is good at—displaying interconnected information.

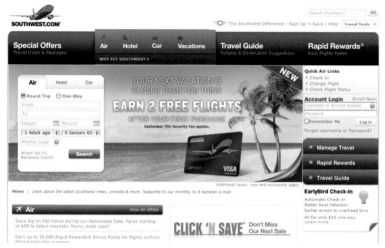

NUIs, Gestures, and the Rise of the Super Real

Natural user interfaces that employ the use of gesture and "super real" qualities are another factor supporting the rise of UIs in which content becomes the interface. While there is something in the human "lizard brain" that possesses a deep affinity for physical objects, networked information is inherently dynamic and ephemeral. Graphical user interfaces play to our love of concrete, physical objects by applying physical characteristics to information through the use of metaphor and analogy (folders, files, documents, etc.). Yet information in a networked space has qualities that physical objects do not. When graphical user interfaces are used to depict information in a networked space, it limits the user's imagination into what is possible.

Natural user interfaces, the rising star of mobile UIs, have several defining qualities that are useful in depicting the ephemeral and dynamic nature of interconnected information. Unlike GUIs that contain information in physical metaphors, successful NUIs extend information objects in a logical way into the world of magic. With features like stretch to zoom, the

UI elements of NUIs not only look real, but we perceive them to be super real as their character can change in a way that is almost magical. The use of gestures and direct manipulation enabled by NUIs allows designers to rely on a user's physical relationship with the information itself, not the UI chrome, to navigate and interact with information. Instead of "clicking on a button," users can actually click on a piece of content to initiate an interaction. The use of gestural UIs for tasks like scrolling an email list on a mobile device allows designers to remove superfluous UI elements like scroll bars, freeing up limited screen space for content. These characteristics inherent in NUIs make it an interface paradigm that is well suited to interactions where content becomes the interface (see Figures 5.42 and 5.43).

> As interaction designers, our role of making UIs familiar as tools has shifted to one of communicating vast amounts of connected information. It tilts the form and function balance from a focus on how things work to how information and meaning is conveyed.
>
> —Mike Kruzeniski

FIGURE 5.42
Content is the star of Cover Flow, an animated UI pattern integrated within iTunes and other Apple products. Content becomes the interface, allowing users to browse through snapshots of documents, Web site bookmarks, album artwork, or photographs.

FIGURE 5.43
Like many experiences where content becomes the interface, the iPad application created for Popular Science+ by London-based design studio BERG *feels* fundamentally different than consuming information in a paper magazine or on a Web site.

The mobile platform that has undeniably pushed the notion of content as the interface the farthest in recent years is Windows Mobile (as seen in Figure 5.44). Instead of drawing inspiration from the PC or other mobile platforms, the design team took inspiration from the design work of graphic design legends Josef Müller-Brockmann and Massimo Vignelli. The result: an elegant and inspired mobile UI. The following principles, courtesy of Window's Mobile team lead, Mike Kruzeniski, were used to guide the design and development of the Metro UI system.

FIGURE 5.44

People "hub" of the Windows 7 mobile platform.

DESIGN PRINCIPLES FROM WINDOWS 7 MOBILE

Clean, Light, Open, and Fast

The design team for Metro applied an approach of "fierce reduction" to remove any elements in the UI that were unnecessary—both visual elements and feature bloat. This approach allowed the team to shine a focus on the primary tasks of the UI and make the UI feel smart, open, fast, and responsive.

Alive in Motion

The transitions between screens in a UI are as important to the design as the screens themselves. Motion gives character to a UI but also communicates the navigation system, which helps to improve usability.

Celebrate Typography

The design inspiration for Metro was very typographic. It was time for user interfaces to be uncompromising about type. Type is information; type is beautiful.

Content, not Chrome

It's the content on the phone that people want, not the buttons. Reducing the visuals on the phone that aren't content creates a more open UI, and it also promotes direct interaction with the content.

Authentically Digital

A user interface is created of pixels, so in Metro the team tried to avoid using the skeuomorphic shading and glossiness used in some UIs that try to mimic real-world materials and objects.

MOBILE PATTERN #4:
Use Uniquely Mobile Input Mechanisms

Despite the seductive qualities of touchscreen devices, the keyboard and mouse remain a hard habit for most users to break. Mobile devices offer a variety of unique input mechanisms that could be more intuitive and effective in the mobile context. Unfortunately, these uniquely mobile input mechanisms have historically been left largely unexplored by designers. Until now…

Observation: Text and numeric input is difficult on a mobile device.

Extension: Whether entering a mobile number or attempting to type an email response, text and numeric input is challenging on modern mobile devices, especially touchscreen devices. The small physical size of a mobile device coupled with the mental focus required to spell correctly or enter the right number makes alphanumeric entry an uncomfortable and unpleasant part of most any mobile experience.

FIGURE 5.45
Regardless of the mobile platform or the quality of the design of the keyboard, text input on a mobile device is tough for users.

While numbers have long been associated with phones and voice communication, text input through a keyboard has not. Keyboards are in fact an input mechanism borrowed from the PC paradigm. Because the context of use for laptops and computer workstations is usually seated in a relatively predictable environment, text input through a keyboard feels comfortable and relatively natural and is a highly efficient way to create and communicate information. Mobile is different. As established in earlier chapters, the mobile context is highly variable and unpredictable, making mobile experiences that require text input challenging (see Figure 5.45).

Design Strategies: While text input often feels awkward on a mobile phone, most mobile devices are equipped with a palette of input mechanisms that are easy to use in the mobile context yet remain largely unexplored by designers. Too often, designers turn to a keyboard out of habit or convenience when other mechanisms could likely do the job better. This is a habit/pattern worth breaking.

The following list of mobile inputs has great possibilities: video, photos, voice, sound, GPS, sensors, and near-field communication. Our over-reliance on QWERTY keyboards causes these mobile inputs to be often overlooked when crafting mobile experiences. Unlike keyboards, which are mini replications of the PC experience, these inputs are inherently sympathetic to the unpredictability of the mobile context because they are a natural extension of the device. They are underutilized and definitely worthy of consideration.

Video

Whether it's capturing your toddler's first steps or video chatting with a friend who lives far away, the video functionality found on most mobile smartphones is a great way to capture and share slices of time. While the world has seen success with real-time video communication applications like Skype and FaceTime, we've only begun to scratch the surface of video (see Figure 5.46). It's an effortless form of input that feels natural and intuitive in the mobile context.

Photos (Photos, RFID/QR Codes)

Similar to video, still images captured through the camera of a mobile device are an easy and intuitive way to input information without a keyboard and mouse. Snapping a picture of yourself in a new outfit and sending it to a friend for her opinion, for example, is an interaction that's perfectly suited for a mobile device. In addition to capturing photos of your daily life or using images to communicate, QR code readers, activated by taking a photo of the codes found

FIGURE 5.46
FaceTime is a video-calling application that allows users to both *see* and *hear* the recipients of their phone calls.

FIGURE 5.47
A QR code (Quick Response code) is a specific matrix barcode (or two-dimensional code) that is readable by dedicated QR barcode readers and camera telephones. The code consists of black modules arranged in a square pattern on a white background. The information encoded may be text, URL, or other data.

on many consumer goods (as seen in Figure 5.47), allow users to gather information about products they encounter through a simple point-and-click interaction. The image-capturing capability found in most mobile devices is an instinctive way to input information and trigger interactions without the hassle of a keyboard and mouse.

Voice

Voice is a natural way to interact with mobile devices because of the telephone legacy—telephones and mobile phones are close cousins, so talking into a mobile phone feels intuitive. There is more that users can do with voice than simply communicate. Voice is emerging as a powerful way to trigger interactions on mobile devices. While voice-driven interfaces have been around for quite a while, it's only been in recent years that we've seen voice as an input mechanism for interactions increase in popularity. In all fairness and honesty, voice and sound-driven interfaces are difficult to pull off because of the following reasons:

- Speech recognition is often inaccurate (users get incorrect results 5% to 20% of the time).

- Speech UIs are hard to learn. (Example: How do users explore the interface? How do users find out what you can say?)

The mobile devices' voice-call legacy means that mobile devices contain all the mechanisms necessary to enable voice interactions (microphone, speaker) and make talking into the tiny devices less socially awkward and uncomfortable. As accuracy and familiarity with voice interfaces improve, voice (like the example shown in Figure 5.48) is near perfect for mobile input.

FIGURE 5.48
Powered by TellMe, voice search in Bing for the iPad works well, providing users with Bing's smart "decision engine" search results mixed with movie listings, news articles, trending topics, and local business information.

Sound

Mobile devices with voice capability have built-in microphones, making them prime candidates for capturing an often-overlooked information type: sound. Similar to video, sound is a great way to capture a moment in time, activate a music or television search (such as Shazam and IntoNow), or capture sound bites that can be strung together to make music (such as Smule's MadPad), as shown in Figure 5.49. Largely unexplored, sound is relatively easy to capture through a mobile device and is a compelling way to convey messages, capture information, and express your creativity.

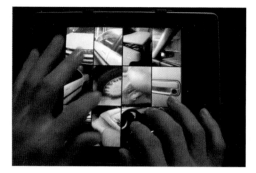

FIGURE 5.49
MadPad, an iPad app created by Smule, allows users to turn everyday sights and sounds like the hum of a car's engine, crushing an empty soda can, or conversation bits into the ultimate percussive instrument.

FIGURE 5.50
Mobile devices with GPS (global positioning system) functionality allow users to locate themselves in space and time, allowing them to add that dimension of information to their interaction.

GPS

Maps and mobile devices are perfect complements to each other because a mobile device with GPS can do something a paper map can't: It can tell you where you are! Users don't need to enter the address of where they're located, because GPS can do it for them (see Figure 5.50). A mobile device's GPS enables users to locate themselves in space and time, allowing them to add that dimension of information to their interactions. Whether it's checking in to social networking applications like Gowalla or Foursquare, tagging photos with location data, or filtering search results with proximity to a user's physical location, information through GPS input opens up a whole new world of experiences for users.

Sensors

Most modern smartphones and mobile devices are embedded with a myriad of sensors (see Figure 5.51). Accelerometers (used to measure the orientation or vertical and horizontal positioning of the phone through linear accelerations), multitouch sensors, ambient light sensors (light/dark awareness), and gyroscopes (used to measure the orientation or vertical and horizontal positioning directly) are just a handful of the types of sensor technologies being used in mobile devices today. These sensors provide the means to gather information seamlessly and use it to create novel new experiences and interactions that are unique to mobile devices.

FIGURE 5.51
The Sleep Cycle alarm clock uses the accelerometer within the iPhone to wake users up at the right time to prevent grogginess during the day. Once the application determines you are in a phase of light sleep, it wakes you up.

FIGURE 5.52
NFC lets users hover their mobile phone or other device over a compatible receiver to access content or complete a transaction.

Near Field Communication (NFC)

NFC (near field communication) is a technology that allows for simplified transactions, data exchange, and wireless connections between two devices in close proximity to each other, usually no more than a few centimeters (see Figure 5.52). It's been used for years with keycard door access and contactless credit card machines but recently has found its way into most modern smartphones. NFC is a great example of an easy, seamless way to input information into a mobile device based on location without the hassle of a keyboard and typing into a mobile device.

MOBILE PATTERN #5:
Say Good-Bye to Done

One mobile user experience trend I've been tracking is the slow erosion of a task-based interaction model. Increasingly, I've been thinking that to create great mobile experiences, designers need to say good-bye to tasks, say good-bye to done…and explore new or different interaction models that leverage the things that mobile is good at: exposing possibilities.

Observation: People want do more with mobile devices than simply complete tasks.

Extension: Most software, Web sites, and Web-based products used today have evolved around the task-based model. Because PCs are great tools for efficiency and "getting stuff done," this is a model that has served the PC well. Designers are well armed with a vast set of tools and processes that support this approach—use cases, task flows, task analysis—just to name a few.

Unfortunately, mobile isn't a great platform for accomplishing tasks. The small screen and variability of the mobile context leaves most users attempting to complete complex tasks on a mobile device with the feeling of being lost in a labyrinth of menus and screens. In addition, reducing the wide scope of activities for which people use mobile devices to one model—completing tasks—feels reductive and fails to capture much of the nuances that mobile user experiences offer. If PCs are great for getting stuff done, mobiles are good at exposing possibilities.

Design Strategies: Here are three emergent interaction models that support the idea of exposing possibilities in the mobile context, as shown in Figures 5.53–5.55.

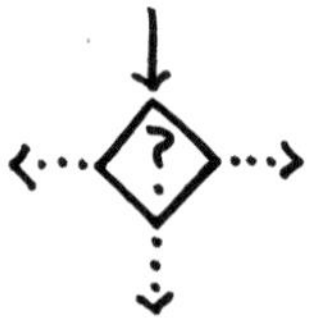

Interactions That Accrue Value Over Time

This interaction model shifts the focus from task completion to surfacing information and making it easy for people to participate. A great example is Twitter. I've long heard folks who have never used Twitter ask, "What's the point?" Compared to a similar experience that uses a more task-centric model like email, Twitter's value is only revealed as users engage with the service over time (see Figure 5.56). The value of the interaction is not around completing a task—typing a response to "What are you doing?"—but rather the conversation what can happen as a result.

FIGURE 5.53
Interactions that accrue value over time.

FIGURE 5.54
Interactions that facilitate exploration and discovery.

FIGURE 5.55
Interactions that sense user intent.

FIGURE 5.56
Twitter is an example of an interaction that accrues value over time.

FIGURE 5.57
Koi Pond is an example
of an interaction that
facilitates exploration

Interactions That Facilitate Exploration

This is an interaction model that calls to mind two of my favorite iPhone apps: Koi Pond and Bloom (see Figure 5.57). These are open-ended interaction models that are easy to enter and exit. The interfaces usually have built-in affordances that inspire curiosity and play. They typically have some type of clear and immediate feedback, are visually rich and engaging, rely on animation to aid in cognition, and often orchestrate touch, gesture, and sound into the experience. Pointless? Perhaps. However, there is something so completely intriguing and fun about these interfaces that is far more emotionally satisfying than clicking a send or buy button on a Web site.

Interactions That Sense Intent

This interaction model is one I've been tracking for the past 18 months and is perhaps the most exciting of the three. This model uses information from sensors, use patterns, and GPS data and algorithms to anticipate needs and deliver intuitive options that make sense in a particular context (see Figure 5.58). Devices are already doing this today. Sensors and accelerometer data on the iPhone can sense the orientation of the device and adjust the interface and screen orientation accordingly. The mobile Google Maps application anticipates that users will want to use their current location and automatically integrates it into the interaction. This model seems to be less about enabling users to complete discrete tasks and more about sensing what users want and delivering intuitive options.

FIGURE 5.58
Interfaces that adapt
based on device
orientation are an
example of interactions
that sense intent.

Summary

I've long admired the work of Christopher Alexander and the contributions he made to the world of design through his theories of a pattern language. As mentioned earlier, Mobile UX has been a design space riddled with deeply entrenched user experience problems—problems that creative people like you can help solve. At the heart of any new pattern was somebody, somewhere, looking at how things were currently being done and having both the courage to wonder why and the creative impulse to think up an alternative. While the five mobile design patterns captured in this chapter are a good start, there are surely many more to come. As you design mobile experiences, I'm sure you'll identify some of your own and hopefully a pattern language can help you express them

- Mobile UX problems can be attributed to two key issues:

  - Mobile UX has had few well-documented design patterns. Designers too often borrow design patterns from the PC instead of designing and documenting new patterns for mobile.

  - The few design patterns that do exist for mobile are evolving at a very rapid pace.

- "The cloud" and applications are emerging as a natural set point for mobile experiences. The eight emergent applications types are:

  - Core applications
  - Widgets
  - Consumption-focused applications
  - Search/find applications
  - Search/find/transact applications
  - Feed-focused applications
  - Tool applications
  - Game applications

- Good mobile experiences unfold progressively to reveal their nature, allowing users to "top-in" to information and rely on their intuition for interaction and engagement.

- Content that becomes the interface is an emerging and important interface trend that will likely supplant the skeuomorphic design trends of today.

- The mobile context is highly variable and unpredictable, making mobile experiences that require text input challenging. This makes experimentation with uniquely mobile input mechanisms an important part of the mobile UX process.

- People want to do more with mobile devices than simply complete tasks. If PCs are great for getting stuff done, mobiles are good for exposing possibilities. In order to break free from the dominance of the "task-driven" interaction model, designers need to say good-bye to done and explore new interaction models that leverage the things that mobiles are good at.

CHAPTER 6

Mobile Prototyping
Tools and Methods for Designing Mobile Experiences

The Design Process	145
Prototyping	147
Genres of Mobile Prototyping	151
Tactical Prototyping	153
Experiential Prototyping	162
Three Prototyping Truisms	172
Chapter Summary	175
Expert Interview: Julian Bleecker	176

One of my favorite television programs of all times is the reality cooking show *Top Chef* (see Figures 6.1 and 6.2). Food, creativity, competition, drama—it's a show that's got everything. My favorite part of the program is the elimination segment referred to as "Judges' Table." It's the suspenseful finale of each show where the three chefs who performed the worst that week are called before a panel of judges to defend their dish. Time and again, regardless of circumstance, most of them repeat a similar phrase, "…I would have made different choices."

FIGURES 6.1 AND 6.2
Top Chef is an American television show in which chefs compete for the title of Top Chef. Each week a panel of judges (known as the judges' table) must eliminate a contestant.

The act of design, like cooking, is all about choices. Whether designing a meal, a dress, or a mobile Web site, the end product is the result of a million and one design decisions. UX designers are called on to make decisions about interaction, form, function, and style, and these choices are driven by a host of internal and external drivers such as time, personal goals and motivation, client/organizational needs, and social pressure. The ability to make good design decisions in the face of constraints and pressure is perhaps the most valuable skill any designer can possess.

Designers interested in getting into mobile UX often ask these questions:

"What makes mobile design and development different?"

"What modifications to my existing design processes do I need to make to create good mobile experiences?"

"When the rubber hits the road, what do I need to do differently?"

My answer: decision-making. The primary skill that designers new to mobile UX must learn is to calibrate their design decision-making skills to a new medium.

And that's what this chapter is about. It's designed to help you get in tune with your design decision-making so that you can:

- Be confident about your mobile design choices.

- Know how to identify and recover from bad choices and failures.

- Know when you've made good design choices.

The Design Process

Different designers manage their design processes in a myriad of ways. However, a process blueprint I find myself turning to time and again for most mobile design projects is the double-diamond model, as shown in Figure 6.3. Even if you've never heard of this model, it will likely feel familiar because it's a model that many designers intuitively follow during a typical design project cycle. Divided into four distinct phases—discover, define, develop, and deliver—this model maps the divergent and convergent stages of the design process, showing the different modes of thinking that designers use in each phase.

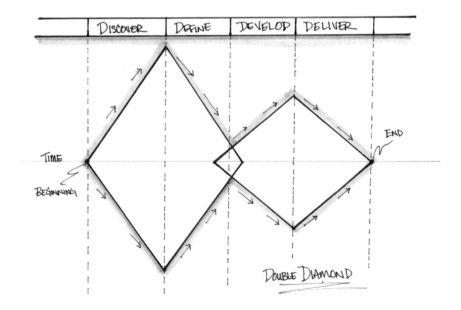

FIGURE 6.3
The double-diamond project model.

Discover

The first quarter of the double-diamond model represents the set of activities conducted at the beginning of a design project. This phase starts with a single point—an initial idea or inspiration—followed by exploratory design activities that fan out and diverge, such as the following:

- Contextual user research
- Secondary research
- Competitive research—data analysis

Define

The second quarter of the model—the definition stage—is the phase of a project that is all about filtering. Unlike the discovery phase, which is divergent, design activities in the define phase are convergent in nature and focus on editing ideas and information on what's most relevant to the given project. Key activities during the define stage are:

- Data synthesis and design principles
- Brainstorming and concept development
- Business alignment

Develop

The third quarter of the double-diamond process is the phase of a project where design solutions are developed, tested, and iterated. Similar to the discover phase, the design activities in the develop phase are divergent and generative in nature. Key activities and objectives during the develop stage are:

- Sketching and diagramming flows
- Interaction and visual design language development
- Prototype development, testing, and interaction
- Prototype testing and iteration

Deliver

The last quarter of the double-diamond model represents the final stage of a design process. This is the key "decision-making" phase of any design project. In this phase, any fine-tuning of the final concept of a product or service occurs before it's launched into the world. The key activities and objectives during this stage are:

- Interaction and visual design language finalized and applied to screen layouts and flow diagrams

- Technical implementation, testing, and fine-tuning design
- Salability testing

Where Things Usually Go Wrong

The two diamonds of this model are not different sizes by accident. The first diamond—the discover and define phase—is bigger because it requires more divergent thinking. While some convergent thought is required in this phase, it's generally regarded as the blue sky/green field part of a project where anything seems possible. The second diamond—the develop and deliver phase—is where you start to see the results of your decisions take form and become concrete.

Fate has a funny way of revealing bad choices at inopportune moments, and the second diamond is no exception. Unfortunately, this phase (the phase where your project's precious time and resources are dwindling) is where most mobile UX projects go sideways or entirely off the rails.

The biggest reason involves bad decision-making. The second diamond is where all the ideas that once seemed brilliant in your mind start to take form—and all their imperfections come to light. It's the place where a series of small assumptions and well-intentioned but poor decisions can accumulate and rear their ugly head, resulting in a bad design.

The second diamond of almost any mobile UX project is where good design decisions matter most. Unfortunately, it's the place that designers new to mobile have the least skill and confidence because they are largely unfamiliar with the subtle nuances of the mobile medium. However, there is something that can alleviate the impact of this common problem. It's a design activity that will help designers new to mobile improve their decision-making skills, build their confidence, and up their chances of success. That activity is prototyping.

Prototyping

We've heard it all before…prototype, prototype, prototype. It's a standard step we've all been encouraged to include in our design processes, but often it's the first step skipped in time- and budget-constrained projects. Although prototyping is considered a luxury for many PC-based experiences, it is an absolutely *essential* part of creating compelling tablet and mobile experiences. The reason is simple. Chances are if you are new to mobile, your design experience and instincts aren't very well tuned to mobile. This often results in bad decision-making. Bad design decision-making will make that last diamond—the develop and deliver phase of your project—feel like a death march. And it doesn't have to be that way if you plan and engage in a lot of prototyping.

Prototypes are like decision-making aids. They are a way of working through a design idea with tangible means, giving other people a chance to experience your idea and provide feedback. Like a list of "if/then" statements of a geometric proof, prototypes are the design equivalent of "showing your work." Unfortunately, they are often sidestepped.

The reason that prototypes are often side-stepped in other design domains is that designers tend to marshal the decision-making skills they've acquired from previous design projects and apply them to the project at hand. Whether it's leaning on already established heuristics, expertise, or instinct, it's not always necessary when designing PC experiences to "show your work"—you can simply make the call.

Mobile is a different animal, though. Designers and UX professionals new to mobile don't have the skills and the confidence to intuitively make consistently good design decisions. Those intuitive design and decision-making skills for mobile take time and experience to develop. Additionally, unlike the PC, the mobile design space is relatively new, and design patterns have yet to be formally codified. In lieu of experience and heuristics, the best way to develop these skills is to practice turning the brilliant ideas in your head into tangible experiences you and other people can engage with. In short, if you want to develop your mobile design decision-making skills, you've got to get into the practice of showing your work. You've gotta prototype.

Aside from accruing mobile UX experience and skills, prototypes can perform important roles in your project and serve a variety of purposes. I've identified four basic reasons I turn to prototyping when designing mobile experiences. There are probably more or variants on these…but these are my four "whys":

1. Communicate a design idea or experience.

2. Gather user feedback.

3. Explore the unknowns.

4. Fine-tune an idea.

Communicate a Design Idea or Experience

While humans are highly verbal, words can be a tricky way to communicate an idea because words can mean different things to different people. Prototypes serve as a powerful communication tool because they are often more precise than words. Whether you're pitching a start-up idea to investors or trying to explain your team's idea to internal stakeholders, prototypes provide people with something more tangible than an elevator pitch or a marketing statement, as shown in Figure 6.4.

FIGURE 6.4
Research scientists at the Nokia Research Center created a concept video that communicated Morph, a product that demonstrated some of the possibilities nanotechnologies might enable in future communication devices.

Gather User Feedback

Most designers are blessed with a solid gut sense of what users will like, tolerate, or reject outright. However, even the most skilled designers know there is a time and place when it's important to gut-check their instincts with users (see Figure 6.5). Prototypes provide you with a tangible artifact in which to gather feedback with people outside of yourself and your team. They are the perfect tools for gut-testing your design assumptions.

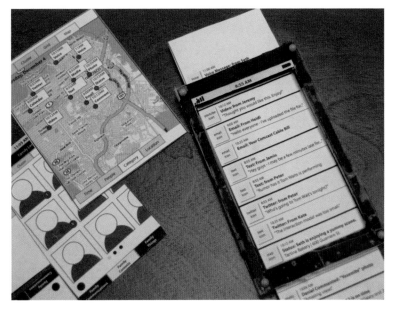

FIGURE 6.5
Paper prototypes are an easy way to gut-check design decisions with users early in your design process.

Exploring the Unknowns

When designing user experiences, there are two types of unknowns: the known and unknown unknowns. Often, designers arrive at a point in the design process when they intuitively sense there's a particular design decision that is crucial to the success of their product or service, yet they're not quite sure about the solution. Or sometimes designers find themselves working on a very future-facing project that requires thinking outside of typical products and contexts. Prototyping is a great way to explore these "unknowns." It allows designers to explore their ideas in the physical world through the creation of artifacts or experiences. Instead of ruminating about a design issue, or laboring through all the possible solutions and "it could be…" in your head, prototypes provide the means to explore tangible solutions. The physicality of prototyping also helps designers see flaws or the unexpected—otherwise known as the *unknown unknowns*—at a better rate than simply "thinking" about the design. Figure 6.6 is a perfect example of this physicality.

FIGURE 6.6
Before starting development of the early Palm Pilot, inventor Jeff Hawkins carried a block of wood, the size of the potential Pilot, in his pocket for a week to explore how the idea felt.

Fine-Tune an Idea

One of the biggest challenges when creating mobile experiences is the discrepancy between the tools used and the static context that exists for most designers during the design process—not to mention the dynamic contexts of use in which most mobile design work is experienced in once it finds its way into the hands of users. There is often a disconnect between creating a design on a large computer screen in a static context and experiencing that design on a handheld device in a dynamic context. Layouts can become too information dense, type may feel too small, or an interaction may not feel intuitive. There is no substitute for getting your work on a mobile device early and often (see Figure 6.7). The devil is often in the details, and prototyping is a great way to fine-tune your work.

FIGURE 6.7
On-device prototypes are a great way to fine-tune important interactions and details of your design.

Genres of Mobile Prototyping

Regardless of the "why" for your particular prototype, selecting the right prototyping method for your mobile UX project is a lot like selecting a good book. There are countless options to choose from, so how do you pick the right one? Similar to asking yourself, "What type of book am I in the mood for?," the first step in identifying the right prototyping method involves asking, "What type of design exploration am I about to embark on?" Unlike selecting the right reading material from countless book genres, mobile prototyping methods tend to fall into two basic genres: "tactical" and "experiential" prototyping.

While I've categorized mobile prototyping into the two genres—tactical and experiential—there's nothing to stop you from "crossing the streams." For example, it's perfectly fine to use an experiential prototyping method, such as storyboarding, in a more tactical-type project and vice-versa. However, identifying the nature of the project you are taking on is the first point in your mobile UX decision-making process. It will help you identify the design prototyping methods that are best suited for your project and will likely prove most valuable to you as you embark on designing for the mobile medium.

Tactical prototyping is best suited for design explorations where:

1. **You are working on a "focused" mobile design project.**

    Examples:
    "I'm creating a mobile application."
    "I'm creating a mobile version of my company's Web site."

2. **Target mobile hardware and software platform options are perhaps not decided, but the scope is known.**

    Examples:
    "We're targeting smartphones with a capacitive touchscreen."
    "We're not quite sure which software platform we'll target, but it will likely be either platform X, Y, or Z."

3. **The design space is relatively known. Precursors exist, and other designers have begun to explore the terrain.**

    Examples:
    Mobile/tablet applications
    Mobile Web sites

Experiential prototyping is best suited for design explorations where:

1. **You are working on a "broader" design project where you're thinking about a mobile device's role in a user's device ecosystem experience.**

    Examples:
    "We're thinking about all the touchpoints a customer has with our service: mobile, PC, tablets, and interactive TV."
    "We're trying to understand how we can use mobile technology to improve people's experience with our city's public transportation system."

2. **Target mobile hardware and software platforms are unknown and perhaps in the process of being created.**

    Examples:
    "We're trying to use gestural interactions to make the television experience more intuitive."
    "We're trying to enable mobile payments at a supermarket chain."

3. **The design space is relatively new and unchartered.**

    Examples:
    NFC
    Gestural interfaces
    Service experiences that prism through various devices, such as Netflix (computer, TV, mobile device)

Tactical Prototyping

The three tactical prototyping methods I find myself turning to repeatedly and which have proved to be the most valuable are:

- Sketching
- Paper Prototyping
- Interactive On-Device Prototyping

Sketching

There are few things more direct and efficient than running a pen across paper, and that's what makes sketching such a powerful design skill and prototyping method. Whether it's on a whiteboard, recipe cards, or using custom platform UI stencils and sketchpads, sketching is by far my favorite form of prototyping because it's direct, generative, inexpensive, and allows you to explore ideas with a low level of commitment. Because of its generative properties, sketching is the perfect activity during the divergent phases of any design project. I use sketching to work through rough ideas for screen flows and layouts, and I find that it's an activity best suited for communicating screen-based experiences.

Mobile Templates

Can't draw? Not a problem. Most mobile software platforms have stencils that can be purchased online. These stencils are lifesavers if you are self-conscious about your sketching abilities (see Figure 6.8). For a relatively low financial investment, they come in handy for anyone interested in putting mobile ideas on paper quickly.

FIGURE 6.8
Here's an example of a mobile software stencil that can be used to sketch mobile screen designs quickly and easily.

Sketching and Ruthless Editing

Sketching out your ideas early and often is a key step in creating intuitive interfaces that "speak their power." An intuitive interface, for any medium, has long been the hallmark of a good user experience. However, the inherent cognitive constraints of mobile design make it even more important to create intuitive interfaces. Great mobile interfaces are like a light switch or a shopping cart (see Figure 6.9). They speak their power.

UIs that speak their power have affordances that invite exploration; their very design provides user with interaction cues. Compare the differences between a Web page designed for a PC experience and a similar experience tailored for a mobile device. The large screen real estate of a PC experience enables more room for annotating expectations. In mobile, options have to be readily apparent (see Figures 6.10 and 6.11). The design elements must instantly communicate to the user how to engage with them.

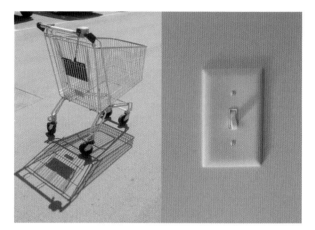

FIGURE 6.9
Similar to a shopping cart or a light switch, a great mobile design provides users with interaction cues.

FIGURE 6.10
The generous screen real estate of a PC experience enables more room for annotating expectations.

FIGURE 6.11
Options in mobile have to be readily apparent.

Tips for Ruthless Editing

After amassing many sketches, the next step is often to work through your mobile Web site or application's system flow. This is where your ruthless editing skills should kick in. Here are some good questions to keep in mind while evaluating your sketches.

1. What is the primary purpose of this screen?

2. What are the three to five secondary actions this screen must provide to a user?

3. What is the most intuitive way to visualize this information?

4. Will users know how to interact with this screen within 3 seconds?

5. Is the information on this screen too dense? What can be removed?

6. How can I get users to the information they are looking for in the least amount of time?

In order to create interfaces that speak their power, designers new to mobile must grow ruthless editing skills. Ruthless editing is about getting rid of extraneous text, visual treatments, and goofy transitions. It's about combining all the design elements—screen design, interactions, transitions, flows, visual treatments, haptics, and sound—in order to guide people through information quickly and intuitively. Just like a topiary artist pruning an overgrown tree into the shape of an elephant, ruthless editing is about taming the chaos and being able to make the cuts necessary in order for a vision to take form. Ruthless editing is about making good decisions. It's about learning to say *no*.

Visualizing Data on a Small Screen

Learning how to visualize data efficiently on a small mobile screen is an important mobile skill to master. Sketching on index cards early in your design process is a practice that will enable you to experiment with different ideas while simultaneously giving you realistic size constraints (see Figure 6.12).

FIGURE 6.12
Sketching on index cards early in your design process will show you how to effectively visualize data for a small mobile screen.

FIGURE 6.13

An example of a mobile paper prototype.

Paper Prototyping

A paper prototype is basically a paper model of your screen-based product or service (see Figure 6.13). Similar to sketching, paper prototyping requires a modest time and small financial investment while providing you with the means to work generatively and iteratively on your designs. Paper prototyping is a great technique for working through the details of screen flows and sequencing, as well as validating decisions about screen layout, button placements, and rough ideas for touch and gesture.

The thing I like best about paper prototypes is that they are a tangible way of testing out your interaction ideas with users and gathering feedback at an early stage in the design process. For designers new to mobile, paper prototyping is an ideal way to take your design assumptions for a test run early and often—and prevent the end of your project from feeling like a death march. A paper prototype can provide the opportunity for a quick iteration of a single concept or the ability to simultaneously work through several design directions.

Paper Prototyping Basics

Paper prototypes are a great way to work through your design ideas early in your design process. The steps outlined below will help you create paper prototypes with ease.

1. **Determine the key interactions.**

   Chances are that it's not necessary to create a paper prototype of a complete mobile application or Web site. Instead, you'll probably want to prototype key interactions. The first step of the paper prototyping process is to identify the key interactions you want to prototype and the central questions you want the prototype to answer.

2. **Sketch screen layouts.**

   Next, determine the types of screen layouts that will best convey information to your users. Whether you use index cards, specialized paper templates, or higher-fidelity comps created on a computer, this step is about determining how to convey information and intuitively pivot people through a series of screens in order to get them to the information they need (see Figure 6.14).

3. **Determine the screen flow/sequencing.**

   Map out individual screen layouts and the flow of those screens. It's the process of identifying what goes where and what the users will see as they navigate through the system you're creating. This process will help you identify primary and secondary navigation elements and how to most efficiently map out the underlying system of the key interactions (see Figure 6.15).

4. **Prepare interactive elements.**

   Paper prototypes allow you to fake some level of interactivity. Feel free to include and create elements like text entry, keyboards, alerts, highlighting, and pickers in your prototype. It will help you get a more accurate sense of the user experience.

5. **Take your prototype for a test run.**

   Once you've created all the elements, take your prototype for a test run with colleagues or friends. Identify what's working and what needs further refinement or modifications (see Figure 6.16).

Paper Prototyping and Touchscreens

In recent times, modern smartphones have moved away from interactions instigated by physical buttons like four-way keys and dial pads in favor of touchscreens and gesture-based interactions. This is a trend that will probably not change anytime soon. Making the move from GUI, mouse-based interactions to touchscreen/gesture-based interactions can pose an unexpected and significant challenge for designers new to mobile. Paper prototyping is a great method for working through the key differences between NUI and GUI paradigms.

FIGURE 6.14–6.16
Sketching screen layouts, determining the screen flow, and taking your prototype on a test run with users are a few of the steps involved in creating a paper prototype.

Interactive On-Device Prototyping

To this day, I still get a little giddy when I see an early on-device prototype of my mobile design work. There's something about seeing all the elements—the screen layout, the interaction flows, the gestures—come together that's…well, it's exciting and a little magical. Part of that magic comes from the fact that unless you have some serious mobile programming skills, actually getting your design work on a device and experiencing it has historically been a challenge. While getting an on-device prototype up and running has its hurdles, there are significant benefits. Aside from that totally awesome feeling of seeing your work on a device, on-device prototypes enable you and others to critically evaluate your design decisions. As mobile UX becomes more prevalent, viewing your early design work on a mobile device will likely get easier. Until then, here are some on-device methods to try:

- In-screen mobile prototype

- Mobile browser prototype

- Mobile prototype using presentation software

- Platform specific prototype

In-Screen Mobile Prototype

An in-screen prototype is basically a paper prototype that's ported into a mobile device by snapping photos of the screens with the device's camera. Creating an in-screen mobile prototype entails creating low-fidelity sketches, importing them into a mobile device, and viewing them through an application such as a slideshow on the mobile device's camera.

FIGURE 6.17

This on-device prototype was created using image maps and viewed through the browser on a mobile device.

Mobile Browser Prototype

A browser prototype is simply a prototype that is rendered by using your mobile device's browser, which is using HTML and other browser-based programming such as JavaScript. Screens can be created using HTML, which is potentially a great option, particularly if you're building a mobile Web site and are proficient in HTML. However, for those less familiar with extensive markup, you can easily upload a series of linked image maps of screen layouts and view them through your phone's browser (see Figure 6.17).

Creating prototypes using presentation software such as Apple Keynote or Microsoft PowerPoint is an efficient way to prototype interactivity and transitions on a mobile device. You can easily download platform components from the Web, build your prototype using the presentation software, fine-tune the interactions and transitions included in the software, and download the file to your mobile device.

While designers use various types of tools to document their wireframe ideas, presentation software is emerging as a favorite tool in the mobile UX realm (see Figures 6.18–6.20). In addition to specifying the placement of design elements on a screen, presentation software enables designers to turn their work into low-fidelity on-device prototypes. Instead of flat, static documents, presentation software offers designers the ability to experiment with transitions and interactivity.

Keynotopia is a fabulous resource for Keynote prototypers. The site's creator, Amir Khella, has put together a truly useful collection of templates sporting a comprehensive collection of standard controls and widgets. Just drag these visual elements into place to build mock-ups that will run on a mobile device. Travis Isaacs also has created a great online resource for creating prototypes with presentation software like Keynote. His Web site, Keynote Kungfu (http://keynotekungfu.com), contains great resources for creating on-device prototypes.

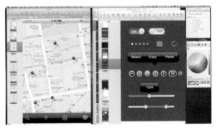

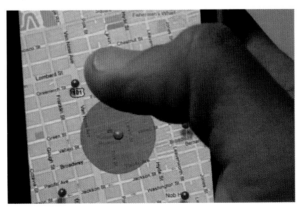

FIGURES 6.18–6.20 Presentation software, such as Apple Keynote and Microsoft Powerpoint, is emerging as a favorite mobile prototyping tool.

- It's super efficient and fast!

- Level of fidelity is high; it gives you an end result that looks and feels like a real app.

- Supports some gestures and transitions.

- It's as close as you can get to the real thing without digging into code.

Platform-Specific Prototype

If you're the type of designer who likes to roll up his sleeves and get into the code, then investing in the SDK (software developer kit) and creating your prototype using the programming language of a target platform might be the way to go. This approach allows you to create prototypes using native code, and while labor intensive, it provides the most interactivity of any prototyping method.

Pros and Cons of Common On-Device Prototyping Tools

Although getting an interactive prototype up and running on a device is no small task, it is possible. Table 6.1 should help you get a sense of the benefits and drawbacks of common mobile prototyping tools, as well as help you determine what type of prototype is best given your project's resources.

TABLE 6.1

PROS AND CONS OF PROTOTYPING TOOLS			
	Level of Complexity/ Difficulty to Create	Level of Interactivity	Level of Programming Required
In-Screen Prototype	Low	Low	None
Browser Prototype	Medium	Low	Low
Keynote Prototype	Medium	Medium	None
Platform-Specific Prototype (example: XCode for the Apple platform)	High	High	High

In-Screen Prototype Basics

I'm a sketcher, not a coder, so in-screen prototyping is my favorite on-device prototyping method. While it's not great for expressing detailed interactivity and transitions between screens, it's an easy way to get your work on a device quickly. Here are the basics as outlined by Diego Pulido in his article published by *UX Magazine* (http://uxmag.com/articles/paper-in-screen-prototyping):

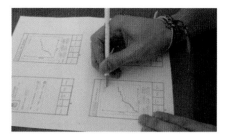

FIGURE 6.21
Sketch.

1. Sketch screen layouts, as shown in Figure 6.21.

2. Scan or photograph the sketches (see Figure 6.22).

3. Make any necessary sizing adjustments to the files (see Figure 6.23).

FIGURE 6.22
Scan or photograph.

4. Save the resized images in a file format supported by the mobile device, as shown in Figure 6.24. Organize all the screen images into the correct order for the scenario. Be mindful of the sequencing of your screens and label files accordingly.

5. Import the files into the mobile device's photo gallery, as shown in Figure 6.25.

6. Click and swipe away, as shown in Figure 6.26.

FIGURE 6.23
Make necessary sizing adjustments.

FIGURE 6.24
Save the resized images in the correct file format.

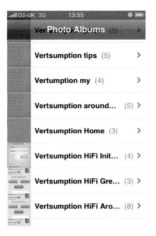

FIGURE 6.25
Import the files into the
photo gallery.

FIGURE 6.26
Click, and you're done.

Experiential Prototyping

One of the realities of mobile user experiences is that they rarely occur in isolation. Mobile technology often interacts with technology in the environment or works in concert with other technology in a device ecosystem. If getting the orchestration of all these elements in sync is critical to the success of your project, experiential prototyping methods can help you explore ideas as well as identify and fine-tune core system elements of the experience.

Five experiential prototyping methods that prove helpful in these types of design explorations are:

- Storyboarding
- Bodystorming
- Speed dating prototypes
- Concept videos

Storyboarding

Storyboarding, the act of creating a set of comics or illustrations and placing them in sequential order to convey a narrative, is a powerful UX technique borrowed from the filmmaking process. Unlike wireframes or system flows, storyboarding is a visual tool for communicating the experiential aspect (the story) of a product or service (see Figures 6.27 and 6.28). Since storyboarding is a form of storytelling, the sequence of drawings you create can help you think through a typical user's life and find clarity on the central user issues your designs should try to solve. I also find the process of storyboarding a great method for working through and identifying interaction vignettes. Vignettes are the key interactions that are central to a user's experience. They are the interactions that communicate "breakthrough moments" and describe how what you are creating will actually work and the impact that it could have for a user. Before diving into detailed screen designs and UI flows, storyboarding is a great tool for identifying these vignettes and beginning to describe how they would (or should) work.

All Your Data In Your Pocket
Concept Name:

BJORN'S PASSION IS PHOTOGRAPHY. IN ADDITION TO OWNING MULTIPLE CAMERAS, HE OWNS MULTIPLE COMPUTING DEVICES.

BJORN STORES ALL HIS PHOTOS ON HARD DRIVES. HE'S BEEN TAKING PHOTOS FOR A LONG TIME – SO HE HAS MANY HARD DRIVES.

BJORN'S CURRENT PROCESS FOR CURATING PHOTOS IS TO DOWNLOAD THE PHOTOS FROM HIS CAMERA TO HIS LAPTOP...

HE THEN EDITS HIS PHOTOS AND COPIES THEM OVER TO A HARD DRIVE, THEN DELETES THEM FROM HIS LAPTOP.

PEOPLE HAVE EXPRESSED INTEREST IN HIRING BJORN FOR FREELANCE PHOTOGRAPHY WORK.

HE'S TRIED USING ONLINE SERVICES LIKE FLICKR TO STORE & SHARE HIS PHOTOS WITH FRIENDS & POTENTIAL CLIENTS...

BUT BJORN LIVES IN AN APARTMENT IN THE HILLS – WHICH MEANS HE HAS POOR CELL & DSL COVERAGE & SLOW DOWNLOADS

PLUS BJORN TRAVELS TO GERMANY FREQUENTLY TO VISIT HIS FA

All Your Data In Your Pocket
Concept Name:

WHICH MAKES "DOWNLOADING TO THE CLOUD" VIA HIS PHONE OR LAPTOP COSTLY

BJORN'S CURRENT PROBLEMS
• FRAGMENTED STORAGE MAKES ACCESSING, ORGANIZING & SHARING PHOTOS DIFFICULT.
• STORING "IN THE CLOUD" IS COSTLY & IMPRACTICAL

BJORN'S NEW MOBILE DEVICE ALLOWS HIM TO KEEP ALL HIS DATA IN HIS POCKET.

IT'S LIKE COMBINING A MEMORY STICK, A COMPUTER, AND A MOBILE PHONE INTO ONE DEVICE.

BJORN CAN ACTUALLY PUT THE DEVICE INSIDE A CAMERA. ALL THE PHOTOS SAVED ONTO THE DEVICE...

WHEN THE DEVICE IS INSIDE THE CAMERA BODY, IT FUNCTIONS LIKE A REGULAR CAMERA

WHEN BJORN'S FINISHED TAKING PHOTOS, HE SIMPLY TAKES THE DEVICE OUT OF THE CAMERA BODY...

HE CAN THEN PLUG THE DEVICE INTO A MONITOR OR A TABLET TO VIEW HIS PHOTOS MORE CLOSELY

FIGURES 6.27 AND 6.28
These storyboards depict how a new-to-the world mobile device concept might interact with other parts of a user's device ecosystem.

Storyboarding is a great prototyping method for helping designers explore experiential aspects of a mobile experience early in the design process. The steps outlined in Figures 6.29–6.31 should prove helpful as you begin to explore this prototyping technique.

1. **Identify the central idea(s) your storyboard should communicate.**

    The purpose of the storyboard is to communicate your story, so identifying and clarifying the central idea(s) your storyboard will communicate is the first and most important step. A common mistake people make when creating storyboards is to try and include too many ideas in a single storyboard. Don't try to communicate more than three key ideas within a single storyboard; otherwise, it will simply be too confusing.

2. **Create a character and identify the key issues he/she currently faces.**

    Just like any good story, your storyboard should communicate how a central character is struggling, as shown in Figure 6.29. Who is this person and what are the problems or issues they are currently dealing with? Do these issues make them frustrated? Angry? Lonely? What are their goals, hopes, and aspirations?

3. **Rough out the basic story.**

    The next step of the storyboarding process is to rough out a basic storyline (refer to Figure 6.30). Using rough stick-figure sketches and scrawling notes, I tend to piece together my first drafts of a storyboard using Post-it notes. The key to creating a good storyboard is to communicate how a product or service will change someone's day-to-day life in a compelling and interesting way. Don't be afraid to express emotion and humor—that's an important part of the storytelling process.

4. **Start drawing.**

    Using a paper template that contains a series of frames or cells, begin illustrating each cell (refer to Figure 6.31). It's not necessary to illustrate every single step of your character's life. Instead use space between the frames to communicate changes of scene and the passage of time. Use "key frames" to depict important changes in the story. Your natural inclination may be to draw every detailed cell in order. Resist! Roughly sketch out the complete storyboard and then go back to fill in the details. This will prevent you from wasting time creating detailed cells that you end up editing out later in the process.

5. **Walk through it.**

    Done with the scene? Go back and walk through it a few times (by yourself and with a colleague or friend). Make sure that your cells make sense and help tell a cohesive story. Can you add or change a shot to increase the dramatic effect? Can you remove a shot to tighten the pacing? Walking through the your storyboard several times and sharing it with a colleague will help you figure out how to tighten the story and make any final edits.

FIGURE 6.29
Identify key issues the character in your story currently faces.

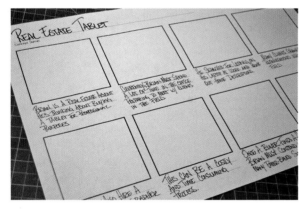

FIGURE 6.30
Rough out a basic story line.

FIGURE 6.31
Done drawing? Walk through your storyboard by yourself and with a colleague or friend to find out where you can tighten the story line.

Bodystorming

Unlike many design techniques that focus on the output of design artifacts, bodystorming focuses on the "performance" of an experience. Bodystorming is a design technique where designers enact the physical performance of an experience in order to gain an understanding of its physical, emotional, and behavioral dimensions. The technique builds on the notion that people must act first in order to know reality (see Figure 6.32). Unlike computer-based technology that is logic based and only makes visible the conditions that existed before it, people are illogical, perceptive, aware, and self-correcting. Bodystorming is a technique that helps capture and harness these messy yet essential aspects of human behavior and account for them in the mobile design process.

FIGURE 6.32
Members of an IDEO design team used bodystorming to prototype for Elmo's Monster Maker iPhone app.

Similar to improvisational theater, bodystorming involves acting out possible scenarios or use cases with actors and props. Five to eight participants are needed to create a bodystorming troupe, making the technique highly collaborative. Through the process of acting out multiple scenarios, the design troupe can capture user expectations and the emotional tempo of an experience. Actors can be people or objects and engage in dialogue—thought-bubble cards are used to show what an actor is thinking versus saying. Acting out several scenarios helps designers get a more complete sense of the various contexts of use. In doing so, designers get a visceral sense of how users feel throughout an experience, so the designers can make adjustments accordingly before any big design decisions must be made. Another great benefit of the bodystorming technique is that it makes the design process more physical. Designers must get up and move, trying things out with their own body, rather than just sitting around a meeting table.

Guidelines for Bodystorming

Use these guidelines for creating an effective bodystorming experience (see Figures 6.33–6.36).

1. Select groups of five to eight participants in a troupe.

2. Identify three to five experience scenarios for your troupe to "perform." For example, purchasing a cup of coffee with an iPhone or selecting which phone to purchase in a carrier's store.

3. Every player must have a role; there should be no "trees" that are just for background. Use large cards that label the roles people are playing.

4. Props can have feelings, thoughts, and the ability to speak. Use thought-bubble cards to show what a participant is thinking versus saying. He may say, "How can I help you?" while someone holds a thought-bubble card above her head showing she is really thinking, "Jerk."

5. Have a narrator or color commentator who can explain things. The narrator can pretend the scenario is like television, using a remote to stop action, rewind, or fast-forward.

6. Run through a scenario with your troupe. When your group is working through a scenario, try to approach the experience with the spirit of improvisational acting: "Yes, and..." rather than "No, but...."

7. Try creating two skits for your scenarios, showing a before and after.

8. Try splitting larger groups into two or more teams that bodystorm the same scenario and observe any differences.

9. Debrief after each scenario. What did the group learn? What was surprising? What seemed important? Capture what you learned from the exercise and discuss how you can integrate it into what happens next.

FIGURES 6.33–6.36
Images of a team of designers bodystorming an iPhone application.[1]

---

1   *Bodystorming as Embodied Design*, pp. 47–51 of November/December 2010, *Interactions Magazine*. Authors: Dennis Schleicher, Peter Jones, Oksana Kachur

Unlike prototyping a mobile application or a Web site, creating convergence or ubiquitous computing experiences (experiences that involve multiple devices such as a mobile device, laptop, television, car sound and navigation system, and so on) presents multiple challenges. From a creative perspective, it's difficult to explore and iterate multiple ideas because the design space is vast and complex. Additionally, it is a relatively nascent design space, and there are few tools and techniques available to designers to explore systems that touch so many facets of a user's life. From a tactical perspective, even though there's a high level of confidence in a concept, "building" a working prototype has a high cost of failure. Prototypes are time-intensive to create, there are few existing interaction design patterns to build on, and there are often unpredictable social consequences.

Scott Davidoff of CMU created the speed dating prototyping method to address these very issues. Like it's romantic counterpart, Scott's theory builds on the following three ideas:

- Abundance brings perspective.

- It's easier to compare something relative to other things.

- Multiple low-cost engagements with a wide variety of concepts enable a broader perspective to emerge.

Using a combination of storyboarding and a form of experience prototyping, Scott's speed dating prototyping technique provides designers of ubiquitous systems with a framework to explore ideas, evaluate multiple design concepts, and quickly identify "showstopper" issues with minimal investment.

Speed dating consists of two main stages: need validation and user enactments. In the need validation phase, designers create multiple storyboards that depict both an unmet need that was uncovered during research and a design solution that addresses that need (see Figure 6.37).

" No signal, I feel so helpless."

The smart home senses that Dad's going to miss Annie, and pings the people the Millers count on in a pinch.

The neighbor's not far from Annie. She agrees to get her.

The tow truck that comes for Dad tells him that Annie is safe and sound.

FIGURE 6.37
Examples of storyboard sketches used in speed dating prototyping activity.

The creation of multiple divergent concepts is encouraged. Next, the design team presents the paper storyboards to a set of target users. This process allows the team to synchronize the needs uncovered during research with users and vet design solutions developed to address those needs with a group of target users. Paper is cheap, so storyboarding is a quick and inexpensive way to validate and prioritize user needs as well as evaluate the potential of multiple ideas.

Next, top-rated concepts and their possible instantiations are inserted into a matrix. Teams then conduct user enactments of the various concepts with research participants. Research participants are asked to enact a specific role they regularly play (like mother or father) as they walk through the scenarios, within an inexpensive, low-fidelity mock-up of the target environment or device ecosystem (see Figure 6.38).

FIGURE 6.38
Research participants are asked to enact a role they regularly play in everyday life as they walk through the scenarios.

Throughout the enactment stage, designers gather feedback from research participants. Building on the idea that it's easier to compare something relative to other things, an essential component of the enactment stage of this process is to "act out" multiple design solutions to an identified user need.

Since the mobile device is a common, if not standard, part of most users' device ecosystems, speed dating is a great prototyping method for exploring the role that mobile devices will play in converged device systems. Speed dating provides a low-cost way for design teams to compare multiple converged or ubiquitous computing system concepts and supply a structure to explore those multiple versions. It's a technique that helps capture how users might react to a concept early in the design process.

Some mobile UX projects are less about creating an experience or product that finds its way into the world and more about communicating ideas about how people will interact with mobile technology in the future. They are about exploring and communicating what is possible in the future. These assignments are best served by a prototyping method known as a *concept video*.

At heart, concept videos are a practice in storytelling. They provide designers with an opportunity to explore how a user might engage with a product or service without actually designing and building out the nuances and details. Concept videos are often short videos (3–5 minutes in length) that highlight several key features of a product or service. Concept videos often focus not only on the design or experience, but also on the impact that experience can have on a user's life.

Concept videos can be powerful storytelling tools; however, they require a wide variety of skills to create. Creating them can be a lot like shooting a movie—they involve art direction, script/narrative development and editing, video, photography, and sound (see Figures 6.39 and 6.40).

FIGURES 6.39 AND 6.40
Creating concept videos often requires video-editing skills. Action shots for this video were taken with a device covered with a green screen. The mobile interface was applied in postproduction using video editing software.

Depending on fidelity, concept videos can be time-consuming to create. However, they are a powerful tool for generating enthusiasm for an idea or communicating the benefits of a technology that is not yet available—and might not be for many years to come (see Figures 6.41–6.46). Table 6.2 shows some tips to help determine whether a concept video is the right solution for your project:

TABLE 6.2

CONCEPT VIDEO PROS AND CONS	
Pros	Cons
High impact	Resource intensive
Highly shareable	Skill intensive
Good for high-level ideas	Not a good cultural fit for all organizations
Good for technology still in development	Don't make bad ideas good

FIGURES 6.41 AND 6.42
These images depict stills from a concept video created by Tamer Nakisci. The video depicts a future product called the Nokia 888 Communicator device, which incorporates a flexible display that can be worn in multiple configurations. The device conveys information—such as an incoming call— by changing shape.

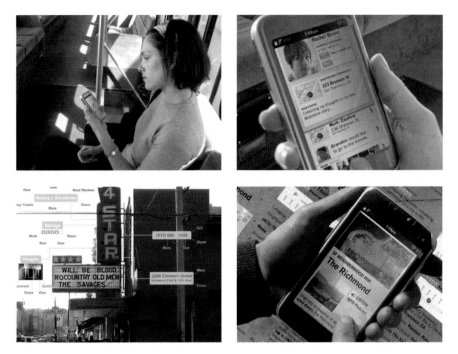

FIGURES 6.43–6.46
These images depict stills from a concept video created in 2008 to
communicate an application-less mobile interface concept. Instead of
applications, the interface relies on the organizing principle of dynamic tiles.

Three Prototyping Truisms

This chapter has hopefully given you insight into the breadth and depth
of prototyping methods at your disposal as you begin crafting mobile
experience. Regardless of the methods you choose to use, there are three
prototyping truisms to always keep in mind:

- Choose the appropriate fidelity

- Embrace failure

- Remember that prototyping is not a panacea

Choose the Appropriate Fidelity

A common reason many folks side-step prototyping during their design process is because it's an activity that has a bad rap for being time-consuming. To be fair, prototyping *does* take time, but I would argue that prototyping has earned this "time-consuming" reputation unfairly. The reason is because prototypes have a sneaky way of becoming a time drain. The culprit really isn't the method as much as it is designer pride.

A funny thing can happen once you start making a prototype. Your designer instincts can kick in, leaving you longing to keep working on a prototype in order to make it "beautiful" or "perfect." Resist this urge!

While the desire to make something "perfect" can be noble, it's often not the best use of your time and can be unfair to your team. The fidelity of a prototype should map to your reason for making it. Prototypes are a means to an end. Be open to what you can learn from them, but don't get too attached. Remember when creating prototypes, perfection is your enemy—not your friend (see Figure 6.47).

FIGURE 6.47
Famous French writer and philosopher Voltaire coined the famous and relevant quote: *"Perfection is the enemy of the good."*

Embrace Failure

One of the best and most valuable things about prototyping is that it can reveal bad ideas—or ideas not worth pursuing—early in the design process. However, identifying ideas not worth pursuing requires objectivity. Throughout my career, I've seen many designers (myself included) lose their objectivity and doggedly invest time and energy continuously prototyping an idea that just won't work.

It's important to stay objective about your prototypes. Just because your idea failed doesn't mean you are a failure. We've all had ideas that seemed brilliant in our head but that turned out to be colossal failures once we prototyped them. Don't be afraid to identify when failure is happening and move on to the next idea. If you're unsure if an idea is working, seek feedback from colleagues or users about the work. Be open to what creating prototypes can teach you, and remember that failure helps you learn.

Prototyping Is Not a Panacea

Any method or process is a means to an end. Prototyping is a useful and important tool for building great mobile experiences. However, prototyping an idea doesn't make an idea great.

Remember that prototyping is a great way to do the following:

- Build your mobile UX skills
- Communicate a design idea or experience
- Gather user feedback
- Explore the unknown
- Fine-tune an idea

Prototyping, however, is no substitute for creativity and great ideas. Those come from you.

Summary

- The primary skill that designers new to mobile UX must learn is to calibrate their design decision-making skills to a new medium. Prototyping is the best way to improve decision-making skills for mobile UX.

- Mobile prototyping methods tend to fall into two basic genres: tactical and experiential prototyping.

- The three tactical prototyping methods are:

  - Sketching

  - Paper prototyping

  - Interactive on-device prototyping

- Five experiential prototyping methods are:

  - Storyboarding

  - Bodystorming

  - Speed dating prototypes

  - Concept videos

- The four key reasons designers should turn to prototyping are:

  - Communicate a design idea or experience.

  - Gather user feedback.

  - Explore the unknown.

  - Fine-tune an idea.

- Don't be afraid to identify when failure is happening and move on to the next idea.

- Prototyping is a useful and important tool for building great mobile experiences; however, prototyping an idea doesn't make an idea great.

Expert Interview: Julian Bleecker

Designer, technologist, and researcher at Nokia Design and co-founder of Near Future Laboratory

Julian Bleecker is an artist and technologist with a history of developing innovative mobile research projects (see Figure 6.48).

Bleecker holds a Ph.D. from the History of Consciousness Program at University of California, Santa Cruz. He's been an artist-in-residence at the Eyebeam Art and Technology Center, exhibited work at Ars Electronica, been a Research Fellow at the Annenberg Center for Communication, and an Assistant Professor at the USC Interactive Media Division. He now works as an interaction designer at Nokia Design (Los Angeles). Bleecker has been active as a researcher in the areas of mobile computing, pervasive networks, near-field interaction systems, and the Internet of Things.

FIGURE 6.48
Julian Bleecker is an artist and technologist with a history of developing innovative mobile research projects.

How did you find your way into the mobile design space?

It was when I was living back in Brooklyn after I had finished my Ph.D. It was right about the time the first dot com thing was taking off, and there was a lot of excitement around technology and the Internet. Cell phones were definitely around, but they were pretty inaccessible.

I remember flipping through the Sunday *New York Times* one Sunday morning and noticed this full page ad for J & R, which is like the geeky kind of technology superstore in New York City. It was an ad for Palm 7, which was the Palm that had a flip-up antenna that would allow it to connect to the Internet. I remember seeing it and thinking, "That's it. That's exactly it." Just the idea of being able to do *Internetty* things while on the go was super, super exciting to me. I saw that as a new range of possibilities for doing networked activities. I literally went out that morning to J & R and picked up one of those so I could begin mucking around with it and seeing what I could do.

Ever since then, I have focused on mobility connected networked experiences.

What was it about mobile networked experiences that enchanted you?

I think to a large degree it was this funny thing where science fiction was collapsing into science fact in a way. I had this naïve sense that those things I'd seen in movies or TV shows that I adored when I was younger could actually happen. It opened up all these creative possibilities in my mind.

We humans are mobile beings. Being tethered to a desk or a computer that has to sit on your lap seems a little archaic in a way. The idea of mobile networked devices opened up a whole new set of contexts and paradigm of use. It adds another degree of freedom that includes all the possible kinds of experiences you could have because you are walking around the world.

In the mobile paradigm, buildings become an interface element, or walking down a street becomes a gesture. It just expands and increases and enriches that range of possibility.

What are some of the biggest changes you've experienced during the course of your career in mobile?

The tools for doing app development for mobile devices have matured so much, especially with the newer, more modern operating systems that it's become much easier and faster to translate your ideas into reality. Making a mobile experience is not trivial by any means, but there's so much support for it now as compared to 10 years ago. Back in the day, the tools were a pain in the butt. They were super arcane, almost wizardry kind of stuff. Now, there's not a huge gap between the idea and its kind of material possibility.

I also think just the sheer number of people interested in mobile is another change from 10 years ago. People didn't used to think about mobile as a possibility; it was more obscure and science fiction-y. That's not the case today. There are a lot of people interested in the mobile space now. The fact that all these people who are interested in mobile can just find each other and support each other and that allowing the community of people interested in mobile to grow and be this Katamari agglomeration of active individuals making and thinking and doing and creating. That didn't exist before like it does now.

The biggest change is that it's become a lot easier to make things. Now, people who have a little spare time can build a mobile application on the side that is just a wonderfully whimsical kind of crazy, kooky, little app that makes people think about what could be possible.

Just being able to translate an idea into the material of the day, which happens to be software and electrical hardware, has become a lot easier.

How has this change in the ease of making things affected your work?

I like the world of ideas and thinking about things and talking about them and writing about them and that kind of thing. Lately, I've come to see how you need an object or the tangible expression of the idea. There's a split between the idea and its representation in the world in some other medium besides words that is super important—not only because the representation communicates the idea to other people, but because you often learn through the process of making the thing.

Making allows you to refine and develop and evolve the idea. It's like if you write something, it's seldom perfect the first time. So you go back and refine it, and as you're refining it, you're not just changing—you're also refining your thinking.

I think you have to start making something in order to really understand what it is that you're trying to do. I think the fact that you can do that so much easier nowadays in mobile really helps people approach the work in this way. Rapid prototyping allows you to rapidly prototype both the material and your thinking.

How did this approach help you when you were working on your project about trust?

Well, that project started out with a provocation: What would provoke us to discuss and think about things we trust and things we don't trust? People don't generally trust things that make them uneasy, so I wanted to know what those things might be. I wanted to create something that would allow people to have a conversation about what trust is in a material, substantive, experiential way, as opposed to a conversation about the philosophy of trust. That's where that design probe started.

Then I started thinking about objects we trust and landed on alarm clocks and how people trust alarm clocks to wake them up every morning.

Then I started playing around with the idea of an alarm clock and the ritual of waking up every morning. I came up with an idea for a clock with two pieces. One piece sits by your bed. It's not plugged in, though. The other piece of the clock is another little secondary device, like a key fob that you would give to a friend. And the friend was meant to wake you up when the key fob clock buzzes. The interesting thing about the clock is that after you've set it and take out the key fob part, the clock sitting by your bed goes blank. You have no idea what time it is. It's a little bit of a joke, but the serious part of the joke is that it's deliberately designed as a sort of theoretical probe. It's a thought experiment made in material so you can see it, you can touch it, and play with it in order to help try to understand what trust is. So it begs that question. Who would you trust with this if you had to wake up at 5 A.M. to catch a flight? See Figures 6.49 and 6.50.

FIGURES 6.49 AND 6.50
The trust clock was designed to have two pieces. One sits by your bed. The other piece is much like a key fob. First, you set the clock, and then you give the key fob to a friend. When the key fob clock buzzes, only your friend can activate the alarm by the clock near your bed.

Often, designing and the thinking about the designed object still happen while you're making it, which is precisely what happened with this clock.

In the design, development, and iteration of the clock, people in the studio ended up asking a number of questions that wouldn't have come up if we had just had a philosophical conversation about trust. We had some disagreement about whether or not the clock should go blank when you give the smaller fob-like device to your friend or the person who you trust the most.

I felt very strongly that it should go blank because I thought otherwise it wasn't doing its job. Some people in the studio would say, "There's no way…I could not find anyone whom I would trust enough to wake me up in that fashion with me not knowing the time that it was. If I happened to wake up in the middle of the night and I just needed to know, it would drive me nuts." So that was, I think, a key turning point in the project. To solve that problem, we gave the clock two modes: It's got dream mode where the face goes blank, and then it's got the coward mode where the face stays on.

When the discussion "Who would you trust?" came up, one person said, "There's no one whom I would trust." In that discussion, we started thinking about an evolution of the clock that would not just wake up to people, say this person you trusted, but would wake up to other things that were happening in the world. That led to the evolution of adding the ability to have things in the world that you trust wake you up. So in addition to having someone you trust wake you up, the clock can wake you up to three things.

One is the activity of Twitter in your kind of area, your geographic area. So that might be for people who want to wake up when the rest of the world starts stretching itself on the Internet. So when people start yammering on Twitter at a certain threshold, the alarm would go off. Then the second one is the flow of traffic and where you designate, and you can decide what that threshold is. So you might be the kind of person who, once traffic starts slightly moving, says "Okay, I'm gonna get up, and I'm just gonna get on the road and get to wherever I need to go without getting caught up in it."

And then, the third one is the height of the surf at a surf beach that you identify. For some people, it's not a question of waking up early, but waking up in time for when the surf is really going off at their favorite surf beach. As opposed to waking up, checking online, and then maybe not being able to go to sleep, the clock can wake you up according to the tides.

All of these ideas came out of conversations about who and what we would trust. If we didn't have the object of the clock to catalyze those conversations, I doubt we would have thought of those things.

CHAPTER 7

Motion and Animation
A New Mobile UX Design Material

Principle 1: Squash and Stretch   184

Principle 2: Anticipation   186

Principle 3: Staging   187

Principle 4: Straight Ahead and Pose to Pose   188

Principle 5: Follow-Through and Overlapping Action   190

Principle 6: Slow In and Out   191

Principle 7: Arcs   193

Principle 8: Secondary Action   194

Principle 9: Timing   195

Principle 10: Exaggeration   196

Principles 11 and 12: Solid Drawing and Appeal   198

Methods for Specifying Motion in Your Work   198

Summary   201

rowing up, weekends were about worship in the Hinman household. Sunday mornings were reserved for a laborious worship ritual dictated by my parents. It required dressing up in uncomfortable clothes, going to church, and pretending to listen to long-winded sermons about Jesus while drawing doodles in hymnals. Saturdays, however, were reserved as my day of worship, and I was a proud and dedicated disciple of the church of Saturday Morning Cartoons. Every Saturday, rain or shine, healthy or sick, I'd jump out of bed, run downstairs to the living room, plant myself in front of the TV, and celebrate the gospel of Wonder Woman, Captain Caveman, Scooby Doo, and Papa Smurf for hours on end (see Figures 7.1–7.3).

While my parents were far from enthusiastic about my choice of religion, they tolerated it as a form of quid pro quo for Sunday church attendance. Little did either of us know that those hours of fanatical dedication to the gospel of Saturday morning cartoon programming would eventually turn into a valuable vocational asset.

FIGURES 7.1–7.3
Animated cartoons such as *Wonder Woman*, *Captain Caveman*, and *Scooby Doo* taught me how movement can breathe life into drawings.

I would imagine many of you reading this book are members of the very same congregation—the group of us who recognize the subtle yet important religious differences between still-frame cartoons (like those found in the "funnies' section of the Sunday newspaper) and the animated TV cartoons where we gladly took communion of orange juice and cereal every Saturday morning. We are the ones who understand what adding movement to something flat and lifeless can do. Movement breathes life into everything it touches.

Adding movement to anything—whether it is a series of drawings or the transitions between the screens in a digital experience—is not a "just-as-easy-as-adding-water" kind of task. It's an art that requires patience, an eye for subtlety, and careful study of how objects and people move through space and time.

Transitions and subtle motion-based animations are emerging as a new and compelling mobile design material worthy of learning to use with efficiency and grace. The addition of movement to mobile experience can provide clarity, information about context, and frankly, a dash of joy and fun. However, too much animation or funky transitions can destroy a perfectly good mobile experience. This makes understanding the guiding principles behind the art of animation the best first step to artfully apply motion to your design work.

The people who understand this better than anyone are the legions of brilliant animators who have worked at Walt Disney. Thankfully for us, two animators by the names of Ollie Johnston and Frank Thomas decided to put pen to paper and share with the world the basic animation principles used by Disney animators during the filmmaking process in their book, *The Illusion of Life: Disney Animation*.

You may wonder what animation has to do with mobile user experience. While the art form of animation was once the providence of animated films and television, it has found its way into the computer and digital user-experience realms. The addition of artful animation has all but invaded the mobile user experience field. Whether it is the transitions between screens of a mobile experience or the behaviors applied to UI elements that can be interacted with using gestures, motion has become a significant mobile design element. It's a design material you can use to help guide you through the mobile experiences you'll create.

Taking cues from Johnston and Thomas, this chapter explains the Twelve Basic Principles of Animation, borrowed from their 1981 book *The Illusion of Life: Disney Animation* (see Figure 7.4). Although originally developed for animated film and television, these principles are completely applicable to screened-based experiences, too. If applied with subtlety and finesse, motion can elevate your mobile work, giving it that little touch of magic you experienced every Saturday morning as a child.

Here are the twelve basic principles of animation:

- Squash and Stretch
- Anticipation
- Staging
- Straight Ahead and Pose-to-Pose
- Follow Through and Overlapping Action
- Slow In and Out

- Arcs
- Secondary Action
- Timing
- Exaggeration
- Solid Drawing
- Appeal

FIGURE 7.4
The Illusion of Life: Disney Animation by Frank Thomas and Ollie Johnston outlines twelve basic principles of animation.

Principle 1: Squash and Stretch

People and objects inherently have a sense of mass. When an object moves, the character of the movement often indicates the rigidity of the object. Manmade, real-world objects, such as bookshelves or a wooden chair, are rigid and have little flexibility. Soft surfaces, like clothing, organic objects, and the leaves of a plant, have less rigidity and a higher level of flexibility (see Figure 7.5). Squash and stretch is the animation principle used to accurately express the rigidity of an object.

FIGURE 7.5
Organic and soft surface objects, such as a balloon filled with water, have some level of flexibility in their shape. Squash and stretch is the animation principle that helps depict this character in animation.

You should consider using this principle when you decide what feeling you want your mobile experience to evoke as users engage with it. Is your mobile experience a world of solid planes, rigid surfaces, and sharp, exact movements? Or is it a world that's more organic, with softer, pliable surfaces with easy, graceful movements? Squash and stretch can help you express your decision through movement.

Figures 7.6 and 7.7 show mobile UX squash and stretch examples.

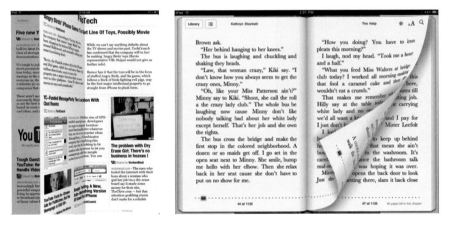

FIGURES 7.6 AND 7.7
Screen transitions on Flipboard use the principle of squash and stretch to express that the surfaces inside the world of the application are rigid and "board-like." In contrast, the screen transitions on Apple's iBook use the principle of squash and stretch to echo the flexible and organic movement of turning the pages of a real analog book.

FIGURE 7.8

The crouching pose of a bowler, winding up before swinging a bowling ball, is an example of the type of pose and motion the anticipation animation principle should capture.

FIGURE 7.9

The aperture animation found on the camera application of many smartphones prepares the user for the action of taking a photograph.

Principle 2: Anticipation

When an illustrator depicts a moving object or character, there are three distinct phases that should be considered to make the object's movement seem realistic:

- The preparation for the action

- The action itself

- The results of the movement

Whether it's a baseball batter winding up before a swing or the recoil of a spring before it's sprung, anticipation is the animation principle used to address the preparation of an object for movement (see Figure 7.8). Anticipation is about orchestrating components of a scene—the lighting, composition, or even manipulating the shape and form of an object or character—in order to give the viewer insight into what is about to happen. It's about giving the viewer a brief clue about what will happen next.

Similar to its application in animated film or cartoons, when applied to the realm of mobile UX, anticipation is all about giving the user insight into what is about to happen next. For example, it's a principle that can be applied to the visual treatment of the interface as a user opens up an application. It can also be applied to transitions between experiences. Because gesture languages are relatively new for users, the principle of anticipation can also be used to provide affordance for gestural UIs. Anticipation gives insight into the speed and direction with which objects within a UI can move and the gestural possibilities of those objects.

Figures 7.9, 7.10, and 7.11 show mobile UX anticipation examples.

FIGURE 7.10
The window shade animation on the home screen of the Windows Phone 7 employs the principle of anticipation by giving users a peek into the phone's dynamic tile UI.

FIGURE 7.11
The way in which the cards of the Palm Pre's user interface move acts as an affordance for users, giving them insight into the gestural language of the UI.

Principle 3: Staging

People keen on selling property often "stage" a home, meaning they arrange each room in such a way that its purpose is completely clear. The principle of staging in animation is similar because good staging makes the central idea of an animation completely clear to the viewer. In the world of mobile user experience, the principle of staging is most relevant when considering the transitions between screens and interactions. Interactions that are well staged combine light, color, composition, and motion to direct the user's eye to exactly where it needs to be as he interacts with an experience. Well-staged mobile experiences have a sense of flow and ease, whereas poorly staged ones feel disjointed (see Figure 7.12).

FIGURE 7.12
The well-staged illustration makes the central idea—two characters engaged in conversation—completely clear. The poorly staged illustration leaves the dynamic between the two characters open for interpretation, making the central idea unclear.

Poor Staging | Good Staging

Staging is a subtle yet important consideration when applying animation and motion to mobile experiences. A key challenge for natural user interfaces is that they lack a strong conceptual anchor. As a result, users new to NUIs often feel anchorless as they navigate touchscreen experiences. If good, strong staging is applied to the animation and transitions of the mobile experience you create, users will likely feel more grounded when they interact with it.

Figure 7.13 shows a mobile UX staging example.

FIGURE 7.13
Good staging used in the iPad version of Keynote enables users to see exactly where the file they are currently working on lives in the application's file structure. This subtle use of staging allows the user to feel grounded in the experience.

Principle 4:
Straight Ahead and Pose to Pose

Straight ahead and pose to pose are animation techniques that refer directly to the animation drawing process. In order to capture fast, dynamic action with unusual movement, animators will use the straight-ahead technique and draw every single frame of an animation. The pose-to-pose drawing technique employs the use of keyframes (the important frames of a sequence) and in-betweens (the intermediate frames that express movement between the keyframes), as shown in Figure 7.14

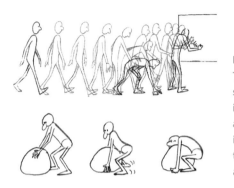

FIGURE 7.14
The first illustration depicts the straight-ahead drawing technique in which every single frame of an animation is rendered. The second illustration represents the keyframes that will be used in a pose-to-pose animation.

The vast majority of animations and transitions used in mobile experiences employ the pose-to-pose animation technique. Pose to pose will usually suffice for transitions that are not overly complex and can be described easily. If you'd like to incorporate unusual or dynamic movement in your experience that can't be achieved using pose to pose, you'll likely need to incorporate the straight-ahead drawing technique in order to capture the motion you are envisioning.

Figures 7.15 and 7.16 show mobile UX straight-ahead and pose-to-pose examples.

FIGURE 7.15
Popular games like *Plants and Zombies* for the iPad employ the use of pose-to-pose animation techniques.

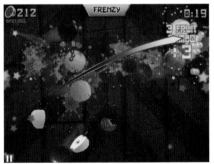

FIGURE 7.16
Games with more complex movement, as in the iPad game *Fruit Ninja*, use straight-ahead animation techniques to capture dynamic motion.

Principle 5:
Follow-Through and Overlapping Action

Imagine a big dog with giant jowls shaking his head side to side. The dynamic movement of the flabby skin on his face as he shakes his head to and fro is an example of the fifth animation principle: follow-through and overlapping action. While anticipation is the preparation of an action, follow-through deals with the end of an action. Actions rarely come to a sudden and complete stop, but are generally carried past their endpoint. Follow-through captures how parts of an object (like the dog's jowls) continue to move even after other parts of that object (like the dog's head) have stopped moving (see Figure 7.17).

FIGURE 7.17
Follow-through captures how different parts of an object move at different rates (such as a dog's head moving at a different rate than his ears or jowls).

Now imagine that dog walking down a sidewalk with his owner. His entire body is moving, but the timing of the movement of his legs is different than the timing of the movement of his tail or head. Overlapping action is the animation principle that captures how parts of an object—such as the dog's head, tail, and legs—move at different rates. Capturing the nature of the movement, as well as the slight variations in timing and speed of these parts, makes objects seem more natural. An action should never be brought to a complete stop before starting another action. Overlapping maintains a continual flow between whole phrases of actions.

While UI elements of a mobile experience should work together to form a whole, follow-through and overlapping action can help you define and communicate the nature of the relationship between UI elements. Transitions and animations are a great way to use movement to express how elements of a UI interrelate.

Figure 7.18 shows a mobile UX example of a follow-through and overlapping action.

FIGURE 7.18
The transition animation to and from the dynamic tiles experienced on the Windows mobile employs the principle of overlapping action. The tiles do not travel as one unit, but rather each tile moves at a different rate.

Principle 6: Slow In and Out

Whether it's a car peeling out from a dead stop, or a sprinter bursting out of the blocks and making tracks in a race, objects need time to accelerate and slow down. The sixth animation principle, slow in and out, deals with the spacing required to accurately depict the inherent law of inertia that governs all objects and people. Objects in the world need time to accelerate and slow down. A strategy for accurately depicting this type of motion when creating an animation is to include more frames of the object near the beginning and end of a movement and fewer in the middle (see Figure 7.19). This principle works for characters moving between two extreme poses, such as sitting down and standing up, and also for inanimate moving objects, such as a bouncing ball.

FIGURE 7.19
Including more frames of the object near the beginning and end of a movement and fewer frames in the middle creates the illusion of inertia in animated work.

While the experiences we create for mobile UX often live in another world—the world behind the glass of our mobile device—allowing some of the laws of physics to exist in that world makes those experiences more relatable to users. Whether it's a subtle timing difference in how a list view of data scrolls or the animated transition that appears as an application opens, slow in and out will make the motion phrases of your experience flow in a way that feels natural to users.

Figures 7.20–7.23 show slow in and out examples.

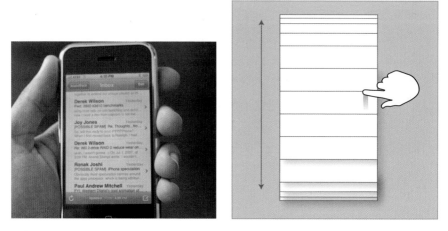

FIGURES 7.20 AND 7.21

The principle of slow in and out is applied to the scrolling lists of many mobile UIs. There are more frames at the beginning and end of the movement. This effect makes the UI appear as if it is governed by the laws of inertia.

 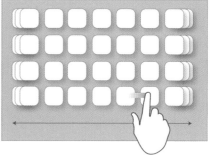

FIGURES 7.22 AND 7.23

There are more frames at the beginning and end of the scrolling transition of the home screen of the iPhone, making the application icons feel as though they follow the laws of inertia.

Principle 7: Arcs

Objects don't move through space at random. Instead, they move along relatively predictable paths that are influenced by forces such as thrust, wind resistance, and gravity. The outline of a sparkler on the Fourth of July or skid marks on the pavement from a braking car are rare examples of the physical traces of these paths; usually an object's trajectory is invisible (see Figure 7.24). While these paths are largely unseen by the human eye, patterns exist for trajectory paths based on whether an object is organic or mechanical. Objects that are mechanical in nature such as cars, bicycles, and trains tend to move along straight trajectories, whereas organic objects such as plants, people, and animals tend to move along an arched trajectory. The object you want to animate should reflect these characteristics of movements for greater realism.

FIGURE 7.24
An object's trajectory lies largely unseen, except in rare occasions, such as the glowing sparks of a lit sparkler that traces the path of where it's been.

When integrating motion into a mobile experience, it's important to consider whether the object being animated should reflect organic or mechanical qualities. If the object possesses organic qualities, the arc animation principle suggests that the object should move along an arched trajectory. An object that is mechanical in nature would move along a straight path.

Figures 7.25 and 7.26 show mobile UX arc examples.

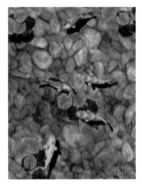

FIGURE 7.25
Natural elements such as fish and water in the iPhone application move along arched trajectories.

FIGURE 7.26
Interface elements in the Android mobile platform tend to move along straight lines, giving the UI a mechanical feeling.

Principle 8: Secondary Action

Imagine a squirrel running across your lawn and then leaping into a tree. The movement of the squirrel's spry legs (considered the primary action) would be animated to express the light, nimble nature of its gate. The agile, undulating movement of the squirrel's tail—considered the secondary action—is a separate and slightly different type of movement that supports the primary action (see Figure 7.27). The squirrel's tail is an example of secondary action, which is an animation principle that governs movement that supports a primary action of an animation sequence without distracting from it. Secondary action is applied to reinforce the mood or enrich the main action of an animated scene. The key to secondary action is that it should emphasize, rather than take away attention from the main action being animated.

Figure 7.28 shows a mobile UX secondary action example. The transition that occurs when a user clicks on a URL in an email, activating the phone's browser on an iPhone is an example of secondary action. The primary action is the browser window emerging forward into the user's view. The secondary action is the email view receding into the background. Both actions occur simultaneously, but the secondary action of the email application supports the primary action—opening a browser window.

FIGURE 7.27
The primary action of this animation is the squirrel's body and legs moving. The shape and character of the squirrel's tail as it moves is the secondary action.Together they make the animation feel more realistic.

FIGURE 7.28
An example of secondary action applied to an animated transition between application windows.

Principle 9: Timing

In animation, as in life, timing is everything. The visceral frustration and awkwardness we feel when objects, characters, or simply the rhythm of life is moving at a pace that feels too slow or too fast is a testament to the innate nature of timing. In the world of animation, timing refers to the number of drawings or frames for a given action, which translates to the speed of the action on film. Timing is an important technique to master because it helps to define the physical characteristics of an object such as weight, size, and scale. It can also make objects appear to abide by the laws of physics— such as how quickly an object moves when pushed.

In addition to expressing physical characteristics, timing helps communicate the emotional state, mood, and personality of an object or character. For example, subtle adjustments in timing can communicate the physicality and mood of the focused and deliberate Wylie Coyote as he feverishly chases the quick, good-natured Road Runner, who in contrast moves with ease (see Figure 7.29).

FIGURE 7.29
Timing—the mere speed at which the Road Runner moves—expresses both the physicality of the character (weight, height, and scale) and the mood of the jovial chase between Road Runner and Wylie Coyote.

Whether it's the speed with which a scrollable list moves or the pacing of a transition between screens within a mobile application, timing is a subtle yet important skill to master. Timing as it applies to mobile UX is an art that requires finesse and practice. Take the time to understand *what* is communicated through the movement and speed of the interface elements in your design. Also, take time for experimentation and trial and error as you begin to work with animation.

Figures 7.30–7.32 show some mobile UX timing examples.

FIGURES 7.30–7.32
The timing used in the iPad's photo application is akin to quickly shuffling a deck of cards. It expresses lightness, buoyancy, and super-real speed.

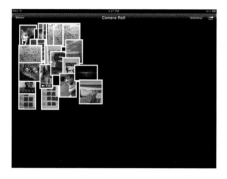

FIGURE 7.33
Canadian animator John Kricfalusi masterfully used exaggeration for the *Ren & Stimpy* animated television series.

Principle 10: Exaggeration

The principle that I personally feel brings the most fun to the animation party is exaggeration. It's the element that makes movement feel dynamic, alive, and just plain fun—much like the iconic characters of *Ren & Stimpy* depicted in Figure 7.33. An animation without some level of exaggeration may look accurate, but will likely feel stiff and mechanical to viewers. Mastering this principle involves identifying a design element, figuring out how that element moves, and then tweaking the shape, scale, or composition of the element in such a way that it reinforces the movement while adding a layer of drama. Exaggeration does not necessarily mean extreme distortion. The classical definition of exaggeration, employed by Disney, was to remain true to reality, but presented in a wilder, more extreme form.

When applying this principle to the movement in a mobile experience, it's important to apply a certain level of restraint. If a scene contains several elements, there should be a balance in how those elements are exaggerated in relation to each other, to avoid confusing or annoying the viewer.

Figures 7.34–7.37 show mobile UX exaggeration examples.

FIGURES 7.34–7.37
The transition between the home screen of the iPad and opening an application is exaggerated. It makes opening an application feel springy and fun, like bouncing on a trampoline.

Principles 11 and 12:
Solid Drawing and Appeal

Of the 12 animation principles outlined by Johnston and Thomas, the last two principles—solid drawing and appeal—are the most specific to the domain of character animation. Subsequently, they have slightly less relevance to mobile UX. Solid drawing is about honoring the rules of three-dimensional space and being sure to give objects and characters appropriate dimensionality through the use of volume and weight. Solid drawing stresses the need for animators to understand the basics of three-dimensional shapes: anatomy, weight, balance, light, and shadow (see Figure 7.38).

FIGURE 7.38
Solid drawing stresses the importance of three-dimensional shapes, accurate anatomy, and animation work that has a sense of weight, balance, light, and shadow.

Appeal in an animated character is similar to the attribute of charisma for an actor. A character that is appealing is not necessarily sympathetic—because villains or monsters can also be appealing. The important thing is that the viewer *feels* the character is real and interesting.

Methods for Specifying Motion in Your Work

While the 12 principles developed by Johnston and Thomas are helpful for providing a vocabulary for motion and giving you a sense of what's possible, the core question around how to integrate motion into your design work still remains. The first step is to be aware of motion as a design material. The next step is to begin to integrate motion into your design process. Three key places in the design process where you can begin working with the magic of motion are the following:

- Sketching

- Wireframing

- Prototyping

Sketching

The first place to begin thinking about motion is during the sketching portion of your design process (see Figure 7.39). Similar to how the movement style of an animated character helps express its personality, the movement styles of screens and interface elements are powerful ways of expressing the "personality" of the mobile experience you're creating. Sketching ideas about transitions and movement phrases early helps get you thinking about the personality you want your mobile experience to convey and how you can use motion to communicate it.

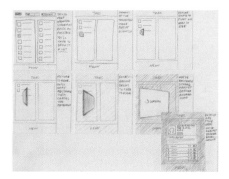

FIGURE 7.39
This photo depicts a motion storyboard sketch for the "Opening iTunes Details" transition using basic Post-it Notes.

Wireframing

Wireframes are yet another place in the design process to specify the desired motion you want to be integrated into a mobile experience. Because wireframes often express screen flow, the specification of transitions—the motion *between* screens—fits naturally and easily into wireframe documents. Using images and illustrations (similar to those depicted in Figure 7.40), you can begin to call out the nature of the movement you have in mind. Since wireframes are documents used to communicate design ideas to both developers and stakeholders within an organization, simply including motion specifications in the document gets everyone on the design and development team aware of and talking about motion.

SNOW GLOBE GESTURE
Shaking the phone allows users to see, refresh, or update the semantic clusters.

FIGURE 7.40
This image depicts a motion specification in a wireframe document using images and illustrations.

Prototyping

Sketching and wireframing motion are good first steps, but nothing beats the real thing. Using prototyping tools in which motion is part of the vocabulary is perhaps one of the most powerful ways to begin to foster your own fluency with motion as a design medium. Software tools such as presentation software (Keynote, PowerPoint, etc.) include motion as part of the tool's vocabulary (see Figure 7.41). Instead of sketching motion, creating low-fidelity prototypes using software tools will help you experiment with motion and specify and communicate your animation ideas more accurately to your design team.

Tips for Applying Animation Principles to Your Mobile UX Project

1. **Practice restraint.**

   There are few things more annoying than a mobile experience with too much animation "zazz." While animation is a fun and exciting design material to add to your arsenal of skills, don't overapply it to the experiences you create. Doing so can turn a great experience into a train wreck. Instead, practice applying motion with subtlety and finesse.

2. **Complementary principles.**

   Whether it's a scene in an animated movie or the transitions between screens in a mobile experience, animated principles rarely occur in isolation. Instead, most successful animations are an orchestration of many principles applied at once to achieve a desired effect. As you grow your animation skills, you'll learn how to artfully combine these principles in a complementary fashion. These combinations will become like great recipes you can apply to your work.

3. **Animation as a supporting role.**

   In film, animation is used to support the story. The same is true for mobile UX. Animation should be a complementary element to a mobile experience, not the star. Make sure that the animation you add supports the interactions within your experience and doesn't detract or cause confusion.

Summary

Once reserved for animated cartoons and movies, motion is a new and powerful design material in the mobile UX landscape. In addition to adding focus and clarity to your work, it can add a bit of character and even magic to the experiences you create. While learning to use any new design material can be time consuming, getting up to speed with animation and motion probably won't feel like a chore. Instead, it will likely feel intuitive, and it will make all those hours of watching Saturday morning cartoons as a child seem like a wise investment of time.

- Transitions and subtle motion-based animations are emerging as a new and compelling mobile design material worth learning how to use with efficiency and grace. The addition of movement to mobile experience can provide clarity, information about context, and frankly, a dash of joy and fun.

- Although originally developed for animated film and television, the Twelve Basic Principles of Animation from the 1981 book *The Illusion of Life: Disney Animation* are applicable to screened-based experiences.

- The twelve basic principles of animation include:

  1. Squash and Stretch

  2. Anticipation

  3. Staging

  4. Straight Ahead and Pose to Pose

  5. Follow-Through and Overlapping Action

  6. Slow In and Out

  7. Arcs

  8. Secondary Action

  9. Timing

  10. Exaggeration

  11. Solid Drawing

  12. Appeal

- Three key places in the design process where you can begin working with the magic of motion are sketching, wireframing, and prototyping

CHAPTER 8

Awakening the Senses

Touch, Gesture, Voice, and Sound

Touch   205
Gestures: Let's Get Physical!   215
Voice and Sound   226
Swing for the Fences When Thinking about
  the Senses   232
Summary   233

I t's a sad but common sight in modern society—a person walking around in the world, utterly disengaged, head buried in a mobile device—a victim of the visually greedy mobile interface, as aptly shown in Figure 8.1.

FIGURE 8.1
Victims of the
visually greedy
mobile interface are
a common sight in
modern society.

Sure, one might argue there's more to blame than the interface, like our growing Pavlovian response to phone calls and messages and the "always on" expectation, or our strange and ravenous human need to consume more and more information and media.

But as designers, how much control do we really have over those issues?

What we do have some semblance of control over are interfaces, and it is curious that we rely so heavily on the sense of sight to guide users through technology experiences. Ask anybody with a vision impairment who uses a computer or a mobile phone, and you'll find that visually driven interfaces dominate the technology landscape.

On the PC, we can get away with it. But the dominance of visually driven interfaces becomes especially problematic in the mobile context. Design principles and conventions like WYSIWYG and GUI become brittle and broken on small devices. The screens are simply too small, and the requirements of the mobile context too great to support interfaces that are visually demanding. Even the lauded and successful iPhone demands that we disengage with the world and worship its visual luster during use.

The thing is, humans are actually pretty good at knowing where things are even when we can't see them. The sound of a fire truck, the smell of garbage, the vibration of an earthquake... our senses are tuned to innately tell us about the world around us. Unfortunately, these instincts haven't been finely tuned with regard to our behaviors around information and technology. We rely heavily on sight.

Breaking with this pattern is not an easy task. It requires designers to engage innate human senses when crafting digital experiences. Fortunately, advances in mobile technology are allowing us to do just that. Modern smartphones equipped with touchscreens, accelerometers, gyroscopes, sensors, speakers, and a host of other cool technologies are the raw materials you can use to create mobile experiences that engage a sense of touch, gesture, and sound.

This chapter covers the three most underused senses that you should consider when creating a mobile experience: touch, gesture, sound and voice. It will provide you with insight into how to integrate these innate senses into mobile experiences you will create.

Touch

The design and development of mobile devices outfitted with touchscreens has exploded since the release of the first iPhone in 2008, bringing with it the opportunity for users to experience firsthand the magic of touch interfaces. Sure, people may have had experiences with clunky touch interfaces on ATM machines or train ticket kiosks before the iPhone came along. However, there was something so special and so right about the combination of a mobile phone and a touchscreen interface that it created a fundamental shift in mobile user experience. The trend in touchscreen mobile devices doesn't appear to be stopping anytime soon.

Why? Touch interfaces feel so completely intuitive because the sense of touch is quite possibly the most innate and intimate sense we humans possess. Our sense of touch develops before all other senses in embryos, and it is the main sense that newborn infants use to learn about their environment (see Figure 8.2). It's the sense that never turns off or takes a break, and it continues to work long after the other senses fail in old age. Throughout life, people use their sense of touch to learn, protect themselves from harm, relate to others, and experience pleasure.

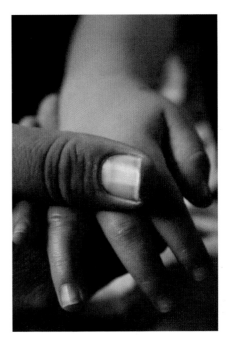

FIGURE 8.2
The sense of touch develops before all other senses in embryos, and it's the main way that infants learn about their environment.

What's magical about touch interfaces is their use of the essential human sense of touch to guide people through technology experiences. They allow people to feel like they're actually "touching" information. Unmediated, direct manipulation of digital content through touchscreens is as close as you can get to tangible experiences in the digital world.

One of the key challenges of creating touch interfaces is ensuring they are…well, touchable. While touch interfaces enable more intuitive and direct manipulation of information, there are three important design considerations to take into account when creating a mobile touch UI:

- Optimize for generous touch targets.

- Map the screen for touch.

- Lead with the content, not the interface.

Optimize for Generous Touch Targets

While touchscreens are great, fingers are…well, human. They're often big, kinda clunky, highly variable in size, and less precise than a cursor. Unlike screen designs optimized for the PC with tiny hyperlinks of text or the "any size goes" approach to button sizes and icons that activate interactions in most screen-based software, the size of touch targets becomes an important design consideration for touchscreens. If the targets are too small, your experience will be so difficult to interact with that your users will want to kill you (see Figures 8.3 and 8.4). If the targets are too big, you'll waste valuable screen real estate and run the risk of making your experience feel childish or unpolished.

FIGURE 8.3
The *New York Times* PC Web site is optimized for the precision of the indirect interaction of a mouse.

FIGURE 8.4
The *New York Times* mobile application is optimized for mobile with generous touch targets.

So how big should you make the touch targets on a touch UI?

The MIT Touch Lab study of "Human Fingertips to Investigate the Mechanics of Tactile Sense" found that the average human finger pad is 10–14mm and the average fingertip is 8–10mm.

That means the magic number is 10mm.

Most users can comfortably and reliably hit a 10mm by 10mm touch target. Different mobile platforms express this size recommendation differently, however.

For example, in the iPhone Human Interface Guidelines, Apple recommends a minimum target size of 44 pixels by 44 pixels (88px on retina display) or about 8mm round. Since physical pixel size can vary by screen density, Apple's pixel specifications apply best to the iPhone's 320 by 480 pixel, 3.5-inch display (164ppi). Since the release of the iPhone 4's retina display (326ppi), Apple has updated these specs to points instead of pixels. In the "Windows Phone UI Design and Interaction Guide," Microsoft suggests a recommended touch target size of 9mm/34px, and a minimum touch target size of 7mm/26px. Since different phone platforms will have different guidelines, it's best to check with the platform's specifications and design accordingly. However, regardless of platform, a minimum touch target of 10mm × 10mm is a good estimate/rule of thumb to apply to all your touchscreen designs (see Figure 8.5). For desktop designers, this

18 mm

15 mm

10 mm

FIGURE 8.5
Research indicates the average human finger pad is 10 × 14mm and the average fingertip is 8–10mm, making 10mm × 10mm a good minimum touch target size.

will feel ridiculously large—toy-like even! But have faith, it's important to make touch targets easy for users to engage with.

Before you start designing for a touchscreen experience, it's helpful to first understand exactly which type of touchscreen your experience will be rendered on. Currently, there are two types of touchscreen technologies that enable touch interface experiences on most mobile devices. Each has subtle design considerations that could have a big impact on how users interact with your experience.

RESISTIVE TOUCHSCREEN

A resistive touchscreen is composed of two thin, electrically conductive layers separated by a narrow gap (see Figure 8.6). When an object, such as a finger or a stylus, presses down on the panel's outer surface, two metallic layers become connected at that point. This causes a change in the electrical current, which is registered as a touch event. Both touch and pressure are required to interact with a resistive touchscreen. A major benefit of resistive touch technology is that it is extremely cost-effective. One disadvantage of resistive technology is its vulnerability to being damaged by sharp objects

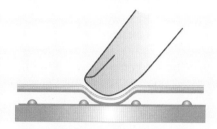

FIGURE 8.6
Resistive touchscreen diagram.

CAPACITIVE TOUCHSCREEN

Capacitive touchscreens are made from an all-glass material with a transparent metallic conductive coating (see Figure 8.7). An electrode pattern printed along the edges distributes a low voltage field over the conductive layer. When a finger touches the screen and draws a minute amount of current to the point of contact, it registers a touch event. Unlike a resistive touchscreen, a capacitive touchscreen can be activated with a very light touch—no pressure is required. A key and significant advantage of capacitive touchscreens is that they produce experiences that feel very responsive. People often describe capacitive touchscreen experiences as "sharp" and "slick" because of this very attribute. Some disadvantages of capacitive touchscreens are that they are more costly to produce than their resistive equivalent, and they generally cannot be used with a mechanical stylus or a gloved hand.

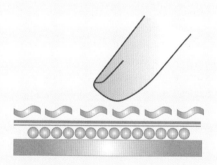

FIGURE 8.7
Capacitive touchscreen diagram.

Mapping the Screen for Touch

Unlike personal computer experiences, which involve many physical buttons like keyboard keys and mice with scroll wheels, most mobile touchscreen experiences involve a device that is nothing more than a flat screen of glass. While there are few physical buttons, the nature of touchscreen interactions is highly physical because interactions are explored through human hands. Subsequently, it's important that your touchscreen layouts not only offer generous touch targets, but also accommodate the ergonomics of fingers and thumbs (see Figure 8.8).

FIGURE 8.8
Touchscreen layouts should offer generous touch targets and accommodate the ergonomics of fingers and thumbs.

Smartphones and the "Thumb Zone"

Smartphones are often used one-handed. Touchscreen interfaces must not only be aesthetically pleasing, but also should be organized for the fingers, especially the thumb. It's the finger that gets the workout and the reason why most major interface elements are located at the bottom of the screen instead of the top.

Interfaces designed for the desktop experience typically follow the design convention of placing major menu items across the top of the screen. The reverse is true of mobile experiences. Major menu items of your mobile experience should reside in "the thumb zone"—the screen area navigable using just a thumb (see Figures 8.9 and 8.10).

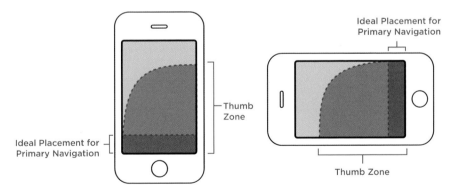

FIGURES 8.9 AND 8.10
Ideal navigation for "thumb zone" placement. The thumb zone is slightly less important when a mobile device is in landscape mode since most users hold the device with two hands while the device is in this orientation.

What About Tablets?

While they have many similar characteristics (few physical buttons and user interactions with a piece of glass), the ergonomic considerations for tablets are quite different than smartphones, mostly because one-handed use isn't possible. Instead, people use tablets in a variety of ergonomic configurations. From curling up with it like a book, to holding it like a clipboard, to propping it up in a kitchen while cooking—the variety of ways people use tablets makes it difficult to recommend heuristics about navigation placement.

Instead, it's better to think about the ways that a user will likely configure his body when using your tablet application. Then you can determine the area of the screen that makes the most sense, given the user's typical stance during use, and you can place the primary navigation elements accordingly, as shown in Figures 8.11–8.16.

FIGURES 8.11 AND 8.12
Curling up. Tablet experiences that encourage the "curling up" user stance opt for navigation at the top and consider incorporating horizontal gesture controls.

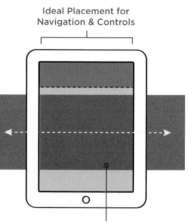

Ideal Placement for Navigation & Controls

Well Suited for Horizontal Gesture Controls

Ideal Placement for
Navigation & Controls

FIGURES 8.13 AND 8.14
The clipboard. For tablet experiences in which the user will often be holding the tablet like a clipboard, consider placing the navigation at the top where it's easy to see.

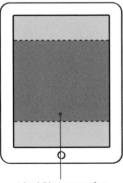

FIGURES 8.15 AND 8.16
Multitasker. For active tablet experiences where the user will likely be multitasking with other objects or devices, opt for placing the primary navigation at the top and/ or bottom. Tablets used in this configuration are often resting on tables/ desks/hard surfaces, making placement along the bottom of the screen a viable space for navigation and controls.

Ideal Placement for
Navigation & Controls

Ideal Placement for
Navigation & Controls

Ideal Placement for
Navigation & Controls

Lead with the Content, Not Interface Elements

Unlike GUI interfaces that make users interact with mechanism-like elements such as scroll bars, buttons, and UI chrome (like the example depicted in Figure 8.17), NUI/touchscreen interfaces allow users to interact directly with the content. Instead of UI chrome, images and blocks of text can serve as triggers for interaction. Since most mobile experiences come with the built-in constraint of limited screen real estate, embracing this aspect of touchscreen UIs can buy you some much needed pixel real estate for your designs. This will require a fundamental shift in the approach and thinking of most designers. You'll have to learn how to lead with the content, not the interface.

FIGURE 8.17
"The pointer" is a prevalent affordance in most GUI experiences, indicating clickable interactive elements.

Leading with the content means creating screen layouts that focus less on iconography and buttons and more on the content itself (images, videos, and text). Text and images are given visual prominence instead of interface elements. Interfaces that lead with content make content the star by celebrating its richness and giving it greater scale within a screen layout, while de-emphasizing the weight and visual presence of the UI controls—sometimes even hiding them from view until an action, such as a gesture, triggers them to appear (see Figure 8.18).

FIGURE 8.18
Content elements in a touch UI must often convey both a message and the affordance for interaction. The folded corner of this iPad Google Map is a great example of a touch UI affordance.

Part of learning to lead with the content requires designers not only to consider how a design element, such as a photo, communicates a message, but also how it can convey affordances for interaction. The mouse, prevalent with most GUIs, provides a lot of great affordances for interaction that designers can't rely on when designing for touch.

Five Touchscreen Affordance Strategies

Banishing GUI elements from touchscreen experiences is no easy task. It requires subtle communication through design. I've identified five emerging strategies that when applied artfully and appropriately will likely make your work inviting to the human touch.

1. Rely on real world metaphors, as shown in Figure 8.19.

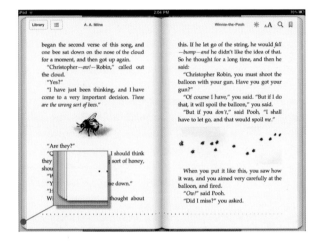

FIGURE 8.19
Many mobile applications rely on the book metaphor for navigating the experience. Screens are rendered like the physical pages of a book. This affordance gives users an indication of how to interact with the screen.

2. Render subtle UI elements (see Figure 8.20).

FIGURE 8.20
The application Flipboard is a great example of an experience that leads with the content. The app provides subtle UI affordances but allows content to be the star of the experience.

3. Spell it out or provide directions, as shown in Figure 8.21.

4. Hide the UI elements until they're needed, as shown in Figure 8.22.

5. Rely on visual clues (see Figure 8.23).

FIGURE 8.21
Some touchscreen applications simply take the direct route and spell it out for the user. This iPad version of *Popular Mechanics Magazine* incorporates instructions into the design.

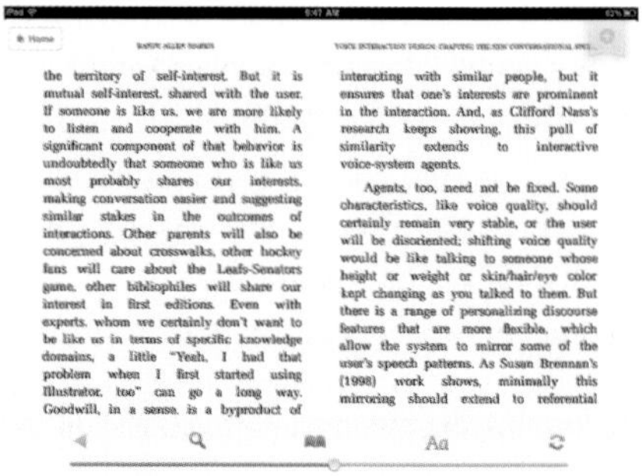

FIGURE 8.22
Several consumption-oriented mobile applications simply hide the touch UI elements. Tapping the bottom of the Kindle application makes the UI elements viewable. The UI controls remain hidden from view until they are needed, allowing the user to focus on the content.

FIGURE 8.23
Typography that spans past the viewing dimensions of the screen in the Windows Mobile UI is a great example of a touchable affordance. This affordance hints that there is more content, and scrolling right allows the user to access it.

Haptics

In addition to touchscreens, mobile haptics are another "sense-related" design material that can be incorporated into the mobile experiences you design. Derived from the Greek word *haptikos*, meaning to contact or to touch, haptics refers to tactile feedback given from a device to communicate with a user. Even if you haven't heard of the term "haptics," you've likely experienced it. The most common and widely used example of haptic feedback is the "setting your phone to vibrate" feature prevalent on most mobile phones.

Haptics are often overlooked in the design of mobile experiences because most designers aren't as proficient with touch/tactile feedback as a design language as they are with the design language of other senses, such as sight and sound. Another drawback is that haptics are challenging to prototype. Experimenting with haptics often requires software coding and insight into the hardware of a device. For all its challenges, however, dipping your toe into the "pond of haptic feedback" is worth the time and energy. There are few senses stronger and more innate than the human sense of touch, making haptics a topic worthy of greater understanding and a place for skill development. Make experimentation around this topic part of your mobile design process (see Figure 8.24).

FIGURE 8.24
Artist Masayo Ave's haptic touch panel—The Sound of Materials.

Gestures: Let's Get Physical!

For decades, digital experiences have mainly occurred at arm's length, mediated by a mouse and a keyboard. Gestural interfaces—UIs that trigger interactions with a digital system through human movement—are fundamentally changing this model. They are enabling new ways for people to interact with technology through movement of the human body. It took the widespread success of gesture-based experiences such as the Nintendo Wii, Microsoft Kinect, and a multitude of other devices to introduce the world to this new and more intuitive model of interaction. Now that they've arrived, it's hard to imagine how we lived so long without them (see Figures 8.25–8.27).

"Human beings possess a wide variety of physical skills—we can catch baseballs, dodge projectiles, climb trees—which all have a sort of 'underlying computational power' about them... But we rarely take advantage of these abilities in the realm of computing. The most nearly muscular mentality that we use (in computing) is pointing with a mouse. In retrospect, that seems strange and not very obvious why it should be that way."

—David Liddle[1]

FIGURE 8.25
Gesture-based UIs found in the Nintendo Wii and Microsoft Kinect introduced the world to a new breed of home video game experiences.

FIGURE 8.26
Girl playing Dance Central on a Microsoft Kinect.

FIGURE 8.27
Teen heartthrob, Justin Bieber, demonstrating the universal gesture for "talking on the phone."

---

1   *Wired* "Dogs Don't Do Math" by Tom Bestor, November 1993.

Gestural UIs have found their footing in the digital landscape because they're inherently intuitive: They build on our innate sense of movement to trigger interactions. From physically nudging a friend to get their attention to gracefully swiping the physical pages of a book, the gesture-based digital interactions that lean on experiences with real-world objects inherently feel natural and intuitive.

Gestures are definitely *not* visually greedy. You can't see them; you have to feel them. That's because they leverage our kinesthetic intelligence— the same intelligence that helps us learn how to ride a bike and shoot a basketball. While this reliance on kinesthetic intelligence makes gestural UIs intuitive, it's what also creates many of the challenges that both designers and users face when designing and interacting with these types of systems. It's the learning that makes them difficult.

Think of any physical movement you learn—from an infant learning to walk, to a child learning to ride a bike, to an adult learning the tango. Physical movement is largely learned through an observational learning process known as *modeling*. We observe someone performing the movement and then attempt to retain it through practice (usually failing a little). Then we finally master the movement through replicating it successfully several times. When a movement is repeated over time, a long-term muscle memory is created for that task, eventually allowing it to be performed without conscious effort (see Figure 8.28).

FIGURE 8.28
Physical movement is largely learned through modeling. When a movement is repeated often enough, eventually the physical task will be performed without conscious effort.

What makes gestural interactions difficult is that devices can't model the movement for us. Even when it does—through step-by-step instructions, etc.—it feels akin to learning to ride a bike through written instructions. Awkward.

This is why the most successful gestural UIs are those that leverage movements we have already learned. Gestures like sliding or flicking a page in a digital application, nudging a digital object, or rotating a digital photograph with our fingers feel intuitive because we have real-world experience with those movements. They're committed to our long-term muscle memory so we don't have to learn them. We simply have to associate the movement with the experience and proceed. The most discoverable UI gestures are those that build on existing experience.

It's the unnatural gestures—those that have no real world equivalent—that are truly troublesome. Unfortunately, not all the actions in a digital system have a corresponding gesture to lean on. Common interactions from the PC experience such as "copy and paste" have no clear and obvious real-world gestural equivalent. So if you're a designer keen on integrating gestures into your mobile experience and you stumble onto an interaction that has no analog gesture to rely on, there are three strategies you can apply:

- Introduce new gestures with the help of familiar ones.

- Provide feedback with an additional sense.

- Be creative and patient!

Introduce New Gestures by Building on Familiar Ones

Unlike GUI elements, such as a button that looks clickable or arrows attached to scroll bars that indicate the directions it can move, gestural interfaces have few or no visual affordances. They are largely invisible, and this is why discovery of gestures can be a difficult obstacle for users to overcome. One strategy for grappling with this design challenge is to introduce new gestures by building on familiar ones.

Some gestures such as tap, drag/slide, flick, and press are easy for users to grasp because they build on existing experiences in the world. Josh Clark, Joshua Kaufman, and David Maulouf have all documented the clever way developer Loren Brichter extended the gesture of "swipe to scroll," used to navigate a list, to encompass the gesture that triggers a refresh of the results of that same list. Once the user reaches the end of the list, simply tugging on the list activates a query to refresh the results of the list. "It's discoverable because you already know how to scroll a list, and as you scroll up, the gesture reveals itself." This gesture is now an emerging standard for scrolling through lists on many iPhone applications, as shown in Figure 8.29.

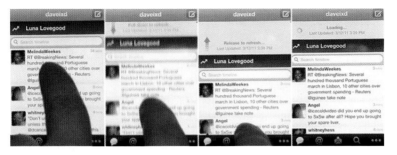

FIGURE 8.29
The now standard "spring to refresh" gesture for list views on iPhone and iPad applications. *Image courtesy of Dave Malouf.*

Another example of building on familiar gestures to introduce new ones is the touchscreen equivalent of a "rollover." Rollovers are a common interaction convention used in PC-based experiences. They provide users with additional information about a link. A user simply rolls his cursor over a clickable image, icon, or text link, and a "preview" of information is displayed. Rollovers are common on Web-based experiences and also on PC-based software. They're nearly impossible to implement on a touchscreen experience, however. Touchscreens only register direct contact with the screen, not hovering.

Although the "tap" gesture is most commonly used to select an item and trigger an interaction on most touchscreen experiences, some touch applications are using the "tap" gesture not only to trigger an interaction, but also to trigger a preview (the equivalent of a rollover state) on clickable interface elements (see Figures 8.30 and 8.31). It's yet another example of building on the familiar to introduce new meaning to a user's new and evolving gesture vocabulary.

FIGURES 8.30 AND 8.31
The "tap" gesture does double duty in the Trip Advisor application for the iPad. Depending on the context, "tap" either initiates an interaction or displays a preview of information about an active element. It's a clever way to build functionality into a well-understood gesture.

Provide Feedback with an Additional Sense

Another way to help users grasp new gestures is to provide feedback through an additional sense. Several keyboard experiences on mobile devices provide both visual and audio feedback for users by increasing the size of the key being tapped and registering a "tock" sound each time a keystroke is registered. In some instances, an image of a magnifying glass appears when the "press" gesture is performed on the iPhone (see Figures 8.32 and 8.33). Not only does this magnifying glass allow greater precision for selecting an element on the screen, but it's also a great example of providing visual feedback for a gesture that's not particularly intuitive. Providing this type of feedback can increase the user's confidence with the gesture, as well as improve the UI's efficacy.

FIGURE 8.32
The keyboards on most smartphones display a magnified version of each tapped key.

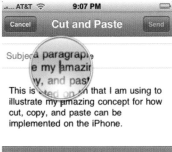

FIGURE 8.33
After a user performs the "press" gesture, a magnifying lens appears on many smartphone applications, providing both precision for selecting the text and a form of visual feedback for a somewhat lesser-known gesture.

Be Creative and Patient!

Finally, and most importantly, remember that gestural UIs are a relatively new addition to the world of interaction design and mobile experiences. Unlike GUIs with 40 years of history, a ton of research, and tried-and-true conventions and heuristics to lean on, gestural UIs are still in the formative stages. Few standards and heuristics exist yet, which can simultaneously be creatively liberating and immensely frustrating. Be sure to follow the established standards for the mobile platform you are building for and if you have an idea for a new-to-the-world gesture, test it with users to make sure it feels intuitive not only to you, but to them as well. Coming up with new gestures for digital experiences is definitely challenging but worth the work. There's no doubt that gestural UIs will play an important role in the future of mobile experiences.

Table 8.1 represents the most commonly used mobile gestures at this time. An important note: I consider these to be the *most common* mobile gestures; there are *many* additional gestures not included in this collection. Most mobile platforms have their own unique gesture library that you should reference before fine-tuning the detailed design of your experience. However, this collection should prove helpful as you start getting the hang of integrating gestures into your mobile experiences (see Figures 8.34–8.66).

TABLE 8.1

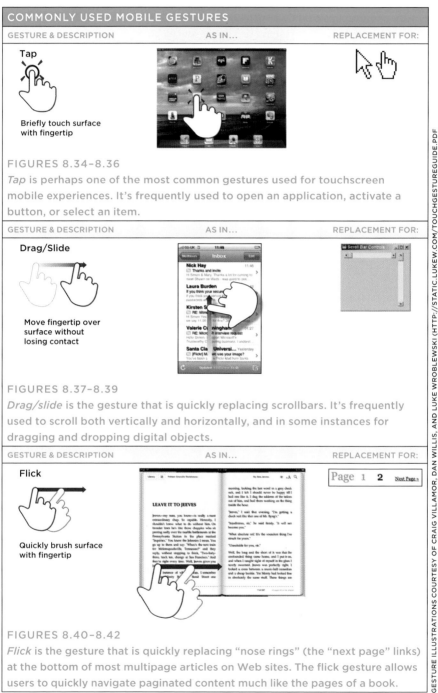

COMMONLY USED MOBILE GESTURES

GESTURE & DESCRIPTION	AS IN...	REPLACEMENT FOR:
Tap Briefly touch surface with fingertip		

FIGURES 8.34–8.36

Tap is perhaps one of the most common gestures used for touchscreen mobile experiences. It's frequently used to open an application, activate a button, or select an item.

GESTURE & DESCRIPTION	AS IN...	REPLACEMENT FOR:
Drag/Slide Move fingertip over surface without losing contact		

FIGURES 8.37–8.39

Drag/slide is the gesture that is quickly replacing scrollbars. It's frequently used to scroll both vertically and horizontally, and in some instances for dragging and dropping digital objects.

GESTURE & DESCRIPTION	AS IN...	REPLACEMENT FOR:
Flick Quickly brush surface with fingertip		

FIGURES 8.40–8.42

Flick is the gesture that is quickly replacing "nose rings" (the "next page" links) at the bottom of most multipage articles on Web sites. The flick gesture allows users to quickly navigate paginated content much like the pages of a book.

TABLE 8.1

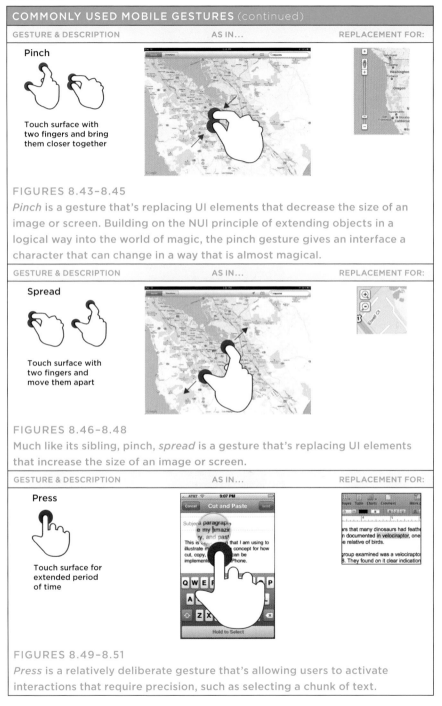

COMMONLY USED MOBILE GESTURES (continued)

GESTURE & DESCRIPTION	AS IN...	REPLACEMENT FOR:
Pinch Touch surface with two fingers and bring them closer together		

FIGURES 8.43–8.45

Pinch is a gesture that's replacing UI elements that decrease the size of an image or screen. Building on the NUI principle of extending objects in a logical way into the world of magic, the pinch gesture gives an interface a character that can change in a way that is almost magical.

GESTURE & DESCRIPTION	AS IN...	REPLACEMENT FOR:
Spread Touch surface with two fingers and move them apart		

FIGURES 8.46–8.48

Much like its sibling, pinch, *spread* is a gesture that's replacing UI elements that increase the size of an image or screen.

GESTURE & DESCRIPTION	AS IN...	REPLACEMENT FOR:
Press Touch surface for extended period of time		

FIGURES 8.49–8.51

Press is a relatively deliberate gesture that's allowing users to activate interactions that require precision, such as selecting a chunk of text.

TABLE 8.1

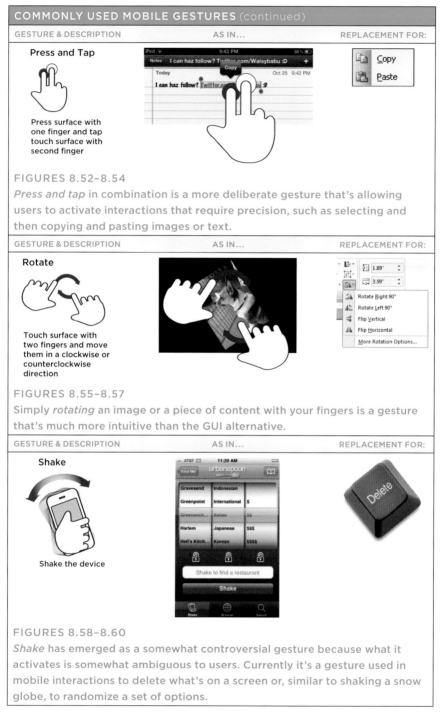

COMMONLY USED MOBILE GESTURES (continued)

GESTURE & DESCRIPTION	AS IN...	REPLACEMENT FOR:
Press and Tap Press surface with one finger and tap touch surface with second finger		Copy Paste

FIGURES 8.52–8.54

Press and tap in combination is a more deliberate gesture that's allowing users to activate interactions that require precision, such as selecting and then copying and pasting images or text.

GESTURE & DESCRIPTION	AS IN...	REPLACEMENT FOR:
Rotate Touch surface with two fingers and move them in a clockwise or counterclockwise direction		Rotate Right 90° Rotate Left 90° Flip Vertical Flip Horizontal More Rotation Options...

FIGURES 8.55–8.57

Simply *rotating* an image or a piece of content with your fingers is a gesture that's much more intuitive than the GUI alternative.

GESTURE & DESCRIPTION	AS IN...	REPLACEMENT FOR:
Shake Shake the device		Delete

FIGURES 8.58–8.60

Shake has emerged as a somewhat controversial gesture because what it activates is somewhat ambiguous to users. Currently it's a gesture used in mobile interactions to delete what's on a screen or, similar to shaking a snow globe, to randomize a set of options.

TABLE 8.1

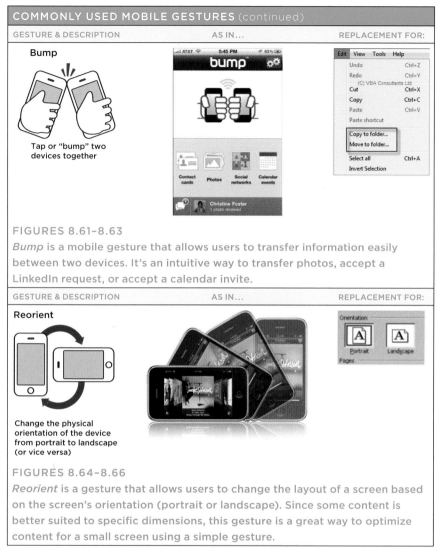

COMMONLY USED MOBILE GESTURES (continued)

GESTURE & DESCRIPTION	AS IN...	REPLACEMENT FOR:
Bump Tap or "bump" two devices together		

FIGURES 8.61–8.63

Bump is a mobile gesture that allows users to transfer information easily between two devices. It's an intuitive way to transfer photos, accept a LinkedIn request, or accept a calendar invite.

GESTURE & DESCRIPTION	AS IN...	REPLACEMENT FOR:
Reorient Change the physical orientation of the device from portrait to landscape (or vice versa)		

FIGURES 8.64–8.66

Reorient is a gesture that allows users to change the layout of a screen based on the screen's orientation (portrait or landscape). Since some content is better suited to specific dimensions, this gesture is a great way to optimize content for a small screen using a simple gesture.

Voice and Sound

Voice UIs are likely the least greedy interface type of all because they are largely invisible. Instead of sight, they harness one of the most natural forms of communication between humans: speech.

It's their invisibility, however, that makes voice-based interfaces challenging to design and use. While speech is one of the most natural forms of communication between humans, most people find using speech to communicate with machines anything but natural.

Voice user interfaces (known as *VUIs*) aren't terribly common because they're actually very difficult to pull off successfully (see Figure 8.67). There are a lot of reasons to consider them as a viable UI approach for mobile experiences, though. As direct decedents of landline phones, mobile devices have a rich legacy of voice interface that designers can lean on. VUI's invisibility is also a great foil to the limited screen real estate dilemma most mobile designers must contend with. And while sound can require a high level of cognitive processing, VUIs offer users a hands-free way to interact with information. The trick to taking advantage of all the good things that voice interfaces can bring to a mobile experience is in knowing when to use a VUI and how to create a good one.

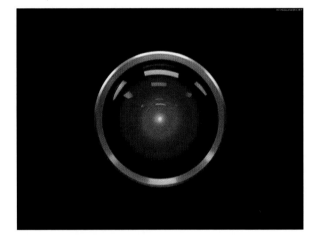

FIGURE 8.67
Voice interfaces can go to the creepy "Hal" place if not done well. (Hall was the notorious rogue computer enhanced with artificial intelligence that was operated by a VUI in the movie *2001: A Space Odyssey*.)

When to Use Voice

Part of creating a successful mobile VUI is using it as a solution to the right design problem. Not all mobile experiences are well suited for speech UIs. *Speech input* is generally well suited to circumstances in which the user's hands are busy. *Speech output* is generally well suited to circumstances in which the user's eyes will be busy. *Voice UIs* in general are best suited to mobile experiences where the data input (voice) and output (sound) are constrained. It's an information flow question.

For example, a poor candidate for a voice UI would be an experience such as mobile email. Even though a user's hands and eyes are often busy in a mobile context, email is an experience that has both a legacy of text-based interaction and a vast quantity of different types of information (Sender, Subject Line, Date, Time, message, and so on). The information input and output is high.

Other experiences, such as some banking tasks, are well suited for a mobile VUI because of the amount and flow of information. Tasks such as checking an account balance, transferring funds, and paying a bill have constrained and manageable amounts of information exchanged between the user and the application. Plus, the "invisibility" of voice can be desirable in a mobile context for privacy reasons. Generally speaking, low-input (a low information flow from user to system), low-output (system to user) uses are the best candidates for voice-based interfaces; high-input, high-output uses are the most difficult to pull off successfully (see Table 8.2).

TABLE 8.2

INFORMATION FLOW OF TYPICAL TASKS			
	Low System Output	Moderate System Output	High System Output
Low User Input	Checking a bank balance	Internet search	Credit history
Moderate User Input	Pizza order	Vehicle navigation	Online encyclopedia
High User Input	Survey	Auto mechanic	Purchasing an insurance policy*

* Table adapted from Harris, *Voice Interaction Design: Crafting the New Conversational Speech Systems* (Morgan Kaufman, 2004) p. 208.

Flattening Menus

The following is an example dialogue between a user and a voice interface:

System: *Please state the type of cuisine served by the restaurant you are attempting to locate. Some examples would be Thai, Italian, Indian, or Chinese.*

Caller: *Mexican.*

System: *You chose "Mexican." If this choice is correct, say "Yes" or press the pound key. If you did not intend to choose Mexican cuisine, say "No" or press the star key now.*

It requires little imagination to see how this type of interface would drive a sane person to the brink of craziness within 30 seconds. It's an example of a fundamental difference between voice interfaces and GUI interfaces. While menus are a standard part of most graphical user interfaces, they can be one of the most troublesome aspects of VUIs.

Arrangements of options, known as *menus*, are the thorn in the side of every voice-based UI experience. They are the presentation of options, similar to the example dialogue, which drives users bonkers and generally kills the joy of the experience. The serial perception of options should be minimized or eliminated, if possible. Since clusters of options such as these are virtually unavoidable in any voice-based interaction, the real design of a VUI is ridding the perception of these types of serial menus from the experience for the user. The clusters of options still exist within the system, but it's making them seamless or invisible to the user that makes for a good VUI experience.

The following diagram in Figure 8.68 is an example call flow, voice-based pizza ordering service.

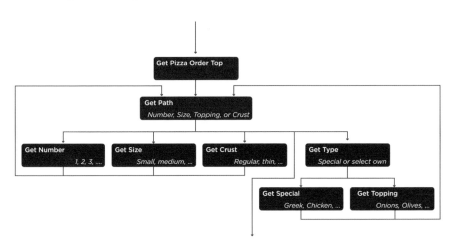

FIGURE 8.68
A stepwise VUI flow for ordering a pizza. If users can't bypass or consolidate option nodes, they'll feel like they're caught in an endless cycle of questions.[2]

Designing a voice UI that doesn't allow users to bypass option nodes forces them to answer *each and every question*, making users feel like they are caught in an endless cycle of questions.

Designing a system that enables users to bypass option nodes allows users to collapse or flatten two or more steps into one response, thereby "flattening"

2   Figure adapted from Randy Allen Harris, *Voice Interaction Design: Crafting the New Conversational Speech Systems* (Morgan Kaufman, 2004) p. 459.

the interaction. Menu flattening does not require the users to collapse all the steps; it simply *allows* them to. But that allowance demands good design—in particular, good vocabulary management and good task management. Good vocabulary management allows the system to accept scores of words instead of a small limited set of words. Good task management allows the user to combine steps instead of forcing users to answer each question serially. Compare the diagram in Figure 8.69 to the previous one. It demonstrates how a user can navigate a voice UI system by combining menus.

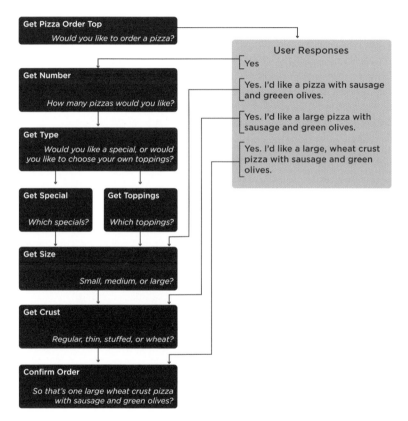

FIGURE 8.69
This diagram illustrates how a user can bypass menu options with their responses, thereby flattening menus and avoiding an endless cycle of questions.[3]

Although voice-based UIs have been around for many years, they largely failed to gain widespread acceptance because they were unwieldy, difficult

---

3   Figure adapted from Randy Allen Harris, *Voice Interaction Design: Crafting the New Conversational Speech Systems* (Morgan Kaufman, 2004) p. 462.

to design well, and difficult for people to use. That's changing. The recent success of well-designed VUIs in the mobile space has opened up the possibilities for voice-based interactions on a larger scale. Mobile VUIs are exposing both users and designers to the possibilities of voice and leading the way for VUIs to soon become a natural and intuitive part of the way that humans interact with technology.

Mobile UX Sense Case Study: iPhone's Siri

Siri is a VUI personal assistant application released for the Apple iPhone (see Figures 8.70–8.73). Part VUI, part artificial intelligence, Siri is an integrated part of the iPhone's operating system introduced to consumers through iPhone 4S, launched in October 2011. The application uses natural language processing to answer questions, make recommendations, and perform actions by delegating requests to an expanding set of Web services. The application provides conversational interaction with many applications, including reminders, weather, stocks, messaging, email, calendar, contacts, notes, music, clocks, and a Web browser.

One of the greatest aspects of Siri is that it reveals how well suited voice commands can be for certain essential tasks, such as scheduling an appointment or texting a friend. After using this feature for a while, it can feel almost like an unnecessary hassle using anything but voice activation.

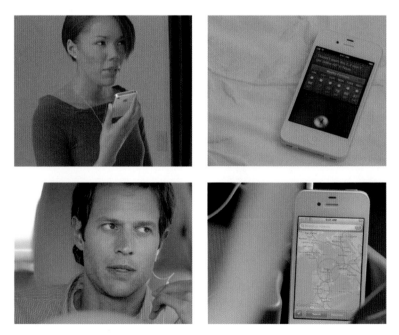

FIGURES 8.70–8.73
Images of Siri in use from an Apple commercial.

Some VUI Fundamentals

Here are some things to keep in mind when designing VUIs:

- VUIs are single-mode interfaces. In a practical sense, the only input method is sound, which can sometimes be the output medium (there are exceptions to this, however). It's more difficult for single-mode interfaces to communicate effectively as compared to multimode interfaces. Subsequently, not all mobile experiences are well suited for speech UIs. Apply VUIs wisely.

- All UIs should be somewhat task-focused, but the inherent limitations of VUIs demand a simple workflow with minimal branching. Compact, task-focused application VUIs keep users engaged and prevent users from feeling like they are trapped in a phone tree.

- VUIs are used in environments that compete for users' attention and cognitive processing. Applications used while driving, walking, and even working should be simple and designed to require as little of the user's memory as possible.

- There are currently no standard VUI elements that correlate to GUI elements such as Home, Back, error dialogs, and online help. This will require designers to build in correlating structures within VUI applications.

Additionally, unlike sci-fi equivalents, Siri isn't creepy. In fact, she's packed with personality. Many users enjoy talking to Siri, often to laugh. The feature is capable of delivering a proper reply while simultaneously keeping the responses light and even funny. There's even a blog (www.ShitSiriSays.com) dedicated to documenting some of Siri's most humorous responses (see Figures 8.74–8.76).

FIGURES 8.74–8.76

The Web site (www.ShitSiriSays.com) is dedicated to documenting some of Siri's most humorous responses to random user questions.

Swing for the Fences When Thinking about the Senses

This chapter has been all about our forgotten senses and how to use them to avoid the visually greedy mobile UIs that are so prevalent today. Admittedly, thinking about interfaces that engage our sense of touch, movement, sound, and voice may at times feel wonky, weird…preposterous even. It's largely unchartered territory without the guideposts and maps of the typical, visually driven approach to interface design.

However, swinging for the fences when thinking about senses seems like the only way we can start to break the dominance of the greedy, visually driven interfaces and deliver mobile experiences and interactions that dissolve into natural behavior.

Take the mobile UX sense case study, Ocarina. Modeled after its namesake (Ocarina is an ancient flute-like wind instrument), the Ocarina mobile application developed by Smule allows users to turn their mobile device into a musical instrument. Users simply blow into the phone's microphone and press the "holes" in the touchscreen UI to make music in touch mode. Tilting the phone activates sensors that allow the user to change vibrato rate and depth (see Figures 8.77 and 8.78).

FIGURES 8.77 AND 8.78
Ocarina turns a mobile device into a musical instrument.

Summary

While humans have a variety of senses (touch, taste, sight, and smell), we rely heavily on our sense of sight to navigate technology experiences. The result = greedy mobile interfaces. Touch interfaces enable more intuitive and direct manipulation of information.

There are three important design considerations to take into account when creating a mobile touch UI:

- Optimize for generous touch targets

- Map the screen for touch

- Lead with the content, not the interface

Gestural interfaces are UIs that trigger interactions with a digital system through human movement and are unmediated by a mouse and keyboard.

If you're keen on integrating gestures into your mobile experience, three strategies you can apply are:

- Introduce new gestures with the help of familiar ones.

- Provide feedback with an additional sense.

- Be creative and patient!

Voice UIs are likely the least greedy interface type of all because they are largely invisible. Speech input is generally well suited to circumstances in which the user's eyes and hands are busy and data input (voice) and output (sound) are constrained.

Remember to swing for the fences when thinking about senses. It's the best way break the dominance of the greedy, visually driven interfaces.

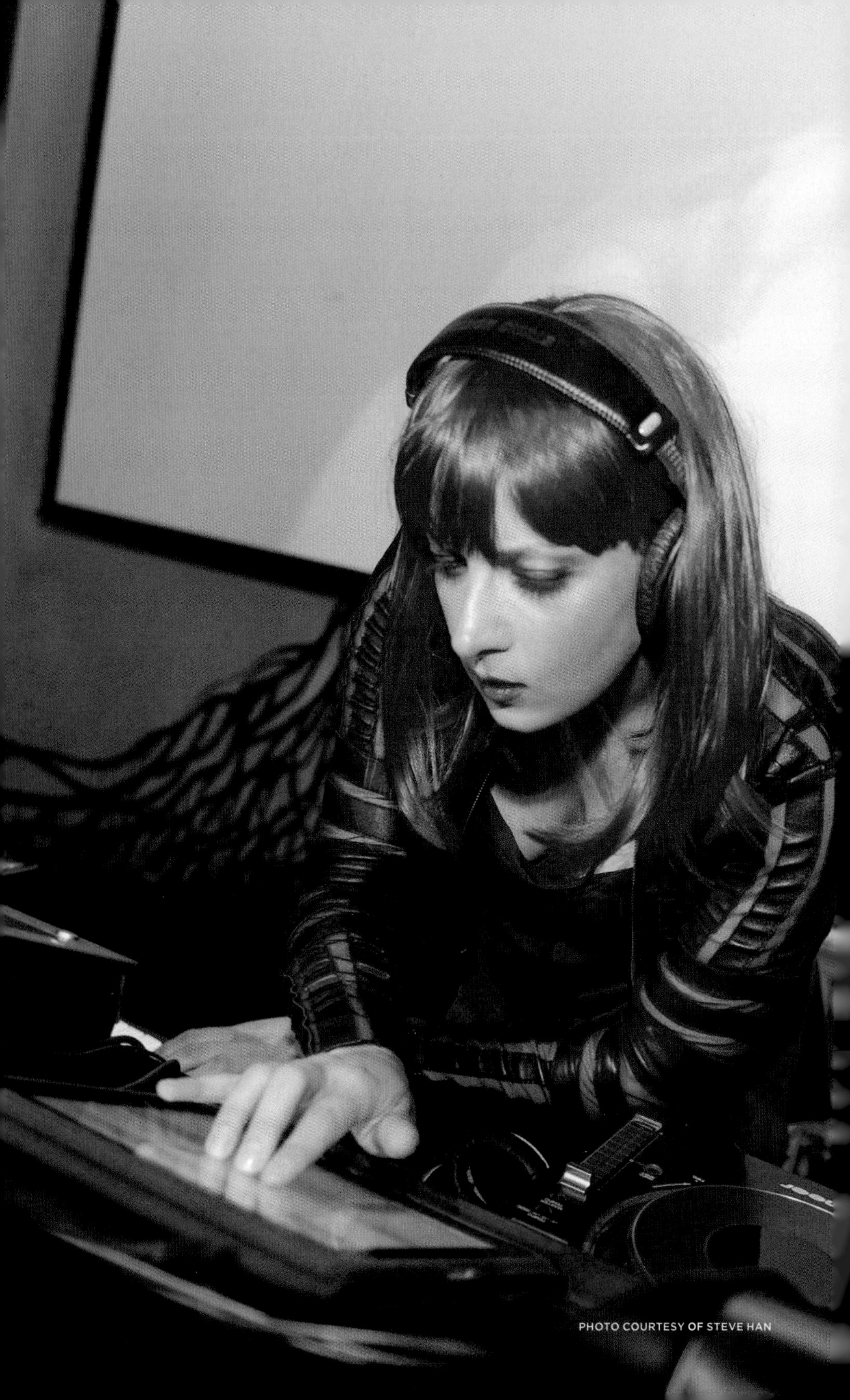

PHOTO COURTESY OF STEVE HAN

CHAPTER 9

New Mobile Forms
Pioneering the Mobile Frontier

The Shifting Boundary Between Computers and
  the Human Body   237
The Shifting Boundary Between Computers and
  the Environment   239
Mobiles and Emerging Markets   242
Pioneering the Mobile Frontier   247

In 1991, PARC scientist and grandfather of ubiquitous computing, Mark Weiser published a seminal article in *Scientific American* entitled, "The Computer for the 21st Century." In the article, Weiser predicted a future where computing would occur on three scales: the inch-scale ParcTab, the foot-scale ParcPad, and the yard-scale Liveboard. Today, some 20 years later, that vision has become a reality with the mobile phone as the handheld inch-scale computing device, the foot-scale ParcPad implemented as the iPad, and the yard-scale wall-mounted Liveboard performed by the television. In short, the future predicted by Mark Weiser 20 years ago has arrived today.

Rapid advancements in the mobile industry have ushered in an age where ubiquitous computing is no longer a heady, academic topic only discussed at obscure conferences by techies and research scientists. Mobile devices have, in many ways, become the "gateway drug" for ubiquitous computing. They are allowing people to experience firsthand what it means to have information follow you wherever you go. Leaving everyone to wonder…if the future is here, what's next? What disruptions and transformations lie in store?

People will continue to shed their desktop computing mentality, trading it in for one that is more distributed and empathetic with the demands of the mobile context. However, mobility will likely look very different in the future than it does today. Mobile will take on new forms, similar to those pictured in Figure 9.1.

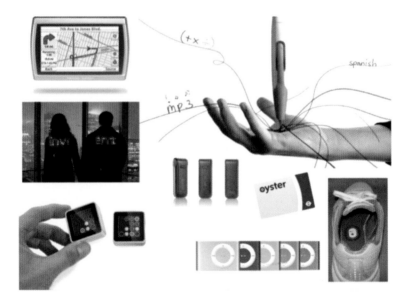

FIGURE 9.1
Nike Plus, FitBit, Apple iPod Shuffle, Oyster Transit Car, Siftables, Leapfrog Fly Pen, and Garmin Navigation System are all examples of emergent mobile forms.

In the near future, many designers and UX professionals will focus on pioneering the parts of the mobile frontier that have already been discovered. And that is a good place to be. But there's a vast space just beyond what's been discovered that some brave souls have already begun to explore. Just as Marc Weiser had a vision for computing before his time, many experts in the mobile and ubiquitous computing fields of today are hypothesizing how the "mobile-led" future will take shape. There are three mobile trends I believe will have a profound impact on the future. These themes will not only redefine mobility, but they'll also irrevocably alter the relationship we have with computing.

Those three trends are:

- Shifting the boundary between computers and the human body

- Shifting the boundary between computers and the environment

- Mobile experiences for emerging markets

The Shifting Boundary Between Computers and the Human Body

Computers used to be huge, room-sized objects that could only be operated by highly trained people. The advent of personal computers brought a smaller, more compact form factor to computers, enabling people to take them into their offices and homes. The portable form factor of today's smartphones has enabled us to bring the functionality of a computer into the palm of our hand, turning computers into portable objects that we carry in a pocket or a purse. Even though it's packed with tons of functionality and considered to be a tool for efficiency and communication, smartphones are so personal that many people see them as a fashion statement. It's an accessory—an expression of their personality, as shown in Figure 9.2. However, while we clearly adore these small devices, they are decidedly separate objects from us. Today, there is a clear boundary that exists between the object (a mobile device) and our body.

Trends are indicating that this boundary is shifting, though. Tiny mobile devices with focused functionality, like the iPod Shuffle

FIGURE 9.2
Mobile devices are being used for personal expression. A bejeweled iPhone is an example of mobile technology being used as a fashion accessory.

FIGURE 9.3
Electronic sensing jewelry,
designed by Philips design, is
made from stretchable electronic
substrates and sensors. By
changing color and shape
according to your mood, it
explores how mobile technology
worn close to the body can be
playful, sensual, mood-affected,
and bioactivity-stimulated.

FIGURE 9.4
The Fitbit Tracker is a wearable
device that measures data such
as the number of steps walked,
quality of sleep, and other
personal metrics.

or the FitBit, are not only lighter and more portable than a typical smartphone, but they're also bringing technology closer to the body. Instead of separate objects that are carried in a purse or a pocket, these examples represent mobile technology that sits on or near the body like a piece of jewelry. Humans have a decidedly different, more intimate relationship to objects that are worn on the body than objects they carry. There's an emotional component to these "jewelry-like" objects that is inherently more personal, more expressive, more sensual, and simply closer to the stuff that makes us human. Sure, jewelry is largely used to make a fashion statement. But it often serves as talismans and mementos of the people and things we cherish most. This trend of "mobile devices we wear on the body" opens up opportunities to create more sentimental, even spiritual experiences, as well as playful, sensual, mood, and bioactivity-driven experiences (see Figure 9.3).

Widespread (and legislated) use of headsets is also suggesting another mobile body boundary trend—mobile devices as an extension of the body. What if, instead of a singular mobile device packed with features and functionality, people could break up the phone's functionality into a system of smaller devices worn on the body. Trends in hardware and software could open up the possibility for low-cost, custom-built systems for individuals.

Philip van Allen of the Media Design Program at the Art Center College of Design has researched and written extensively about a future where users will have a system of devices tailored for their individual needs. In the same way that one can have a bespoke suit tailored to a perfect fit and style, Philip envisions a future where it will be possible to have a bespoke object with the hardware, software, and interaction design tailored to the perfect fit and style for you and your intended use (see Figure 9.4). He argues that rapid advances in 3D printing, system-on-a-board components, open-source software and hardware, open-source 3D parts libraries, and the DIY culture will turn designers into digital tailors.

Whether it's jewelry-like devices worn on the body that collect and reflect information, or highly customized bespoke systems tailored for individuals, trends indicate that the boundary between devices and the body is clearly shifting (see Figure 9.5).

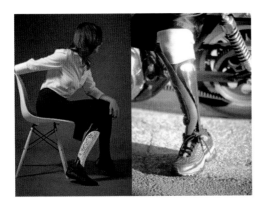

FIGURE 9.5
Bespoke prosthetics provide tailored designs to meet each customer's individual needs.
www.bespokeinnovations.com.

The Shifting Boundary Between Computers and the Environment

Today, if a user wants to access digital information about a book, a vacation spot, or simply information about a topic, the de facto "place" to search for and access that information is the Web. While we think of the Internet as a "place," the World Wide Web is nothing more than an abstract information space that stores our digital content. The Web is basically a giant bucket of disembodied information, as shown in Figure 9.6. Today, digital information has no physical relationship to the objects, places, and people it is attached to—it's only connected by a keyword or a URL. However, new mobile technologies are causing this assumption to shift. Widespread experimentation and development of new mobile technologies such as radio-frequency identification (RFID), near field communication (NFC), and augmented reality are giving us glimpses of a future where digital information is embedded in the world.

RFID tags are making it possible to attach information to objects, making way for a

FIGURE 9.6
The Web is a giant, abstract information space that stores our digital information, disembodied from what it represents.

future where information can be embedded in objects and the environment (see Figures 9.7 and 9.8). Similar to a bar code, RFID tags allow information about an object to reside in a tag that can be affixed to an object. Instead of firing up a browser, the objects themselves can trigger interactions. Interactive objects allow for more tangible interactions; people can interact directly with digital information through objects and the environment.

Similar to RFID, NFC (near field communication) allows for simplified transactions, data exchange, and wireless connections between two devices in close proximity to each other, usually by no more than a few centimeters. Shoppers who have their credit card information stored in their NFC smartphones can pay for purchases by waving their smartphones near or tapping them on the reader, rather than bothering with the actual credit card.

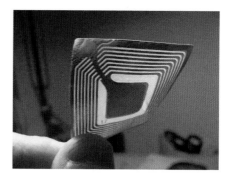

FIGURE 9.7
Radio-frequency identification (RFID) is a technology that uses radio waves to transfer data from an electronic tag, called an *RFID tag* or *label*, attached to an object, through a reader for the purpose of identifying and tracking the object. Some RFID tags can be read from several meters away and beyond the line of sight of the reader.

FIGURE 9.8
Electronic vehicle registration, payment by mobile phones, transportation payment, keyless entry, and e-tolling are just a few of the experiences being enabled by RFID technology. Because of decreased cost of RFID equipment and tags, the technology is finding its way into increasingly more mobile experiences.

Augmented reality (AR) has come of age thanks to mobile technology (see Figure 9.9). Once reserved only for video game addicts and scientists who would bravely don the giant geeky glasses and funky gloves hooked up to computers, AR is now something anyone with a smartphone can experience. Augmented reality browsers such as Layar and applications like Wikitude turn the camera on almost any smartphone into an information lens for the world (see Figure 9.10). Instead of accessing information about a place through a Web browser, these augmented reality applications allow users to actually "see" information in the environment.

FIGURE 9.9
Augmented reality isn't just for geeks anymore. AR applications that run on almost any smartphone let you experience all the benefits of augmented reality experiences without having to endure the humiliation of wearing the dorky glasses.

FIGURE 9.10
Layar is an augmented reality browser that enables users to actually "see" information attached to objects in the world. Making use of a smartphone's built-in camera, compass, GPS, and accelerometer, Layar allows information to appear as if it is actually connected to the physical environment.

The impact of all these technologies is that they're blurring the line between computers and objects and computers and the built environment. In his book, *Shaping Things*, science fiction author and futurist Bruce Sterling coined the term *spime* to describe an object that could be tracked through space and time throughout the lifetime of the object. Technologies such as RFID and NFC, as well as augmented reality, are enabling spimes to take shape in the form of information shadows (information that's associated with an object, such as its name, number, and position in space and time). These information shadows will profoundly change how we interact with and design objects. They'll allow designers to make objects simpler, to reduce the size of interfaces, and to reduce the display requirements of an object. The blurring of boundaries between computers and the environment has the potential to fundamentally change our relationship and interactions with the built environment. It will open up new opportunities for urban spaces and architecture, and will affect the organization of cities themselves.

Mobiles and Emerging Markets

Ever since I began my career in mobile, I've been deeply interested in the topic of mobility in emerging markets—the study of how people in areas of the world such as Africa, India, South America, and China are using mobile technology—and how the use of mobile devices in these markets differs from usage in places like the United States, Europe, and more economically developed areas of Asia (see Figure 9.11)

FIGURE 9.11
Fishermen along the banks of Lake Victoria in rural Uganda using mobile technology.

While the topic of emerging markets is usually married in some measure with philanthropy and a desire to "make the world a better place" (and while I hold a great deal of respect for people working in the field of development), my personal passion for the mobile technology in emerging markets is driven by an interest in the following two topics: leapfrogging the PC and cultural practices and technology.

Leapfrogging the PC

In Western cultures and many developed parts of the East, the primary piece of technology that most users interact with is a PC. Subsequently, it's become the universal reference point for most experiences with technology. This notion of the PC as a reference point doesn't exist for most people in emerging markets. For them, the universal reference point is often a mobile device. What fascinates me about emerging markets is that they are largely unburdened by PC baggage. They are, in some sense, mobile purists. What happens when an entire set of the world's population can essentially leapfrog 30 years of computing legacy?

Cultural Practices and Technology

Secondly, I'm interested in emerging markets because of their cultural specificity. I long held the belief that technology had a simple and universal role in our lives: to improve the human condition. Regardless of race, education level, or socio-economic status, people inherently used technology to fulfill needs and solve problems. While many human needs and problems are universal, the ways that people solve those problems often varies wildly based on culture. As technology-like mobile devices spread throughout the world, it is becoming increasingly apparent that technology reflects our cultural practices. It's this aspect of culture and the ways it influences the shape and form of the design of technology experiences that fuels my curiosity for emerging markets.

While there are an ample number of products and services from emerging markets that epitomize leapfrogging the PC and illustrate the concept of technology as a cultural practice, there are three examples that I feel best represent these ideas most succinctly. They are the mobile money service, M-PESA, the crisis crowd sourcing platform, Ushahidi, and Project Masiluleke, a mobile health program focused on AIDS awareness and prevention.

M-PESA

A key problem throughout the African continent is the problem of moving money. Many people don't have bank accounts, so the process of sending money over long distances to family or friends is a truly arduous task. In addition, many people live in rural areas that have limited access to the types of banking services with which readers of this book are likely familiar. It is these conditions that set the stage for a wildly successful product known as *M-PESA*.

M-PESA (M for mobile, pesa is Swahili for money) is the product name of a mobile phone-based money transfer that was entirely developed by Kenyans to solve the problem of moving money (see Figure 9.12). Initially, M-PESA was conceived as a service that would allow microfinance borrowers to conveniently receive and repay loans using the network of airtime resellers. But when the service was tested in a field trial, customers adapted the service for a variety of alternative uses, namely sending remittances home across the country and making payments.

FIGURE 9.12
M-PESA enables users to complete basic banking transactions through a mobile device.

M-PESA emerged as a branchless banking service, meaning that it was designed to enable users to complete basic banking transactions without the need to visit a bank branch.

The service enables its users to:

- Deposit and withdraw money.
- Transfer money to other users and non-users.
- Pay bills.
- Purchase airtime.

The continuing success of M-PESA in Kenya has been due to the fact that the service is a highly affordable payment service with only limited involvement of a bank. Since its launch in March 2007, M-PESA's popularity has grown. The number of users grew from 6.1 million in 2009 to 9.4 million in 2010 and to 13.8 million users as of March 2011.

Ushahidi

Ushahidi.com (Swahili for "testimony" or "witness") was a Web site created in the aftermath of Kenya's disputed 2007 presidential election. The Web site collected eyewitness reports of violence sent in largely by text-message through mobile devices and placed them on a Google map. The Kenyan site was developed and run by several bloggers and software developers, all current or former residents of Kenya. The site was developed cheaply and put online within a few days. International media, government sources, NGOs, and Kenyan journalists and bloggers were used to verify eyewitness testimony.

The success and impact of the first Ushahidi Web site inspired several of the initial creators to form Ushahidi, Inc.—a nonprofit software company that develops free and open-source software for information collection, visualization, and interactive mapping (see Figures 9.13 and 9.14). With roots in citizen journalism during times of crisis, the software platform has been developed with a robust set of tools through which users can easily crowd-source information using multiple channels, including SMS, email, Twitter, and the Web—providing mobile users with the opportunity to share their stories of place as they are occurring in space and time.

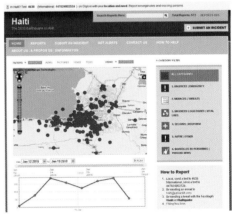

FIGURES 9.13 AND 9.14
Ushahidi is a nonprofit software company that develops free and open-source software for information collection, visualization, and interactive mapping. Users can easily crowd-source crisis information using multiple channels, including SMS.

The software has since been used to map violence in eastern Congo, to track pharmacy stock-outs in several East African countries, and to support humanitarian endeavors after the 2010 earthquakes in Haiti and Chile. It was also used by Al Jazeera to collect eyewitness reports during the 2008–2009 Gaza War.

Project M (short for *Project Masiluleke*, which means "lend a helping hand" in Zulu) is using mobile technology to tackle the worst HIV epidemic in the world in KwaZulu Natal, South Africa, where infection rates are more than 40 percent (see Figure 9.15).

FIGURE 9.15
Project Masiluleke is using mobile technology to tackle the worst HIV epidemic in the world.

South Africa has more HIV positive citizens than any country in the world. In some provinces, more than 40% of the population is infected. Yet only 2% of South Africans have ever been tested for HIV.

Of those who are HIV positive, a mere 10% are receiving anti-retroviral therapy, leaving 90% untreated, infectious, and likely to die. HIV/AIDS carries a huge social stigma in South Africa, preventing many people from getting tested or pursuing treatment, and there is widespread misinformation about how the disease is contracted. Further complicating matters, the nation's overburdened healthcare system is incapable of providing care to the millions in need—many of whom enter the system with end-stage HIV or full-blown AIDS.

> **NOTE** **"PLEASE CALL ME" × 1 MILLION × 365**
>
> The first stage of the project was built around the use of specialized text messages, delivering approximately 1,000,000 HIV/AIDS and TB messages each day to the general public. These messages were broadcast in the unused space of "Please Call Me" (PCM) text messages—a special, free form of SMS text widely used in South Africa and across the continent. The messages connected mobile users to existing HIV and TB call centers where trained operators provided callers with accurate health care information, counseling, and referrals to local testing clinics.
>
> Since the project's launch, over 685 million PCM messages have been sent throughout South Africa, driving over 1.5 million calls to the National AIDS Helpline.

TXTALERT: KEEPING PATIENTS CONNECTED
TO CARE

Only 10% of South Africans with AIDS are currently receiving
anti-retroviral (ARV) therapy, and of those who begin treatment, more than 40% do not remain on the lifesaving drugs
past two years. Project Masiluleke addresses this critical problem through the Praekelt Foundation's TxtAlert technology,
which uses text messaging to remind patients of scheduled
clinic visits, helping to ensure they adhere to ARV regimens.

HIV SELF-TESTING WITH MOBILE PHONE SUPPORT

Ultimately, with more HIV+ citizens than any other country in
the world and infection rates topping 40% in some provinces,
South Africa demands a radical solution to truly reverse its
HIV/AIDS and TB crises. The project partners are developing a
breakthrough distributed diagnostics model: low cost HIV self-
testing with counseling support via mobile phone. Analogous
to a pregnancy test, these distributed diagnostics will provide
a free, private, and reliable way for anyone to take the critical
first step of knowing his or her status, with high-quality information provided via mobile devices.

While I believe these three trends will shape the future of mobility, there are
likely many more. Even though the exact form the future of mobile will take
remains foggy, it's unmistakably clear that the idea of what a mobile device
is and how it interacts with other devices has already started to change. As
new mobile forms replace and redefine mobility, it's likely we'll reflect on
the mobile devices we use today with the same feelings of nostalgia that we
currently feel toward floppy disks and the original brick-like mobile phones.

Pioneering the Mobile Frontier

As I mentioned at the beginning of this book, I've long thought of the
mobile design space as a frontier where people can explore and invent new
and more human ways for people to interact with information. A frontier
represents more than a piece of land—it's a word that symbolizes optimism,
unlimited opportunity, and the shedding of current restraints. Frontiers
inspire in us the sense that anything is possible.

As a designer or UX professional interested in mobile, you've got a vast
landscape at your feet, which is full of opportunities. And make no
mistake—you're very much a pioneer in an emerging form of personal
computing that we're just beginning to understand. Much like the personal

computer and the Internet, mobile technology is poised to fundamentally change how humans do things in profound ways that we can't even imagine—and you are poised to be a part of shaping that future.

The goal of this book was to provide you with existing knowledge about mobile user experience and insights, tips, and tools that can be of service as you explore the frontier that lies ahead. There's a lot about mobile that we still don't understand, that's still unknown, and waiting to be discovered by people like you. And while journeys into the unknown can be scary and unpredictable, I wake up most days excited to be part of this industry and part of inventing the future. I hope this book has given you both the knowledge and information necessary to begin designing mobile experiences with ease and the inspiration to be part of this new and evolving form of design. I hope this book has convinced and inspired you to be a true pioneer of the mobile frontier.

Index

A

accelerometers, 137
acting out scenarios, 166
activity convergence, 73, 74, 75
Alexander, Christopher, A Pattern
    Language: Towns, Buildings,
    Construction, 108
"always-on" communication
    technologies, 50
Amazon Kindle, 15, 93
Amplitude iPad application, 129
anchors
    for hub-and-spoke pattern, 125–126
    for PC design patterns, 122–123
Android operating system, 104
    3.0 Honeycomb user interface, 129
Angry Birds, 121
animated cartoons, 182
animation principles
    anticipation, 186–187
    arcs, 193
    exaggeration, 196–197
    follow-through and overlapping
        action, 190–191
    secondary action, 194
    slow in and out, 191–192
    solid drawing and appeal, 198
    squash and stretch, 184–185
    staging, 187–188
    straight ahead and pose to pose,
        188–189
    timing, 195–196
anticipation in animation, 186–187
aperture animation, on camera
    application, 186
appeal for animation, 198
Apple
    Airplay technology, 95
    email application, 75
    Keynote, 159
    Macintosh, 17
applications
    development for mobile devices, 177
    as set point, 111–121

application types, 116–121
    consumption-focused, 118
    core, 117
    feed-focused, 117–118
    games, 121
    search/find, 119
    search/find/transact, 119–120
    tool, 120
    widgets, 117
arcs in animation, 193
Art Center College of Design, 238
art, evolution of, 19
augmented reality, 241
auras, NUI objects with, 27

B

Bento Box pattern, 127
Bespoke prosthetics, 239
Bleecker, Julian, 176–179
Bloom iPhone app, 25, 140
bodystorming, 166–167
book metaphor, 213
brainstorming in the wild, 56–57
Bravo cable television, 75
Brichter, Loren, 218
brochureware Web sites, 43
browser prototyping, 160
Bump, 60
bump gesture, 61, 225
buttons
    decline in physical, on
        smartphones, 157
    in interface, 129

C

capacitive touchscreen, 208
career, in mobile design industry, 34
cartoons, animated, 182
CCS Insight, 16
cell phones. *See also* smartphones
    for escape, 12
    estimated growth, 98
    impact of change, 10
    sales estimates, 16

choices, 144
Clark, Josh, 218
cloud
  key design considerations, 114
  as set point, 111, 113–115
clue to future event, 186
cognitive load reduction, 51–53
coherence, in screen ecosystem
    relationship patterns, 91–92
"comfortable computing," tablets for,
    82–83
command line interfaces (CLI), 20
complementary principles, animation
    for, 200
complementary screen strategy, 96
computers
  boundary shift between environment
      and, 239–242
  boundary shift between human body
      and, 237–239
  predictions, 236
computing paradigms, 13, 28–30
  computers as media, 29–30
  computers as person, 28
  computers as tool, 29
  future, 30–32
concept video, 170–172
  pros and cons, 171
connectivity, non-network, in cloud
    design, 114
constraints
  destop paradigm and, 14
  of mobile experience, 45–48
consumption-focused applications, 118
content
  design, vs. Web page design, 105
  as interface, 37, 128–133
  interface elements vs., 212–215
content-out strategy, 106
context
  applying PC assumptions to mobile
      experience, 59
  empathy development for, 42–50
  impact on daily experience, 41

impact on mobile device use, 84
  in mobile UX design, 40
contextual environments principle, for
    NUIs, 26
contextualism, 22
continuous partial attention, 50
convergence, 102
  basics, 70–71
  levels of, 73–76
core applications, 117
Cover Flow, 133
Crowley, Dennis, 64
CSS media queries, 100
cultural practices, technology and, 243

D

daily lives, computer infiltration, 14
data
  focus on, 31
  moving between mobile devices, 60
Davidoff, Scott, 168
decision-making, 147
  prototyping as aid, 148
Define phase, in double-diamond
    model, 146
Deliver phase, in double-diamond
    model, 146–147
design. See mobile UX design
design factor, structure of, 108–110
design patterns, 108. See also mobile
    design patterns
design process, 145–147. See
    also prototyping
desktop metaphor, 29
desktop paradigm, 14, 17
  mobility vs., 7
Develop phase, in double-diamond
    model, 146
device ecosystem, 76–81
device shifting, 95
direct manipulation principle, for NUIs,
    25, 132
Discover phase, in double-diamond
    model, 146

discovery, 7

distractibility, and cognitive load, 52

DocsToGo, 115

document conversion to Web pages, 17

Dorsey, Jack, 47

double-diamond model for design process, 145–147

drag/slide gesture, 222

Dropbox, 113, 114

E

ecosystems, 76

designing for, 80–81

identifying relationships through participatory design, 85–90

significance of, 78–79

situated cognition theory and, 84

UX design for, 72–73

editing, when sketching, 153–155

electronic sensing jewelry, 238

email

mobile application development, 44

text messaging vs., 44

voice UI and, 227

emerging markets, mobile devices and, 242–247

empathy, development for context, 42–50

Engstrom, Yuri, 32

environment

boundary shift between computers and, 239–242

constraints for mobile experience, 46, 47

in digital ecosystem, 78

dynamic and unpredictable for mobile, 41

identifying for users, 87

escape, mobile phones for, 12

Evernote, 92

evolution of human expression, 19

exaggeration in animation, 196–197

experiences that scale, 90–97

experiential prototyping, 151–152, 162–172

exploration, interaction model facilitating, 140

eyewitness testimony, 245

F

Facebook app, 118, 126

FaceTime, 135

failure, prototyping and, 173

feedback

for touch, 220

prototype for gathering, 149

feed-focused applications, 117–118

fidelity, for prototyping, 173

Filtered View pattern, 127–128

fine-tuning, prototype for, 150–151

FitBit, 238

flick gesture, 222

Flipboard app, 126, 213

flow, in paper prototypes, 157

follow-through in animation, 190–191

form factors, representations of, 88

form, meaning embedded in, 14

foursquare, 64, 65, 126, 137

fragmentation, 105

frames

for animation acceleration and slow down, 191

in-between, 189

keyframes, 164, 189

frontier, 2

mobile industry as, 3, 247–248

Fruit Ninja, 189

G

games, 121

GeoLoqi, 61

geotagged reminders, 61

gestures, 26, 215–225

commonly used, 222–225

creativity and patience, 221–225

introducing new, 218–219

in NUIs, 131–133

glance-ability, designing for, 54

Google Docs, 113, 115

Google Maps, 140
Google search, 59
Gowalla, 137
GPS (global positioning system), 137
  smartphone capability, 16
graphical user interfaces (GUIs), 21–22,
    29, 122, 131
  characteristics, 20
  in desktop paradigm, 14
  natural user interfaces vs., 24
  reaching limits, 17–18

H

haptics, 215
Hawkins, Jeff, 150
HBO Go, 118
headsets, 238
HIV epidemic, mobile technology to
    battle, 246
HTML, 98, 130
  for prototype, 158
hub-and-spoke pattern, 125–126
human constraints, for mobile
    experience, 46, 47
Human-Machine Reconfiguration: Plans
    and Situated Actions (Suchman), 82

I

iconography for interface, 129
ideas, prototype for
    communicating, 148–149
ideation in the wild, 56
Illusion of Life: Disney Animation
    (Johnston and Thomas), 183
in-between frames, 189
index cards, for prototype design, 155
inertia, creating illusion of, 191
information
  density reduction, 54
  focus on, 31
  interconnected, 130–131
  as objects, 27
  sharing, 58, 67
information collection, mapping for, 245

information shadows, 242
infrastructure, computers as, 31–32
input mechanisms, in mobile design
    patterns, 134–138
input/output, with OUIs, 23
in-screen prototyping, 158
  basics, 161–162
  pros and cons, 160
intent, interaction model sensing, 140
interacting with information
  new opportunities, 3, 59, 61
  phones for, 16
interaction design
  interface design vs., 37
interaction model
  accruing value over time, 139
  decline in task-based, 138
  facilitating exploration, 140
  sensing intent, 140
interactive on-device prototyping,
    158–162
interconnected information, 130–131
interface. See also graphical user
    interfaces (GUIs); natural user
    interfaces (NUIs); user interfaces
  content as, 128–133
Internet
  access to, 105
  content, 130
  information space and, 239
interoperability, 90
interruption, 50
  cognitive load and, 52
  ease of returning after, 55
interviews
  Julian Bleecker, 176–179
  Mike Kruzeniski, 34–37
  Alex Rainert, 64–67
  Stephanie and Bryan Rieger, 104–106
IntoNow, 60, 136
intuition, NUIs and, 124
iPad
  iBooks, 15
  research on use, 17
  Scrabble on, 96

iPhone, 5–6, 23–24, 35, 106
  Human Interface Guidelines, 207
  retina display, 207
  Scrabble on, 96
  Siri for, 230–231
  touch interfaces, 205
iPhone voice memo, 130
iPod Shuffle, 237
Isaacs, Travis, 159
iTunes/iPad relationship, 85

J

jewelry, electronic sensing, 238
Jobs, Steve, 5
Johnston, Ollie, 183
Jones, Matt, 26
Junkyard Jumbotron, 94

K

Kaufman, Joshua, 218
Kayak application, 127
Kaye, Jofish, 82
Kenya
  M-PESA, 244
  Ushahidi.com, 245–248
keyboards, 134
  for GUIs, 25, 27
keyframes, 189
  in storyboards, 164
Keynote Kungfu, 159
keynote prototyping, 160
Keynote, staging in, 188
Keynotopia, 159, 200
Khella, Amir, 159
Kin, 35
Kindle application, 15
  controls visibility, 214
Koi Pond iPhone app, 140
Kruzeniski, Mike, 34–37, 132

L

landscape screen orientation, 225
laptops, 18
LastFM, 113
Layar, 241
layout, content-based, 106
Liddle, David, 216
LinkedIn, 60
location-aware sensors, mobile
  devices as, 67
Lock-in, 90

M

MadPad, 137
manufacturer, diversity in user
  choices, 90
mapping
  for information collection, 245
  screen for touch, 209
maps, 61, 62
  of user device ecosystem, 80
Marcotte, Ethan, 100
marketplace
  fighting the tragedy of, 90
  for mobile applications, 116
Maulouf, David, 218
McLuhan, Marshall, 14, 42
meaning embedded in form, 14
mechanical feeling, straight path for, 193
media, computers as, 29
media convergence, 73, 74, 75
memory, working, 51
menus
  avoiding deep structures, 55
  in voice user interfaces, 227–230
Metro (typography-based design
  language), 36, 133
Metro UI system, 132
Microsoft
  Kinnect, 215
  PowerPoint, 159
  Surface Table, 22, 26, 27
  Windows Mobile 7, 35
  Windows Phone design studio, 34

"Windows Phone UI Design and
    Interaction Guide", 207
Word UI, 18
MIT Touch Lab study, 207
mobile browser prototype, 158
mobile context
  brainstorming in the wild, 56–57
  nouns and relationships for
      framework, 57–59
  opportunity cost in, 52
mobile design patterns, 110–111
  cloud and applications as set
      points, 111–121
  content as interface, 128–133
  progressive revelation of nature,
      121–128
  task-based interaction model
      decline, 138–140
  unique input mechanisms, 134–138
mobile devices. *See also* cell phones;
    smartphones
  app development for, 177
  constraints, 46, 47
  emerging markets and, 242–247
  evolving, 72
  increase, 16
  moving data between, 60
  networked, 176–179
  personal expression with, 237
  physical form factors, 34
  sensors in, 137–138
  synching to PC, 90
  trends, 104
mobile industry
  as frontier, 3
  Golden Age, 4–6
mobile money service, 243–248
mobile NUI paradigm, 23–27
mobile-optimized Web site, 98
mobile user experience
  applying PC context assumptions, 59
  artful animation, 183
  constraints, 45–48
  sense case study, 230–231
  set points and, 112–116

storyboarding basics, 164–175
tips for applying animation, 200
unfolding, 124
  design considerations, 125–128
  uniqueness, 42–48
mobile UX design
  cognitive load and opportunity cost
      reduction, 51–53
  context in, 40
  multitasking and task switching,
      49–50
  tips, 54–55
mobile Web app, 99
mobility
  convergence and, 72–76
  desktop paradigm vs., 7
mobility trends
  boundary shift between computers and
      environment, 239–242
  boundary shift between computers and
      human body, 237–239
modeling, 217
Moggridge, Bill, 28
money service, mobile, 243–248
Morgan Stanley, 98
Morph, 149
motion, methods for specifying,
    198–200
motivation of user, 51
Motorola DynaTAC, 16
mouse, 25, 27
movement, 183
moving data between mobile
    devices, 60
M-PESA, 243–248
Müller-Brockmann, Josef, 132
multidevice experiences, 82–84
  defining moments in, 86
multitasking, 49–50
muscle memory, 217
musical instrument, mobile device as, 232
mutual reconfiguration theory, 82

N

Nakisci, Tamer, 171

native app for mobile phone, 99–100

natural user interfaces (NUIs),
  20, 22, 212
  challenge for, 188
  gestures and "super real"
    qualities, 131–133
  graphical user interfaces vs., 24
  intuition and, 124
  mastering fundamentals, 24–27
  mobile paradigm, 23–27
  qualities, 131

navigation elements, placement on
  tablet, 210

near field communication (NFC),
  138, 240

need, solution vs., 44–45

need validation phase, in speed dating
  prototype, 168

Nested Doll pattern, 125

Netflix, 55, 93, 113, 115

New Guinea, organization of homes, 111

new technology, introduction, 42

New York Times, 206

New York University, Interactive
  Telecommunications Program, 64

NFC (near field communication),
  138, 240

Nielsen, Jakob, 35

Nintendo Wii, 215

Nokia, 106

Nokia 888 Communicator, 171

Nokia Research Center, 149

non-network connectivity, in cloud
  design, 114

nonverbal cues, in participatory
  design, 89

nouns and relationships for mobile
  context framework, 57–59

numeric input, 134

O

object-centered sociality, 32

objects, information as, 27

observation, in design factor
  structure, 108

Ocarina sense case study, 232

online media, 15

opportunities, for interacting with
  information, 3

opportunity cost reduction, 51–53

organic material, computers as, 30–31

organic user interfaces (OUIs),
  20, 22–23

overlapping action in animation,
  190–191

Owen, Charles, 108

P

Palm Pilot, 150

Pandora, 113, 114

paper prototyping, 149, 156–157

paradigms, 13–14
  computing, 28–30
  desktop, 7–8, 14, 17

paradigm shift, 14–18

partial attention
  continuous, 50

participatory design
  assumptions, 86
  identifying ecosystem relationships
    through, 85–90
  role play and, 86–90

pattern language, 108

Pattern Language: Towns, Buildings,
  Construction (Alexander), 108

patterns. See also mobile design patterns
  from paradigms, 13

"Patterns for Multi-Screen Strategies"
  presentation on Slideshare, 91

PC environment
  blindside, 60
  context assumptions applied to mobile
    experience, 59

design patterns' anchors, stacking and recognition, 122–123

early set point for, 112

leapfrogging, 243

peanut butter, 58–59

people, in digital ecosystem, 78

perfection, prototypes and, 173

performance aesthetics principle, for NUIs, 25

personal computer, 90

person, computers as, 28

photos, as input, 135

Photosynth, 37

physical form factors of mobile devices, 34

pinch gesture, 26, 223

place relationships, 60

Plants and Zombies, 189

platform-specific prototype, 160

Popular Mechanics Magazine, 214

portrait screen orientation, 225

pose-to-pose animation technique, 188–189

PowerPoint (Microsoft), 159

Praekelt Foundation, TxtAlert technology, 247

Precious Design, 91

presentation software, for prototyping, 159–162

press and tap gesture, 224

press gesture, 223

print design principles, 35

prism effect, for cloud, 114

processes, in digital ecosystem, 78

Project Masiluleke, 246, 246–247

props, in participatory design sessions, 88

prototyping, 147–151
  basics of in-screen, 161–162
  concept video, 170–172
  embracing failure, 173
  genres, 151–152
  high cost of failure, 168
  interactive on-device, 158–162
  motion in, 199
  platform-specific, 160
  presentation software for, 159–162
  pros and cons of tools, 160–162
  purposes, 148–151
  speed dating, 168
  storyboarding, 162–172
  as tool, 174
  truisms, 172–174
psychological functions
  intuition, 124
  recall, 20
  recognition, 21, 123

Q

QR (Quick Response) codes, 135

R

radio-frequency identification (RFID), 135, 240

radio stations, Web access, 114

Rainert, Alex, 64–67

rear-view mirror effect, 42–43

recall, psychological function of, 20

recognition
  in PC design patterns, 122–123
  psychological function of, 21, 123

relationships
  identifying in ecosystems through participatory design, 85–90
  for mobile context framework, 57–59
  with mobile devices, 65

religious paradigms, 13

re-orient gesture, 225

research
  exercise on user ecosystem, 81
  on tablet use, 82–83

resistive touchscreen, 208

responsive Web design, 100–102

restraint, in animation use, 200

RFID codes, 135, 239

Rieger, Bryan, 104–106

Rieger, Stephanie, 104–106

rigidity of object, squash and stretch to express, 184

role play, participatory design and, 86-90

rollover, touchscreen equivalent, 219

rotate gesture, 224

S

scaffolding principle, for NUIs, 25

scenarios, acting out, 166

Scientific American, 236

Scrabble, on iPad and iPhones, 96

screen ecosystem relationship patterns, 91

coherence, 91-92

complementary, 96

device shifting, 95

screen sharing, 94

simultaneity, 97

synchronization, 93

screens

layouts in paper prototyping, 157

orientation, 225

variation, 100

visualizing data on small, 155

scrolling, 25

transition, 192

seamless experience across devices, 90

seamlessness principle, of NUIs, 27

search/find applications, 119

search/find/transact applications, 119-120

secondary action in animation, 194

semantic relationships, 59

senses

creative possibilities, 232

touch, 205-215

sensors, 137-138

embedded, 30

sequencing, in paper prototyping, 157

set points

cloud and applications as, 111-121

applications, 116

cloud, 113-116

mobile experiences and, 112-116

shake gesture, 224

shapeshifting, 70

Shaping Things (Sterling), 10, 242

sharing information, 58, 67

sharing screens, 94

Shazam, 48, 60, 120, 136

shifting paradigms, 14

Shrinky Dinks, 122

Simon Collision Web site, 102

simultaneity, 97

Siri for iPhone, 230-231

situated cognition, 84

sketching

for prototyping, 153-155, 156

specifying motion, 199

skeuomorphic user interfaces, 129

design strategies, 130

slide gesture, 222

Slideshare, "Patterns for Multi-Screen Strategies" presentation, 91

slow in and out in animation, 191-192

smartphones, 205

decline in physical buttons, 157

touchscreens on, 6

SMS, 66

Smule, 232

social currency, computers as, 32

social graph, 66

social interaction principle

for NUIs, 26

sharing screens and, 94

social networking, GPS and, 137

social paradigms, 13

social relationships, 58

software, rising importance for mobile devices, 34

solid drawing in animation, 198

solution

need vs., 44-45

sound, 226-231

as input, 136

South Africa, HIV epidemic, 246

Southwest Airlines Web site, 131

spatial relationships principle, 27, 58

spatial–temporal relationships, 60

speech. *See also* voice

speech recognition, 136

speed dating prototyping, 168

spime, 242

spread gesture, 223

Square for iPhone, 120

squash-and-stretch animation principle, 184–185

stacking, for PC design patterns, 122–123

staging in animation, 187–188

stencils, for sketching, 153

Sterling, Bruce, Shaping Things, 10, 242

stimuli, in participatory design sessions, 89

Stone, Linda, 50

storyboarding, 162–172

basics for user experiences, 164–165

straight ahead animation technique, 188–189

Suchman, Lucy, Human-Machine Reconfiguration: Plans and Situated Actions, 82

super real principle, for NUIs, 26

synching

mobile devices to PC, 90

in screen ecosystem relationship patterns, 93

T

tablets

growth estimates, 24

research on use, 17, 82–83

touch on, 210–211

tactical prototyping, 151–152, 153–162

paper prototyping, 156–157

tap gesture, 219, 222

task-based interaction model, decline, 138–140

task focus, for VUIs, 231

task management in VUIs, 229

task switching, 49–50

technology platform, 98–99

convergence, 73, 74

cultural practices and, 243

decision on format, 99–100

templates, for sketching, 153

temporal relationships, 58

text input, 134

text messaging

email vs., 44

on HIV/AIDS, 246

Thomas, Frank, 183

three-dimensional shapes, 198

through-line, 76

time

as organizing principle, 55

requirements for prototype, 173

timing for animation, 195–196

tool applications, 120

tool, computers as, 29

Top Chef, 144

topping in to information, 124

touch, 205–215

feedback for, 220

mapping screen for, 209

optimizing for generous targets, 206–208

on tablets, 210–211

touchpoints, 77, 78

relationship of friends and Internet to, 85

touchscreens, 6, 18, 25, 212

affordance strategies, 213–214

paper prototyping and, 157

rollover equivalent, 219

types, 208

transitions, 183

trends for mobile devices, 104

trust alarm clocks, 178–179

Twitter, 47, 139

Twitter/Twitter community relationship, 85

typography, 214

Metro for, 133

U

ubiquitous computing, 236

unfolding, 124

design considerations for, 125–128

unknowns, prototypes for exploring, 150

user experience. *See also* mobile user experience

user interfaces. *See also* graphical user interfaces (GUIs); natural user interfaces (NUIs); voice user interfaces (VUIs)
  content as, 133
  evolution, 19–23
  skeuomorphic, 129
  subtle elements for touch, 213
  voice and sound, 226–231

users
  expectations for convergence, 73, 76
  in digital ecosystem, 78
  motivation, 51
  prototype for gathering feedback, 149
  research exercise on ecosystem, 81

Ushahidi.com, 245–248

utilities, information access as, 31

V

van Allen, Philip, 238

verbal cues, in participatory design, 89

Verplank, Bill, 28

video
  concept, 170–172
  as input, 135

viewport, size changes, 105

Vignelli, Massimo, 132

vignettes, 162

visually driven interfaces, 204

visual UI design, new approaches, 35

vocabulary management in VUIs, 229

voice, as input, 136

voice-driven interfaces, 136

voice user interfaces (VUIs), 226–231
  design basics, 231
  menus in, 227–230
  when to use, 226–227

W

Walt Disney, 183

Web pages
  design vs. content design, 105
  print content transfer to, 17, 42

Web sites
  brochureware, 43
  mobile-optimized, 98
  responsive design, 100–102

Weiser, Mark, 236

Wesch, Michael, 111

widgets, 117

Wikitude, 241

Windows 7, design principles from, 133

Windows Mobile, 35, 132

"Windows Phone UI Design and Interaction Guide" (Microsoft), 207

wireframes, for specifying motion, 199

Wireless Intelligence, 16

Wixon, Dennis, 19–20

work environments, context and, 56

working memory, 51

worlds, mobile devices as, 12

WYSIWYG (what you see is what you get), 21, 123, 204

Y

Yiibu, 104

Z

zoom gesture, 26

FIGURE CREDITS

Figure 1.4	Courtesy of Ed Yourdon
Figure 1.5	Courtesy of Marco Ophof
Figure 2.1	Courtesy of Kathy Slamen Photography
Figure 2.2	Courtesy of *Walt Disney Pictures*
Figure 2.3	Courtesy of Stephanie Klocke
Figure 2.6	Courtesy of Muireann Carey-Campbell
Figure 2.7	Courtesy of Newsweek Magazine
Figure 2.8	Courtesy of Motorola
Figure 2.15	Courtesy of Microsoft Research
Figure 2.16	Courtesy of SONY CSL
Figure 2.20	Courtesy of Microsoft Research
Figure 2.22	Courtesy of Matt Jones and BERG
Figure 2.23	Courtesy of Microsoft Research
Figure 2.25	Courtesy of Charlie Schuck
Figure 3.1	Courtesy of Will B via Flickr
Figure 3.2	Courtesy of Greg Braaten
Figure 3.4	Courtesy of Zac Peckler
Figure 3.5	Courtesy of John Blough
Figure 3.7	Courtesy of Helen Morgan
Figure 3.9	Courtesy of Marie Kåstru
Figure 4.1	Courtesy of DC Comics
Figure 4.2	Courtesy of Twentieth Century Fox Film Corporation
Figures 4.4–4.11	Courtesy of NFL Mobile
Figure 4.18	Courtesy of Gary Dawson
Figure 4.51	Courtesy of A Book Apart
Figure 5.1	Courtesy of Oxford University Press
Figure 5.2	Courtesy of Charles Owens
Figure 5.5	Courtesy of Michael Wesch
Figure 5.18	Courtesy of Daily Grommet
Figure 5.19	Courtesy of Andrea Lam
Figure 6.4	Courtesy of Nokia Research Center
Figures 6.21-26	Courtesy of Diego Pulido
Figure 6.32	Courtesy of IDEO
Figures 6.33-35	Courtesy of Christian Crumlish
Figure 6.36	Courtesy of Scott Davidoff
Figure 6.37	Courtesy of Scott Davidoff
Figures 6.40–41	Courtesy of Nokia and Tamer Nakisci
Figure 7.1	Courtesy of DC Comics
Figure 7.2	Courtesy of Hanna-Barbera /Warner Animations Inc
Figure 7.3	Courtesy of Hanna-Barbera /Warner Animations Inc
Figure 7.4	Courtesy of Disney Editions
Figure 7.17	Courtesy of Naz Hamid
Figure 7.24	Courtesy of snowdrop88 via Flickr
Figure 7.29	Courtesy of *Looney Tunes* and *Merrie Melodies* cartoons
Figure 7.30	Courtesy of Alan Cleaver
Figure 7.33	Courtesy of John Kricfalusi/ Nickelodeon
Figure 7.34	Courtesy of Sarah Dotson
Figure 7.39	Courtesy of Gred Nudelman
Figure 8.2	Courtesy of Zurest via Flickr
Figure 8.8	Courtesy of Virtual Worlds
Figure 8.11	Courtesy of Shawna Lemay
Figure 8.13	Courtesy of IDG UK B2B via Flickr
Figure 8.15	Courtesy of Steve Han
Figure 8.24	Courtesy of Masayo Ave
Figure 8.26	Courtesy of Jacqueline Connor
Figure 8.27	Courtesy of the Ellen DeGeneres Show
Figure 8.28	Courtesy of DeAnn Marston-Gronvall
Figure 8.29	Courtesy of Dave Malouf
Figures 8.34–8.66	Courtesy of Craig Villamor, Dan Willis, and Luke Wroblewski (http://static.lukew.com/TouchGestureGuide.pdf)
Figures 8.78–8.79	Courtesy of Smule
Figure 9.3	Courtesy of Phillips Design
Figure 9.4	Courtesy of FitBit
Figure 9.5	Courtesy of Bespoke Prosthetics
Figure 9.6	Courtesy of The Opte Project
Figure 9.7	Courtesy of Jakob Smith
Figure 9.8	Courtesy of Timo Arnall
Figure 9.9	Courtesy of the UCL Bartlett School of Graduate Studies
Figure 9.13	Courtesy of Ushahidi
Figure 9.15	Courtesy of PopTech

ACKNOWLEDGMENTS

While I am listed as the author, I couldn't have written this book without the support of many people.

First and foremost, I must thank Louis Rosenfeld for taking a chance on me. Thank you, Lou, for your support throughout the writing process and your flexibility around the design of this particular book. The user experience community is lucky to have you as an advocate.

Marta Justak—you are just an awesome human being. Whether kind, supportive feedback or come-to-Jesus tough love, you always knew just what to say to keep me moving forward. Thank you, Marta. This book wouldn't have happened without you. I'm thankful to have had you as an editor and now as a friend.

Next, I feel a great sense of gratitude to the entire faculty of professors, instructors, staff, and students at the Institute of Design in Chicago where I received my masters in Human-Centered Design. From the legacy of Moholy-Nagy and the Bauhaus to the early beginnings of design planning and strategy cultivated by Jay Doblin—my experience at ID taught me the power design can have in the world. There was no professor who inspired me more than Larry Keeley. Larry, it was truly an honor to be one of your students. Thank you for writing the beautiful foreword to this book.

I often think my career in design wouldn't have happened if it weren't for my very first design mentor, the late Gino Lee. Thanks for taking a chance on me all those years ago, Gino. You showed me the ropes of being a professional designer and started me on this path. Your wisdom and mentorship sticks with me to this day. The world is a little darker without you here.

In 2008, I met a man named Bob Ianuuci, and that meeting radically changed both my thinking about mobile user experience and the trajectory of my career. Thank you, Bob, for teaching me the importance of thinking big picture in this rapidly changing design space. I'd feel lucky to have even a measure of your vision and integrity. You are a priceless mentor and friend.

Thank you to Josh Clark, Jon Kolko, and Oliver Weidlich for being generous, honest, and constructive with your early feedback of this book. Your comments made a huge difference, and this book is much better because of them.

262

It was a joy and pleasure to interview the experts for this book. Thanks to Julian Bleeker, Alex Rainert, Mike Kruzeniski, as well as Stephanie and Bryan Rieger for your expertise and generosity. Both this book and the world are better with your perspectives in it.

Dr. Jillian Kleiner, thank you for your patience, wisdom, and care…and for helping me find my way out of the bog.

Thanks in spades go to my two dear friends, Mirjana Spasojevic and Sharon Priest. You've saved me from drowning in the undertow of life more times than I can count. Thank you, for being cheerleaders and shoulders to cry on during this process and throughout our friendship.

John Shen and Quinn Jacobson at the Nokia Research Lab in Palo Alto are two men I will be indebted to for many years to come. They gave me, quite possibly, the most precious gift anyone can give a writer: the gift of time. Thank you for providing a supportive environment from which to create this book. It continues to be a privilege to work for you both.

I have two friends and former colleagues to thank for the title of this book—Brian Cronin and Rachel Glaves. Your creation didn't go to waste.

While I concede it may seem odd to thank a pet in the acknowledgements of a book, I don't think I would have survived the 14 months it took me to complete this publication without the unconditional love and companionship of my dog buddy, Stanley. Thanks, little guy. I owe you some much needed hikes and beach frolicking.

I was fully warned that writing a book can feel like a never-ending slog. At times, it truly was. I also gladly assumed the risk of writing a book about a technology subject that's changing faster than any technology subject before it—almost ensuring that much of what I wrote would be out of date before the book was published. I have my father, David Hinman, to thank for showing me the virtues of hard work, stepping up to risk, and following my instincts. I am glad I inherited your tenacity and optimism, Dad.

Finally, I dedicate this book to my mother, Patricia Tiffany-Hinman. When you went to college, most women had two career options: nursing or teaching. Yet you raised me to believe I could do anything. I believed you and without that belief, both my career in mobile and this book would not exist. Thank you, mom, for your unwavering support and love—and most importantly for raising me to believe a woman can do anything she sets her mind to.

—Rachel Hinman, April 23, 2012, San Francisco, California

ABOUT THE AUTHOR

Rachel Hinman is a researcher, designer, and a recognized thought leader in the mobile user experience field. Her passions for cultural study, art, and design coupled with the belief that people can use technology to improve the human condition have been the driving forces in her career for nearly two decades.

Currently, Rachel is a Senior Research Scientist at the Nokia Research Center in Palo Alto, California. There she focuses on the research and design of emergent and experimental mobile interfaces and mobile experiences for emerging markets. Prior to joining Nokia, Rachel was an experience design director at Adaptive Path and a mobile researcher and strategist for Yahoo's mobile group. Rachel's innate sensitivity to people and culture have proven to be powerful skills in the field, enabling her to successfully lead research studies on mobile phone usage in the US, Europe, Asia, and Africa.

Rachel writes and speaks frequently on the topic of mobile research and design. She is the creative force behind the *90 Mobiles in 90 Days Project*, and her perspectives on mobile user experience have been featured in *Interactions Magazine, Business Week* and *Wired*.

Rachel received a Masters Degree in Design Planning from the Institute of Design in Chicago.